Sometimes I Act Crazy

Living with
Borderline Personality Disorder

Jerold J. Kreisman, M.D.
Hal Straus

WILEY
John Wiley & Sons, Inc.

*In memory of my father, Erwin Kreisman,
and for my mother, Frieda Kreisman,
who taught us that—with unconditional love—all things are possible.*
—JEROLD J. KREISMAN, M.D.

For Lil and Lou
—HAL STRAUS

Published by John Wiley & Sons, Inc., Hoboken, New Jersey
Published simultaneously in Canada

The information contained in this book is not intended to serve as a replacement for professional medical advice or professional psychological counseling. Any use of the information in this book is at the reader's discretion. The publisher specifically disclaims any and all liability arising directly or indirectly from the use or application of any information contained in this book. The appropriate professional should be consulted regarding your specific condition.

For general information about our other products and services, please contact our Customer Care Department within the United States at (800) 762-2974, outside the United States at (317) 572-3993 or fax (317) 572-4002.

Wiley also publishes its books in a variety of electronic formats. Some content that appears in print may not be available in electronic books. For more information about Wiley products, visit our web site at www.wiley.com.

Library of Congress Cataloging-in-Publication Data:

Kreisman, Jerold J. (Jerold Jay)
   Sometimes I act crazy : living with borderline personality disorder /
Jerold J. Kreisman and Hal Straus.
      p. cm.
Includes bibliographical references and index.
   ISBN-13 978-0-471-22286-6 (cloth)
   ISBN-10 0-471-22286-0 (cloth)
   ISBN-13 978-0-471-79214-7 (paper)
   ISBN-10 0-471-79214-4 (paper)
   1. Borderline personality disorder.   I. Straus, Hal.   II. Title.
RC569.5 .B67K743 2004
616.85'852—dc22   2003017775

Printed in the United States of America

SKY10047329_050823

Contents

A Note to the Reader

Most books on health follow a number of guidelines (e.g., *The Publication Manual of the American Psychological Association*), which are designed to minimize the stigma of disease and to employ politically correct gender designations. Specifically, referring to an individual by an illness is discouraged; instead, reference is made to an individual who expresses symptoms of the disease. Additionally, gender-specific pronouns are avoided; instead, sentences are structured in a passive syntax, or "he/she, him/her" constructions are employed.

Though laudable in some respects, these recommendations complicate the communication of information. Although we abhor the implied disrespect and dehumanization of referring to people by their medical conditions ("Check on the gallbladder in the next room!"), we have nevertheless chosen, for the sake of clarity and efficiency, to often refer to individuals by their diagnosis. For example, we use the term "borderline(s)" as a kind of shorthand to represent the more precise designation— "human being(s) who exhibit(s) symptoms consistent with the diagnosis Borderline Personality Disorder, as defined by the American Psychiatric Association's *Diagnostic and Statistical Manual, 4th edition, text revision (DSM-IV-TR)*." For the same reason, we alternate pronouns throughout, rather than burden the reader with the "he/she" requirement. We trust that the reader will grant us this liberty to streamline the text.

The information in this book is true and correct to the best of our knowledge. The book is intended only as a general guide to a specific type of personality disorder and is not intended as a replacement for sound medical advice from the reader's personal physician. The stories that begin many chapters, and other case history material throughout the book, have been developed from composites of several people and do not represent any actual person, living or dead. Any resemblance to any actual person is unintentional and purely coincidental. All recommendations herein are made without guarantees by the authors or the publisher. The authors and the publisher disclaim all liability, direct or consequential, in connection with the use of this information.

Preface

When *I Hate You, Don't Leave Me: Understanding the Borderline Personality* was published in 1989, Borderline Personality Disorder (BPD) was relatively unknown among the general lay public and frequently misunderstood among many mental health care professionals. Only those who suffered from the affliction, their close family and friends, and those professionals who treated them really understood its complexity and pain.

Since then, BPD has become more widely recognized in the professional community and more understood in the general population. A sign of this widening recognition in our society is the increasingly frequent references to the illness in popular books, films, and television shows. On the Internet, many Web sites, bulletin boards, and chat rooms are devoted to exchanging information on BPD.

Over the decade since publication of *I Hate You,* I have received hundreds of calls and letters from readers. Some are from students asking for an update on information. Many are from therapists requesting consultation on a specific case. But most are from patients and the families of patients sharing experiences or asking for help. These communiqués are often desperate, sometimes shocking, and always emotional, relating the personal agonies of living with BPD.

The wide and growing interest in BPD and the responses to our first book validated my goals in its authorship: to increase awareness and understanding of this illness to both general and professional audiences by attempting to make complex scientific issues and data understandable to nonprofessionals, while simultaneously presenting current, well-referenced information for those in the mental health field. I have been pleased to learn that the first book has been utilized as a text in many graduate courses in the social sciences. More profoundly, I have been deeply moved by the communications from those who have struggled with the disease, who want to share their stories and learn more. These correspondents have identified strongly with the case histories and have requested more. We have learned that people don't *have* borderline personality disorder. BPD has *them*!

The increasing interest in BPD over the past decade has prompted significant new exploration in the field. Refinements in diagnosis have improved our conceptualization of BPD. Advances in biochemical, neurological, and genetic research have propelled our understanding of the disorder. Innovative treatment approaches have enhanced prognosis. The interest of our audience and the profound scientific advances of recent years have enticed my coauthor and me to offer this second book. While our first book used case summaries to illustrate didactic text, the case histories in this book are written in the form of personal stories. Each symptom chapter offers a brief glimpse into the mind of a borderline at a crucial life moment, so that the reader can gain insight not only into the principles involved but also *feel* what it's really like to live with—and close to—BPD.

Like our first book, this offering is directed for both the general and professional audiences. I have attempted to digest complex issues and sometimes inconsistent and even contradictory data into a form comprehensible to a nonmedical audience. However, the references for each chapter and a bibliography offer more sophisticated data for those requiring more detailed information. Readers of our first book will discover new information and expanded case material in the second. Readers of this book may be enticed to review our first, for a more historical elucidation of the borderline syndrome. Either work stands alone.

Although I have been deeply gratified by the interest *I Hate You* has generated, I have been disappointed that some have interpreted the material as presenting a pessimistic view of BPD. Although my intent was to instill a more positive perception by explicating the syndrome and describing productive treatment approaches, some readers shared their impression that the depicted outcome for borderlines seemed relatively hopeless. It is my hope that this book will unequivocally dispel that notion. I believe the most significant message of this work is that borderlines, despite tremendous struggles, do, indeed, get better. The pages of this book aspire to promote understanding; to provide comfort; and, most of all, to furnish hope.

— Jerold J. Kreisman, M.D.

Acknowledgments

It is never possible to thank all of those who helped with the usually joyful yet often painful gestation of this work. With delivery comes great postpartum relief that makes it necessary to acknowledge those who were there to get us through the irritability, nausea, and breathing exercises that accompanied the labor and birthing of this book.

Lynne Klippel, the energetic and resourceful librarian at DePaul Health Center in St. Louis was instrumental in helping track down references. Dr. Kreisman's secretary, Jennifer Jacob, tolerated his frustration fits with knowing forbearance and good humor. He feels particularly blessed to be associated with some of the most knowledgeable and talented mental health professionals he has known at Allied Behavioral Consultants in St. Louis. Lawrence Kuhn, M.D., an inveterate friend and colleague, and his other partners were unfailingly supportive of this project.

Dr. Kreisman's wife, Judy, and children, Brett, Jenny, and Adam, did more than merely tolerate his frenzied intemperance. They offered useful suggestions and insights as he attempted to domesticate the often unruly materials with which he was struggling.

Most of all, Dr. Kreisman acknowledges the patients who entrust the medical profession with their very lives, and thus make any project such as this possible. It is his hope that this work is worthy of their courage.

Dr. Kreisman's coauthor, Hal Straus, would like to thank his children, Matt and Sarah, who exhibited more patience than their dad ever did in putting up with his endless hours on the computer.

Both authors wish to express their gratitude to their agent, the late Jane Jordan Browne, of Multimedia Product Development in Chicago, who never wavered in her support of this project, and to Jane's successor at MPD, Danielle Egan-Miller. Finally, Tom Miller, our editor at Wiley, provided wise and helpful suggestions, as did production editor Kimberly Monroe-Hill, all along the way.

1

Borderline Basics

There is in every one of us, even those who seem to be most moderate, a type of desire that is terrible, wild, and lawless.

—PLATO, *The Republic*

Borderline Personality Disorder (BPD), the most common personality disorder seen in clinical settings, is excruciatingly painful to live with—both for the sufferer and those closest to him. Yet despite the prevalence of BPD, it may be the most misunderstood and underdiagnosed mental illness. This chapter provides a broad discussion of the disorder—from biological, genetic, and environmental causes, to the most current *DSM* diagnostic criteria, to the various forms of psychotherapeutic and medical treatments. The obstacles to properly diagnosing BPD, such as its stigma within the mental health profession and the vagaries of insurance coverage, also are examined. A "BPD Checklist" gives the reader a chance to detect BPD's early warning signs in himself and others.

DIANA

In many ways Diana was a typical girl: she loved to play with her dolls and like her friends dreamed of someday marrying her Prince Charming, who would whisk her off to his castle, where they would live happily ever after. But somewhere along the way, Diana veered into a different dimension. She crossed the boundary from "ordinary" into *borderline.*

This change in direction might have been influenced by her mother, who was very close to Diana and who abruptly walked out on the family

1

when Diana was six years old. Her father was left to rear the children, but he was emotionally and often physically distant, leaving Diana and her siblings in the care of a nanny. Diana would be frantically anxious when he was gone, inquiring constantly as to when he would return.

Periodic visits with her mother left both Diana and her mother in tears. During this time, Diana became more moody and insecure. She was afraid of the dark and of being alone. She was very sensitive and would cry easily. She clung to her menagerie of stuffed animals, which she called "my family." Diana tried desperately to please both of her parents, while secretly blaming herself for their divorce. She felt she was not good enough to keep them together and developed a fear that everyone she loved would eventually abandon her.

When she was fifteen, Diana became more concerned about her appearance and, like her older sister, began to induce herself to vomit after eating. She entered into a pattern of anorexia and bulimia, which intermittently plagued her for the rest of her life. The fractures in Diana's personality became more prominent during her adolescence. She could be charming, charitable, and remarkably empathic with friends at times, but on other occasions she exhibited an unpredictably cruel rage when these same friends disappointed her. Sometimes, during stressful periods, she appeared calm and stoic, but at other times she became irrationally emotional, alternating between inconsolable grief and ferocious anger.

At twenty, Diana married her prince—Prince Charles of England. Yet Princess Diana did not live happily ever after. As her fairy-tale marriage disintegrated, so did her manufactured facade of equanimity. She became more overtly impulsive and self-destructive. She threw herself into her charity work, perhaps hoping to derive for herself the kind of caretaking she was bestowing on others. The affliction of borderline personality plagued Princess Diana until her untimely death in 1997.

Advances in Diagnosis and Treatment

Our previous book, *I Hate You, Don't Leave Me: Understanding the Borderline Personality,* originally published in 1989, was one of the first attempts to help those afflicted with Borderline Personality Disorder (BPD) to understand and cope with the condition. At that time, understanding of this disorder was in its infancy. Research studies were scarce, and the few that did deal with the subject lacked the advantage of studying patients over long periods of time. Ideas on the root causes of the disease were more speculation than scholarship. Technology revealing the relationship of brain physiology to behavior and mental illness was still primitive.

The concept of borderline personality was insufficiently understood and accepted—even among those professionals trained to recognize and treat it. Many clinicians were hesitant to accept the newly defined concept and relegated it to the status of "wastebasket diagnosis"—a label to be used when the doctor simply did not understand the patient or could not "fit" the patient's symptoms into any other, more acceptable disorder. In many therapeutic settings the term became a diagnosis of frustration: a difficult patient who was uncooperative; demanding; clinging; confusing; angry; or, most important, failed to respond to the psychiatrist's ministrations was often labeled "borderline."

Structured treatment strategies also were in primordial stages. Psychotherapeutic techniques and medications used to treat related disorders generated inconsistent results when applied to BPD. Outcome studies following therapy interventions were minimal.

It is no wonder, then, that many readers of *I Hate You* came away from the book feeling that the prognosis for borderlines was dismal. Though they could understand what they—or their friends or family—were experiencing, some readers concluded that there was little hope for a cure. One reader wrote that although she found most of the book "informative and helpful, I was still left in tears at the end of it because of the gloomy outcome it suggested."

So what has changed over the past fourteen years? Breakthroughs on many fronts have led to significant leaps in our understanding and treatment of BPD. Geneticists, exploring the effects of individual chromosomes, have connected specific borderline behaviors to discrete locations on the genome. Scientists have discovered biochemical and anatomical alterations in the brain that are correlated with BPD behaviors. Psychotherapeutic techniques have been developed specifically to treat borderline patients, and new medications are more effectively controlling symptoms. Just as the synthesis of therapy and medication has provided relief for those suffering from schizophrenia, bipolar disorder, anxiety disorders, and depression, the same has happened with treatment approaches to BPD. All of these advances have greatly improved the prognosis for these patients. In short, people with BPD can—and do—get better!

Epidemiology and Demographics

BPD is the most common personality disorder seen in clinical settings, both in the United States and in cultures throughout the world. Depending on the study, BPD comprises between 30 and 60 percent of all patients diagnosed with any of the ten defined personality disorders. The prevalence of BPD in the general population, as strictly defined in the fourth and most recent revised edition of the American Psychiatric Association's *Diagnostic and Statistical Manual (DSM-IV-TR)*, is conservatively estimated to be 2 to 4 percent. Many clinicians believe the real percentage to be higher. Most other countries apply the *DSM* in defining psychiatric illnesses and find similar results, confirming that BPD is not confined to Western cultures.

Approximately 10 percent of the entire clinical population evaluated in outpatient mental health clinics, and more than 20 percent of all inpatients, satisfy BPD criteria. Three times as many women as men are diagnosed with BPD, a prevalence that has remained stable over the past two decades. Patients with the diagnosis of BPD are more likely to receive all forms of psychosocial therapy and to utilize more psychotropic medications than patients with depression or any other personality disorder.

The intensity of borderline symptoms may be related to life situations. One large study indicated that more severe pathology was correlated with students or the unemployed, separated (but not divorced) individuals, atheists, people with a criminal record, and those who lost a parent through death or divorce. These associations held for blacks and whites equally. There was no correlation with the level of education.

The Borderline Life Cycle

Typically, borderline behavior is first observed from the late teens to the early thirties, though severe separation problems or rage outbursts in younger children may be harbingers of the diagnosis. A borderline state may emerge from a parental relationship that is at one of two extremes— either too dependent or too rejecting. As described in detail in our previous book, disruption of normal child development, particularly during the crucial rapprochement age (sixteen to twenty-five months), may hinder development of a constant, separate identity, one of the prominent symptoms of BPD.

Most adolescents are *already* grappling with such issues as identity, moodiness, impulsivity, and relationship insecurities that are at the core of BPD. (Indeed, some might argue that the term "borderline adolescent" is a redundancy!) However, normal, volatile adolescents do not exhibit suicide attempts, violent rages, or excessive drug abuse observed in borderline teenagers.

During their third and fourth decades, many borderlines achieve some stability in their lives. Borderline behaviors may be curbed or no longer significantly hamper daily activities. Thus many former borderlines, with or without treatment, may emerge from the chaos of their lives to a relatively stable midlife functioning that no longer satisfies defining criteria for the BPD diagnosis. BPD does persist in the elderly but at a much lower rate.

Crossing the Border: A Brief Historical Background

The term "borderline" was first employed more than sixty years ago to describe patients who were on the border between psychotic and neurotic but could not be adequately classified as either. Unlike psychotic patients, who were chronically divorced from reality, and neurotic patients, who responded more consistently to close relationships and psychotherapy, borderline patients functioned somewhere in between. Borderlines sometimes wandered into the wild terrain of psychosis, doctors observed, but usually remained for only a brief time. On the other hand, borderlines exhibited several superficial neurotic characteristics, but these comparatively healthier defense mechanisms collapsed under stress.

Over the years, such terms as "pseudoneurotic schizophrenia" and "as-if personality" were employed to describe the condition. Revisiting some of Freud's early case histories of neurosis, many theorists reinterpreted such cases as "The Wolf Man" and "Anna O." as examples of borderline functioning. For decades psychiatrists recognized the existence of this "border" illness but were unable to arrive at a consensus definition.

Finally, in 1980, the third edition of the American Psychiatric Association's *Diagnostic and Statistical Manual (DSM-III)* classified the BPD diagnosis, for the first time utilizing specific, descriptive symptoms.

Defining BPD

Borderline Personality Disorder is the most prominent of the ten personality disorders defined and described in *DSM-IV-TR*. A "personality disorder" is defined as a cluster of long-standing, ingrained traits in an individual's demeanor. Typically detectable by the time of early adulthood, adolescence, or even earlier, these traits are relatively inflexible and result in maladaptive, destructive patterns of behaving, perceiving, and relating to others. The diagnoses of personality disorders are separated from those of most other psychiatric illnesses by placement on a separate classification level (Axis II). Other psychiatric illnesses, such as depression, schizophrenia, substance abuse, and eating disorders, are defined on Axis I. Whereas Axis II personality disorders are perceived as long-standing, chronic maladaptations in behavior, Axis I afflictions are traditionally seen as time-limited, more biologically based, and more amenable to medications. Axis I symptoms usually recede, allowing the person to return to "normal" functioning between exacerbations of illness. People with diagnosed personality disorders usually continue to express characteristics of the dysfunction even after the acute problem resolves. Cure usually requires a longer time, since it involves significantly altering enduring behavior patterns. Personality disorders, especially BPD, have been demonstrated to elicit more severe functional impairment in day-to-day living than some Axis I disorders, including major depression.

BPD shares several characteristics with other personality dysfunctions, especially histrionic, narcissistic, antisocial, schizotypal, and dependent personality disorders. However, the constellation of self-destructiveness, chronic feelings of emptiness, and desperate fears of abandonment distinguish BPD from these other character disorders.

The primary features of BPD are impulsivity and instability in relationships, self-image, and moods. These behavioral patterns are pervasive, usually beginning in adolescence and persisting for extended periods. The diagnosis, according to the *DSM-IV-TR* (and generally accepted worldwide), is based on the following nine criteria. An individual must exhibit five of these nine symptoms to receive the BPD diagnosis.

BPD Criteria

1. Frantic efforts to avoid real or imagined abandonment

2. A pattern of unstable and intense interpersonal relationships character- ized by alternating between extremes of idealization and devaluation

3. Identity disturbance: markedly and persistently unstable self-image or sense of self

4. Impulsivity in at least two areas that are potentially self-damaging (e.g., spending, sex, substance abuse, reckless driving, binge eating)

5. Recurrent suicidal behavior, gestures, or threats, or self-mutilating behavior

6. Affective (mood) instability and marked reactivity to environmental situations (e.g., intense episodic depression, irritability, or anxiety usu- ally lasting a few hours and rarely more than a few days)

7. Chronic feelings of emptiness

8. Inappropriate, intense anger or difficulty controlling anger (e.g., fre- quent displays of temper, constant anger, recurrent physical fights)

9. Transient, stress-related paranoia or severe dissociative symptoms (feelings of unreality)

As we will see when we examine these criteria more closely in later chapters, the latest *DSM-IV-TR* makes only minor revisions to defining symptoms. The most significant change is the addition of the ninth crite- rion, which recognizes occasional, fleeting episodes of psychosis.

This constellation of nine symptoms can be subdivided into four pri- mary areas, toward which treatment is directed:

1. Mood instability (criteria 1, 6, 7, and 8)

2. Impulsivity and uncontrolled behaviors (criteria 4 and 5)

3. Interpersonal psychopathology (criteria 2 and 3)

4. Distortions of thought and perception (criterion 9)

Mood changes and impulsivity are the most important factors in risk for suicide.

A collaborative, longitudinal study by researchers from across the coun- try grouped these defining criteria into three categories for classification purposes. After interviewing hundreds of BPD patients and testing and categorizing the criteria, these investigators reestablished the validity of the *DSM* factors that define BPD. The three factor groupings developed are: disturbed relationships, uncontrolled behavior, and mood irregularity (see table 1).

Disturbed relationships encompass problems relating to oneself, as well as to others. Identity disturbance (see chapter 4) will naturally proceed into relationship difficulties (see chapter 3). When identity insecurity persists, there often develop feelings of emptiness and meaninglessness (see chapter 8). When the sense of self disappears altogether, dissociation from reality occurs (see chapter 10).

Uncontrolled behavior covers destructive impulsivity (see chapter 5) and self-destructive behavior (see chapter 6).

Mood irregularity encompasses the remaining criteria. Mood instability (see chapter 7) often leads to frustration and the expression of inap-

TABLE 1   Categorizing BPD Symptoms

Criteria	Disturbed Relationships	Uncontrolled Behavior	Mood Irregularity
1			Abandonment fears
2	Unstable relationships		
3	Identity disturbance		
4		Destructive impulsivity	
5		Self-harming behavior	
6			Mood instability
7	Emptiness		
8			Anger
9	Dissociation from reality		

propriate anger (see chapter 9). These intense emotions alienate others, leaving the individual alone and abandoned (see chapter 2).

These *DSM* criteria define a *categorical* paradigm for defining BPD; that is, a person either *has it* (embracing at least five of the criteria), or he doesn't (with four or fewer symptoms). This conceptualization allows for objective, measurable determinants. However, it embraces all nine criteria as being equally contributory and allows for the seeming paradox that someone with the supposedly enduring diagnosis of BPD could suddenly be "cured" of the illness by overcoming even one defining criterion. In contrast, some authors have argued that personality disorders, which are enduring traits, should be defined in a *dimensional* way. This model proposes that there are *degrees* of personality functioning, much like there are degrees or levels of addiction. Rather than concluding that an individual is borderline or is not, these authors argue that the disorder should be recognized along a spectrum by the *intensity* of exhibited symptoms and by weighting certain criteria and background information proportionately. For example, consider that the determination that one is male or female is categorical, identified objectively by several criteria. Alternatively, designations of masculinity or femininity are dimensional considerations, influenced by personal, cultural, and other less objective criteria. Proposals for the future *DSM-V* include consideration of redefining personality (Axis II) disorders utilizing dimensional models.

Difficulties in Diagnosis: Coexisting and Related Illnesses

Studies over the past decade have confirmed that BPD is linked with other psychiatric illnesses much more frequently than previously thought. Unlike the cheese in "The Farmer in the Dell," BPD rarely stands alone. Some of the defining symptoms are identical to criteria for other illnesses. For example, as with borderlines, many individuals with attention-deficit hyperactivity disorder (ADHD) display impatience, impulsivity, quickness to anger, fractured relationships, poor self-esteem, and frequent substance abuse. Impulsivity and outbursts of anger characterize persons with antisocial personality disorder. The most common "fellow traveler" with BPD is depression. More than 95 percent of BPD patients also satisfy criteria for this disorder. Almost 90 percent of borderlines also meet criteria for anxiety illnesses, especially post-traumatic stress disorder, panic disorder, and social anxiety disorder. Although depression and anxiety are seen equally in both genders, substance abuse and sociopathy are seen significantly more often in male borderlines, while eating disorders and post-traumatic stress disorders are correlated more often in female borderlines. All of these illnesses are found much more often in borderlines than in those with other personality disorders.

Since borderlines usually present with several afflictions, the clinician must address the most disabling symptoms first. And she must juggle the effects that treatment may have on accompanying problems. For example, many borderlines have accompanying ADHD symptoms. If she initiates treatment for the poor concentration and distractibility of the attention deficit with stimulant medicine (such as Ritalin), will the borderline symptoms of rage and mood swings be exacerbated? Conversely, if she engages the patient in an intensive psychotherapy, will he be able to sustain attention adequately to usefully benefit from the treatment? Accurate diagnosis of all disorders is necessary to ensure thorough and balanced treatment.

BPD also can imitate other illnesses. Mood changes may be erroneously diagnosed as bipolar disorder. Transient psychosis may mimic schizophrenia. When an accompanying disorder such as depression or alcoholism is prominent, it may camouflage the significant, underlying BPD.

Although BPD may accompany other illnesses, it is important to differentiate it from other disorders. Borderline depression and mood swings are usually related to environmental situations and, consequently, can change within hours. Major depressive and bipolar disorders more often last for days, or for more extended periods, and may be unrelated to stimuli in the individual's life. Further, between episodes, a person with affective disorder usually functions well, whereas the borderline may continue to engage in destructive behaviors.

Transient, stress-related psychosis in the borderline can acutely resemble paranoid schizophrenia. However, in BPD the psychosis is short-lived and may dissolve, sometimes within hours; schizophrenic psychosis is usually chronic and less related to external stressors.

Although borderlines often experience traumas, post-traumatic stress disorder (PTSD) is defined by characteristic reactions to specific, severe crises. These reactions include recurrent intrusive thoughts about the event, avoidance of associated places or activities, and hypervigilance with exaggerated startle response, which usually are not characteristic of BPD. Physiological distinctions suggest that patients with BPD respond more strongly to themes of abandonment, whereas PTSD patients exhibit a more extreme response to presentations emphasizing trauma.

Diagnostic Bias

Despite its frequency, BPD is often misdiagnosed or underdiagnosed. Primary care physicians, who usually are the first professionals to be consulted for psychiatric problems, are able to accurately recognize and treat BPD less than half of the time.

Coexisting illnesses may contribute to the underdiagnosis of BPD in several ways. When another disorder is primary, many clinicians will ignore Axis II diagnoses, concentrating only on treating the Axis I malady (which usually is easier to treat, since the emphasis is on medication and not on complicated, extended psychotherapy). Additionally, managed care companies sometimes discourage continued therapy for personality disorders, since such patients characteristically require more intensive—and more expensive—long-term treatment. Some insurance companies will disallow coverage for BPD altogether, stating that the required, expensive treatment is not part of the policy. Paradoxically, some insurance case managers refuse certification based on the erroneous assumption that borderline patients never get better, that therapy doesn't help, and therefore treatment attempts waste resources. Thus many doctors avoid the borderline label to minimize hassles with managed care companies.

Finally, many clinicians hesitate to diagnose BPD because of its stigma within the profession. Among many professionals, borderline patients are the most dreaded. They bear a reputation for being overly demanding, with frequent phone calls and agitation for attention. They are the most litigious group of psychiatric patients. When disappointed, their rage is difficult to tolerate. Constant threats of suicide can be difficult to manage. Treatment requires much patience and, even more, much time, which, in today's climate, often is not adequately recognized or reimbursed. Thus many patients with the BPD diagnosis are unable to engage capable clinicians willing to accept them in treatment.

ACTION STEPS: *A Quick BPD Checklist*

Do you have BPD? Or do you think you know someone who does?

Without professional help, of course, there is no way to know for sure if an individual is borderline, but there are "clues" and "early warning signals" for mental illnesses, just as there are for physical conditions. The following life events and behaviors may be clues to the presence of BPD. *Caution: Just as you should not try to diagnose your own heart condition, you should not attempt to diagnose your own mental disorder. If you check more than a few of the following boxes, and they are interfering with your normal day-to-day functioning, you should consult your physician.*

- ☐ traumatic childhood experiences (especially physical or sexual abuse)

- ☐ self-sabotaging behaviors (such as ruining a job interview, destroying a good relationship)

- ☐ history of disappointing relationships, jobs, or other commitments

- ☐ frequent changes in jobs, schools (and majors), relationships (several divorces, separations, and remarriages)

- ☐ history of hurtful relationships (e.g., several marriages to alcoholics who are abusive) or relationships with controlling, narcissistic partners that result in conflict

- ☐ utilization of transitional objects (relying on a multitude of dolls and teddy bears for comfort)

- ☐ dangerous behavior that may be perceived as exciting (such as drug abuse, promiscuity, shoplifting, bulimia, anorexia)

- ☐ frequent conflicts (especially with important figures such as bosses, colleagues, friends, family)

- ☐ repeated history of violence, either as perpetrator, victim, or both

- ☐ severe changes in attitude (e.g., idealizing a friend and later reviling him; purporting to love a book and later declaring it boring)

- ☐ attraction to extremist organizations (such as religious or political cults)

☐ functioning better in structured situations (e.g., performing poorly in college but succeeding brilliantly in the army)

The Roots of BPD

The theoretical precursors in the development of BPD were explored in our previous book. Several methodologies have been used to research the causes and roots of BPD. Family studies have confirmed that most borderlines experienced severe disruption in their development, pointing toward environmental causes.

More recent genetic and neurological studies have theorized that there may be heritable, biological underpinnings. A significant subgroup of borderlines has a history of perinatal or acquired brain injury.

A new line of research posits that predisposing genetic/biological vulnerabilities combine with environmental traumas to produce borderline coping mechanisms. One model suggests that inherited tendencies (called temperament) intersects with developmentally based values (character) to produce personality. Thus temperament + character = personality. Further, specific temperaments can be discerned and correlated with biological imbalances and sensitivities. Models of temperament form early in life and are perceived as instinctual or as habits. Character styles are gradually shaped and culminate in adulthood.

Biological and Anatomical Correlates

Some of the most exciting recent discoveries in BPD research employ modern medical tools to explore the brain's mechanics, such as monitoring chemical changes and observing anatomical alterations. Some researchers have demonstrated that abnormal levels of the neurotransmitter serotonin (a chemical involved in nerve conduction throughout the body but especially in the brain) may result in the increased impulsivity and aggression associated with BPD. Interestingly, such sensitivity is seen more frequently in women, who comprise 75 percent of borderlines. One study utilized positron emission tomography (PET) scanning to demonstrate lower levels of serotonin activity, which correlated with increased impulsivity, in the brains of men and women with BPD. Other neurotransmitters, such as dopamine and gamma-aminobutyric acid (GABA), also may be implicated in the regulation of impulsive aggression. The neurotransmitters acetylcholine and norepinephrine are associated with modulation of mood. Medicines that regulate these neurotransmitter imbalances have been shown to relieve borderline symptoms.

Some researchers have investigated the connection of BPD to autoimmune disorders, in which the body has a kind of allergic reaction to itself and produces antibodies to its own organs. One example, rheumatoid arthritis, is associated with an unusually high prevalence of BPD. One study followed a woman with fluctuating BPD symptoms over a period of nine months while measuring her antithyroid antibodies. These investigators discovered significantly lower levels of the antibodies during periods when her depression and psychosis ratings were low, and higher levels when her symptoms increased. This finding suggests that autoimmune-related inflammation may exacerbate BPD symptoms or vice versa.

Scientists exploring the neurology of BPD have focused on a part of the brain called the limbic system. This section of the brain influences memory, learning, emotional states (such as anxiety), and behaviors (particularly aggressive and sexual). EEG analyses of borderlines have demonstrated disruption in this part of the brain. One study utilized magnetic resonance imaging (MRI) to evaluate changes in limbic system volume in borderline women with a history of trauma. These authors demonstrated significantly decreased volume in the hippocampus and amygdala regions of this brain area. This connection between past physical or emotional trauma and later changes in brain volume that is associated with borderline pathology raises the possibility that child abuse could alter brain functioning, resulting in borderline behavior. What has not been definitively demonstrated is the *direction* of the association. An alternative explanation could be that BPD *causes* (rather than is the result of) changes in brain volume, which are associated, only fortuitously, with past trauma.

Genetic and Environmental Roots

Genome research has exploded over the past few years. Gene mapping, the potential for cloning, and stem cell development have opened up new frontiers in understanding and treating medical illnesses. Some BPD researchers have attempted to establish that specific genes may be responsible for particular types of borderline behaviors. For example, identity instability, mood changes, and aggressive impulsivity have strong hereditary components. Another behavior frequently exhibited by borderlines, novelty-seeking—referring to the pursuit of excitement and sometimes danger, often to avoid feelings of emptiness and boredom—is a characteristic also associated with other BPD criteria, such as impulsivity and aggression. Interestingly, some studies have correlated this observable behavior with chemical dysregulation in the serotonin neurotransmitter system and other studies with a gene locus involving the dopamine neurotransmitter on a specific human chromosome. Although these studies require confirmation, they suggest connections among genetics; internal chemical balance; and, ultimately, behavior.

Family studies have demonstrated that first-degree relatives of borderlines are five times more likely to also fulfill the BPD diagnosis than the general public. Family members of borderlines also are more likely to be diagnosed with related illnesses, especially substance abuse, affective disorders, and antisocial personality disorder.

Throughout one's life, certain genes are, in a sense, "turned on and off," influenced by factors such as parenting. Animal and human research evaluating maternal care suggests that positive parenting can influence genetic predisposition and resulting biochemical balance. Thus an individual may be born with inborn vulnerabilities to impaired brain circuitry for modulating moods and impulsivity, but environmental factors may affect gene expression in a way that determines whether the person will exhibit any or all potential borderline symptoms.

Undoubtedly, genetic contributions—modified by environmental influences—to the development of BPD are dependent on multiple factors and probably engage multiple chromosomal loci. However, further explication of these mechanisms will perhaps lead us to the development of new biotech drugs (see chapter 13), which can target specific genes for adjustment.

Treating the Borderline Patient

Treatment for BPD has advanced considerably over the past decade. Specifically, controlled studies of psychotherapy approaches and medications have yielded important scientific confirmation that has done a great deal to allay previous pessimism. In short, in many cases, therapy works!

Psychotherapy

Psychotherapy remains the foundation of treatment for BPD, comple-mented by symptom-focused pharmacotherapy. When our previous book was released, controlled studies evaluating psychotherapy approaches had not yet been published. At that time, evidence for the efficacy of particu-lar therapy techniques was based on individual case studies rather than on controlled scientific evaluations. Also not yet documented in the literature were studies comparing the efficacy of many medications to the effects of psychotherapy.

The past decade has witnessed the development of new tools that attempt to measure the results of psychotherapy. Two psychotherapy approaches have demonstrated efficacy in controlled studies using these measurement tools: (1) psychodynamic psychotherapy (which follows some psychoanalytic theories) and (2) dialectical behavioral therapy or DBT (which utilizes cognitive and behavioral approaches). Both ap-proaches demand intensive treatment from a team of therapists. Both indi-vidual and group therapies are utilized, and change usually requires at least one year to be discernible.

Our use of SET techniques to communicate with borderline patients continues to be a functional strategy. As we explore in later chapters, there are more similarities among these ostensibly contrary approaches than dif-ferences (for in-depth discussion see chapter 11).

Medication

Pharmacotherapy is an important adjunct to psychotherapy. Medication targets specific symptoms, especially in the arenas of mood instability, impulse dyscontrol, and perceptual distortions. The classes of drugs used are primarily antidepressants, mood stabilizers, psychotropics (antipsy-chotic medicines), and antianxiety drugs (see chapter 11). Occasionally, ECT (electroconvulsive treatment) and opiate antagonists (which some-times have been efficacious in treating self-mutilating behavior) also may be employed.

Prognosis

Make no mistake, BPD is a dangerous—even potentially fatal—illness: about 8 to 10 percent of BPD patients commit suicide. However, over time, most borderlines improve significantly, and almost half enjoy complete recovery (i.e., they no longer satisfy defining criteria for BPD). Despite the many frustrations endured by the patient, close friends and family, and the therapist, the treacherous road that winds out of the horrific, dark forest of borderline personality can lead to a brighter future. If the journey can be sustained, all who experience and confront the pain of borderline personality can arrive at a destination of contentment and acceptance.

2

Fears of Abandonment

Loneliness is the central and inevitable experience of every man.
—THOMAS WOLFE

"Rhett . . . If you go, where shall I go? What shall I do?"
—SCARLETT O'HARA, *Gone with the Wind*

At one time or another, almost everyone worries that her lover is going to leave. But for a borderline, the fear of abandonment—rooted in years of family history—can be excruciatingly painful. The terror involves much more than the simple dread of being alone; abandonment can mean the destruction of the borderline's entire identity. In this chapter you will first read about Arleen, whose childhood panic that her father would abandon her evolves into even greater worries about her husband, Greg, and leads to severe complications in her life. The discussion section explains the psychological basis for these fears, how the borderline deals with threats of abandonment, and how close relations can help calm these anxieties.

ARLEEN: PART ONE

Alone again, the other agents out showing houses or meeting with mortgage brokers or doing God-knows-what busywork, Arleen wonders if Greg is at his desk at Eastland Casualty. She glances at the clock above her desk: 3:10. He damn well *better* be there, but since September 11,

19

Greg's meetings are nonstop. "*Pre*meetings, *post*meetings, meetings to decide if we should *have* meetings," he'd whine in that cute, exasperated tone of his. "We're like some dysfunctional family that has to be together all the time."

Before she can pick up the phone receiver, Eddie jaunts in, the silly cowbell that he had stubbornly installed above the Red Oak Realty door tinkling his entry into her solitude. She had objected strenuously to the bell but to no avail.

"It's so *homey*," he had said with a grin.

"*Hokey* is more like it," she had replied.

Of course, she couldn't complain too much; they both knew the *real* reason for the bell: his childish idea of an early-warning system for their sexual antics in his office, though she couldn't tell him about the real cause of *her* revulsion.

"Hey, doll"—Eddie winks now—"whhhaaaahhhhzzzzupppp?" There it is again—that silly line from the beer commercial. It is so *old*. Why couldn't Eddie just be himself? Short, stocky, balding, with a paunch that threatens to pop the bottom button off his starched white shirt, he is certainly not Arleen's ideal body type, but there is something about him that attracts her. Maybe it's his *own* loneliness, his need for her that he tries to disguise in pretending he doesn't need her at all. Eddie and Doreen have been separated for almost a year, and he's been having a hard time as a single dad. The fact that all three kids are girls does not make it any easier. Eddie just never understood how to relate to women. Worse, he doesn't even know it.

"Hey, where *is* everybody?" he asks mock-grimly, as if he were genuinely surprised by the empty chairs swiveled in every direction. He had come upon this same scene almost every Monday and Thursday for nearly three months now. His question hangs in the air like a punch line to a corny joke.

She sighs, shakes her head, and can't help but smile. Ten years ago, he had been a middle linebacker in high school. She knows that because he tells her every chance he gets. She really has no idea what a linebacker *is*, and she doesn't care. He seems so proud that he was a *middle* linebacker, as if that were supposed to *mean* something to her. "Number fifty-six, *middle* linebacker, Eddie *Miles*," he'd hum, cupping his hands around an imaginary stadium microphone, relishing the echoing alliteration—"*Mid-*

dleton *Matadors*"—and absolutely delighting in his "Aaaaaaahhhhhhhhh" sound effect of the roaring teenage crowd of many years ago.

Eddie seems to be in a particularly jovial mood this afternoon, and she tries to embrace his jolliness, which relieves her frustration with Greg, if only for a moment. As Eddie goes to the Mr. Coffee at the back of the small office, Arleen can sense he is already imagining what they'd be doing in a few minutes. Almost reflexively, she picks up the telephone, dials Greg's number, and fidgets while it rings at Eastland.

•   •   •

She and Greg had met at Ohio State in their junior year. Tall, blond, on the tennis team, he had transferred from a small community college in San Diego. They went everywhere together, to Oxley Library, to Royer Union, she even went with him to Owens Rec Center and watched while he did his step routine in the cardio room. Until Greg, her boyfriends had been a long series of letdowns and disappointments. Maturing early, by the time she was in eighth grade she looked very similar to the way she did now, a decade later: a green-eyed, full-figured brunette with a face one would just stop short of describing as pretty. Something about the gleam in her eye led her girlfriends to call her "Mad"—short for Madonna. It was only a matter of time before the boys were exchanging her coquettish glances with giggling flirtations of their own, which she welcomed openly because they relieved the tension and loneliness at home. Not a week went by when she wouldn't proudly announce to her girlfriends that she had kissed Joey or Billy, her new high school "boyfriend" down the street.

From then on she was never without a boyfriend. Even if she didn't like a boy that much, she always made sure another was waiting in the wings before she broke up. God knows she tried to make it work with all of them. In college she would get close to a guy and then he'd start pushing her away, making a lame excuse about "cracking the books" or "going home to see his parents." After a few dates he'd stop calling altogether, as if he'd fallen off the face of the planet. In her bedroom she laughingly tacked up a picture she had drawn as a second-grader, a crayon drawing of Columbus's boats falling off the "flat" world, and wrote "Boys!" in black letters at the top. Boys were so ignorant, they *belonged* in the fifteenth century!

She was persistent, though, calling her lost sailors at all hours, demanding to know what had gone wrong. Even the ones she gave her body to lost interest. Sure, maybe she *was* demanding at times, but couldn't they see she needed *more?* Not just sex or another date; she needed the confidence that they were sharing their innermost secrets with her, the way she had opened her life to them. They all seemed so *flimsy,* as if they would evaporate into nothingness if she turned away for a moment. It reminded her of a period she had gone through as a child when she believed that she was the only person who really existed and all the rest— her neighborhood, the cars on the street—was an elaborate stage set that God whimsically erased when she wasn't looking and returned to existence when she was. Passersby, she was positive, were really mirages that disappeared the second she turned her back on them. Sometimes she tried to catch God at His tricks. She'd swivel around suddenly, attempting to expose these corporeal beings for what they *really* were: wisps of air. But no, they were always still there, flaunting their existence, walking away from her in the same bodies and the same clothes, exactly as they looked when they approached. It was no use; God was too quick for her.

Thank heavens Greg Petersen had come along; he was different from the other guys she had been with. Greg was so intelligent he didn't need to study much. He was sturdy and reliable—*substantial.* He didn't need family or friends or anything else—just her. For most of their senior year at Ohio State, she hung on his shoulder like a fur stole, and he seemed to love it. For winter and spring breaks, when most of the other kids scattered across the country, he preferred to stay in the dorm. That was the way it was supposed to be.

They had gotten married right after graduation and moved to Middleton, a deteriorating suburb twenty miles from Eastland's headquarters in Indianapolis. It was her first time away from home. Compared to Ohio, Indianapolis was Oz—a bustling metropolis of limestone, lights, and glass. She loved getting dressed up and going into the city with Greg on a Saturday night, to see a movie or go to the Down'n Dirty, a lively nightclub that featured blues bands from nearby Chicago. She felt proud to be with him and knew he felt the same about her.

She often sat at her desk at Red Oak trying to pinpoint precisely when things had changed between her and Greg. Or more like it, when *Greg* had changed. At first, when Greg worked normal hours, everything had been fine. Sure, she wasn't much of a cook, and they wound up going out for dinner or having pizza delivered four or five times a week, but he didn't seem to mind, and she even bought a few cookbooks, hoping to surprise him. But after the attacks of September 11 slashed Eastland's coffers, the company demanded more of Greg's time, and he started working longer hours. The forays into the city that she had anticipated with so much excitement tailed off—the *last* thing Greg wanted to do on a Saturday night was to go back to the city.

So they would spend many Saturday nights watching a rented action movie on the VCR, which would, more often than not, lead to lovemaking before the second act. Afterward, curled in each other's arms on the sofa or living room floor, they would talk while the chase scene or the gunfight blared vaguely in the background.

"You're the love of my life, Greg. You're the sexiest person in the world."

"The *world*?"

"All right, then, the universe."

He would hug her in delight then and she would feel his closeness, the strength in his muscles from years of weight training, but rather than become aroused, she would feel strangely engulfed, almost as if she were suffocating, and pull away, bracing for Greg's inevitable lecture. When she pulls away like this, he has told her, she is like a little kid, one minute boldly reaching out to him, the next running away, back to Mommy. But she can't help herself, she says, she feels like she's suffocating! He would only sigh then, become soft, and gaze blankly at the TV screen. This would enrage her for reasons she could not explain, to herself or anyone else. *The movie stinks!* she would scream. *Why do you always have to get your way about choosing the movie?*

"Then you pick the movie next time—I don't care. We never watch it anyway. And then the damn thing sits around for a week and we wind up paying twenty bucks in late fees for a movie we never watched."

"Why are you so *angry* all the time?"

"*Why am I angry!?*" he exclaims. "*I'm* angry because I never know what you want. You complain I never hold you and then when I do, you complain it's too tight, or I'm suffocating you. What the hell do you want from me?"

"See? There you go! What's *happened* to you?"

And on they would go for ten minutes, until Greg would storm out of the living room. After fights like this, she wouldn't speak to him for a week.

For Arleen, the evenings alone in their apartment dragged on and on, engulfed in an intense emptiness that the TV sitcoms and Internet chat rooms did little to fill. Lying alone in her bed, wearing Greg's soiled "Buckeye Basketball" sweatshirt, the unique Greg "smell" would give her some comfort that indeed they had a *history* together, a history filled with good times, that Greg would eventually come home, that he had not left her forever. But comfort would soon succumb to panic, and she'd recall how she felt when her father had dropped her off at grade school and she was sure *he* was never coming back. Her heart pounding, cheeks flushed, chest tight, she feared she was going to pass out at any moment. The walls of her room seemed almost alive, magnifying her sense of being alone. She wanted frantically to call someone but there was no one to call—she and Greg had made few friends in Middleton, and the only friends she did have were so well adjusted, they would never understand. Helplessness would yield to rage: How could Greg—the world—*do* this to her? She was an innocent pawn who was doing her best to hold up her end. Why was she being neglected like this?

"You asshole!" she would scream at the wall. "I hate you! I hate you!"

Somewhere along the line, she had boarded an emotional roller coaster, and there was no jumping off. Sometimes the only way off was at top speed: she would leap out of bed and do frenetic sit-ups on the floor until her stomach muscles ached and she was too exhausted to feel anything.

One rainy fall night, she drove to the four-block street of shops that passed for downtown Middleton, hoping to find a bar or a nightclub where she could have a drink and just *be around people* for an hour or two. But George and Walt's Lounge, a small, dark saloon with only a pool table and a TV set to offer its sparse clientele, proved even worse than her own bedroom. After sipping a beer and absorbing the suspicious stares of the two old men at the end of the bar, whom she assumed were George and Walt, she left and went home. A few weeks later she visited the bar at the Holiday Inn, just off the interstate. She was afraid to return the shy half smiles beamed across the room by a few of the men there. Only on the way driving home did she allow a grin to break her studied detachment as she contemplated the power that would have accompanied a decision to go upstairs with any of them. Later that memory would be strangely comforting during the very lonely times.

Finally she couldn't take the solitude any longer and applied for the secretarial job at Red Oak and enrolled in a night real estate class at Middleton High School. Greg approved, and for a short while their relationship was almost back to normal. It didn't last long. In a few weeks, when she returned home late in the evening and he still wasn't there, the loneliness set in again. She tried to refrain from calling him at the office again and again. She realized that the more she tried to squeeze the relationship, the more likely she was to crush it—but sometimes she just couldn't help herself.

●   ●   ●

With Eddie now in his window-enclosed office, ensconced in the sports section of the *Indianapolis Record,* she listens impatiently as the Eastland phone rings for the fifth time . . . sixth. . . . Did receptionists have to attend meetings too?

"Eastland." For some reason the receptionist's curt, flip tone raises Arleen's hackles; she knows if she answered the phone like that at Red Oak, Eddie and the other agents would be on her case in a flash.

"Extension two-sixty, please." In the middle of the fourth ring, her hopes soar as the familiar sound of Greg's voice fills her ear. "Hi, Greg? I —"

But it isn't him at all. Eastland's phone system being clear and seamless, she has mistaken voice-mail-Greg for live-Greg. Perfect! Just like real life, she thinks bitterly: *there* but not *really there.* Despite the comfort that Greg's voice gives her, even in recorded form, she bangs the receiver down on the base of the phone without leaving a message.

●   ●   ●

If Greg doesn't tell her he loves her ten times a day, she becomes anxious, panicky. She imagines him sitting at his desk, screening his calls, plotting his escape, just like all the other people close to her in her life. One night she awakens at 3:00 A.M. in a cold sweat and nudges him hard with her elbow. "I swear, Greg, I'll kill myself if you leave me," she blurts out.

Greg stares at her, unbelieving. "What the hell are you talking about?"

"If you want out, tell me. I can take it."

"I'm not going anywhere, Arleen. It's the middle of the night, for God sakes! Are you losing your mind?"

"So that's it! I knew it! You think I'm crazy. I'm crazy and I'm not good enough for you."

"Oh, brother . . ."

"You're right, Greg. I'm *not* good enough. It'll always be that way."

"You need help. Shrink help. Big time."

"There, you see? Fuck you! There's nothing wrong with me!"

"Arleen, look! I know you're hauling around a lot of emotional baggage —"

"You're right. But, you know what, Greg? You're just not much help with it!"

"I'm going back to sleep."

"You never loved me. It was all a sham."

•   •   •

She can hear Eddie washing his hands in his private bathroom, and the splashing water reminds her instantly of the nightmare. It had come again the previous night, and she winces at the memory. When she was just a toddler, her family spent two weeks in July at Knox Lake, a small tributary of Lake Erie, lined on one side by housekeeping cabins and second-rate motels. In the afternoons she would go out on her yellow float, pushed along by her dad, a soft-spoken junior college English instructor. Soon, bobbing on the gentle lapping of the water and the hot summer sun, she would fall asleep—until a gleeful shout or a loud splash of another child would awaken her suddenly and she would realize her father had disappeared. She looked everywhere, but he was gone. She couldn't swim. He had abandoned her, and she had no way to get back to shore. "Daddy! Daddy!" In real life, she had worn her bright orange inflatable "wings," and her father monitored her from a wooden raft only a few yards away, but in her nightmare he was gone, leaving her alone, trapped in her terror.

Shuddering involuntarily, she goes to Red Oak's glass front door, flips over the "Open/Closed" sign, sets the hands on the "Back At" clock for 4:00, and pulls down the shade. As she turns the door latch, the bell tinkles again, this time instantly bringing her back to the old house in which she grew up, to the bell that her mother kept on her nightstand. Pale, sickly, constantly sedated, Mary rarely left her bedroom after Arleen's brother Gordon was born with cerebral palsy. Mary's postpartum grief had turned into severe depression, which was then compounded by headaches, backaches, and stomachaches. Arleen could not a recall a day when her mother did not rattle that little Christmas tree ornament—Arleen's signal to trudge upstairs with one pill or another or to call Dr. Schoenbrun. After months of phone calls, Arleen could detect the exasperation in Dr. Schoenbrun's voice, and she had become savvy enough about medication to understand that the doctor's multiplying prescriptions and increasing dosages were intended more to manage Mary's incessant pestering than her medical condition.

God, how she hated that bell! "Little Mother," the neighbors christened Arleen back then, and at first she enjoyed the title. Even though the chores were endless—changing Gordon's diapers, cleaning the house, cooking for her father—she relished the role, the feeling of being in charge. Over the years, however, responsibility had engendered resentment. From her dark upstairs lair Mary became more demanding, like a sick bear growling for her cub. Medicated, barely coherent, Mary would ask Arleen to lie with her in the bed and tell Arleen how special she was, how she was destined to achieve all the great things that Mary couldn't achieve because of her illness.

Soon her father began to spend more time away from home. One afternoon after school, while walking home to do more chores, she saw him on Folger Street, jumping into his car with a pretty, young coed.

Now Arleen pulls the cord on the old-style venetian blinds, cringing at the musty vinyl slats that no one bothers to clean anymore. It's all part of a script now, a script she knows by heart. As she walks past her desk to Eddie's office, he's back in his chair, already closing the newspaper, a wide-eyed grin starting to spread across his face. She grins back, knowing that in a few moments his smile would be gone, replaced by closed-eye moans of pleasure. When they first started up, he'd buy a bottle of Four Roses bourbon and they'd go to The Four Kings Motel on Jackson Street, a hovel if she'd ever seen one, with X-rated movies on a seventeen-inch tube and cheap plastic lamps chained to the walls. The springs in the king-size bed would squeak as Eddie grinded into her. At first the sleazy motel and the cheap booze added a kind of thrill to their clandestine meetings, and Eddie wanted to take her there almost every day. One afternoon, in his initial exuberance (or his mad rush of hormones, she wasn't sure which), he registered under his own name; Arleen flew into a rage, accusing him of trying to break up her marriage.

But after a few weeks the sex lost its urgency and Eddie would spend long hours telling her about his wife and kids, and she would start to feel a tenderness for him. It was obvious he was still in love with Doreen—no matter how much he denied it—just as she was in love with Greg. When it came right down to it, they had a great deal in common.

Now, with the local housing market severely depressed, he couldn't afford to take her to The Four Kings. Why spend forty dollars when they could do it in the office for free? As she shuts the door to Eddie's office, he is almost bursting with excitement. He enjoys oral sex more than anything, and so does she. She had learned long ago that a guy was like a car with a stick shift—pull it one way and he'd speed up, yank it another and he'd slow down, swirl her tongue in a certain way and he'd go into overdrive—her personal joystick. Men were such babies it was almost comical.

But today it is not the imminent sex that has him so excited. "Guess what?" he blurts, not waiting for Arleen to answer. "We're getting back together!"

At first Arleen is mystified; the sentence is not making a logical impression in her brain. "'We'?" she can only ask.

"Me and Doreen," he declares proudly. "She's willing to give it another shot."

"Oh," she says weakly. "Well, that's great, Eddie." Her emotions surge so quickly, like an unruly mob of commuters trying to crowd onto a subway car, she can't sort them out right away. Jealousy, anger, envy, loneliness all vie for entry. Confusion wins out: the only thing she can think of saying is, "Where does that leave *me*?" but she can't quite get the words out.

"Yup, we're back in business!"

Feeling tears well up behind her eyes, she turns away and is halfway out the door when she whirls around to face him. "You stupid sonofabitch!" she screams. "You tell me this sitting on your fucking throne, waiting for me to bow down on my hands and knees to suck you off! *What about us*?!"

Eddie is so stunned by her outburst, his chair is propelled backward as if by a gust of wind. "I thought we were just having some fun. That's what you always said, Arleen. There was never any 'us.' Just fun. And—and what about Greg?"

Even through her blinding rage, Arleen is fascinated by Eddie's feeble groping. She knows her ranting is over the top. Yet, she cannot, will not (she isn't sure which) stop it. Part of her has become detached, staring down at the scene from the ceiling and marveling at her power to frighten him.

A hesitant tapping on the door glass brings her back to earth. "I better get that," she says and rushes from his office. Despite the "Closed" sign on the door, a tall, thin guy stands outside, squinting through the venetian blinds. She unlocks the door and opens it. He is in his early thirties, his navy blue suit is expensive and nicely pressed, and a curly shock of black hair sits on his forehead that makes her think of Superman.

"Hi, yeah, well," he stammers shyly. "I wasn't sure if anyone was here."

"Oh, we're here, all right," she says through pursed lips, motioning him in. "We're *very* here."

"I was in the neighborhood and thinking of buying a house in town. I was thinking maybe on the north side."

"Well, you've come to the right place," she replies, perhaps a bit too brightly. "Make yourself at home." He sits in the chair next to her desk and she hands him one of Red Oak's Preliminary Info forms. "Just fill this out and one of our agents will be right with you."

"Jim Flaherty," he says.

"Arleen. Arleen Petersen."

As he pulls a pen from his breast pocket, she pokes through some files on her desk, pretending to be occupied. Her hands are shaking, she notices, and she takes a deep breath, hoping to quell the anxiety rising in her chest. She recognizes in the smile he volleys back to her, eyebrows raised, head nodding slowly, that he is silently acknowledging and returning her flirtation. She glances over at the moving pen of Jim Flaherty, Red Oak's newest client, to see if has checked the "Single" box.

Arleen's story is continued on page 133.

The Roots of Abandonment Fears

The desperate fear of abandonment, a core feature of BPD, impacts many other defining behaviors of the borderline. The dread of being alone interferes with the borderline's close relationships, disrupts identity formation, and precipitates severe mood swings, self-destructive behaviors, and outbursts of anger. Feelings of emptiness usually accompany the painful isolation.

Childhood Experiences

The borderline's terror of loneliness often stems from earliest experiences, which may be a landscape of confusing, contradictory road signs. As explained in our first book, the parent (most commonly the mother) of a borderline discourages normal separation and individuation by being too clinging (perhaps because of her *own* fear of abandonment), or too rejecting (perhaps because of her own fear of closeness), or sometimes both simultaneously. Arleen's parents were so self-absorbed, they could not recognize and attend to the needs of their daughter. Bedridden Mary, obsessed with her own maladies and the guilt of producing a palsied son, clung constantly to Arleen, transforming her from a daughter in need of her own nurturing into a mother who was forced to take care of her own mother. To compound the problem, after relentlessly criticizing Arleen's caretaking, Mary would rhapsodize about Arleen's "special destiny," which became to Arleen all the more unreachable the longer Arleen was "trapped" with Mary. And to make matters even worse, Arleen's father, to escape the family agony, virtually disappeared from the household, sparking Arleen's nightmares of abandonment that were more real than imaginary. The radical extremes promulgated during Arleen's development seriously distorted the process of forging her own identity.

Object Relations Theory

According to psychoanalytic and object relations theories, during ideal early development the child experiences consistent, nurturing parenting. He begins to internalize important images. Although Mother may not be in the room, the infant begins to perceive that she still exists and will come when he cries. Within the first $2^{1}/_{2}$ years of life, he develops trust in a world that is reliable and inchoately predictable. These stored reassurances allow the child to function more independently as he begins to develop a persona.

These theories suggest that the borderline frequently experiences a more chaotic upbringing. Trapped in a maze of inconsistent images, the borderline is unable to form a constant, predictable sense of self and the world; unlike the healthy child, the borderline is unable to establish a healthy object constancy—a reliable, comforting, internalized image of her world—that she can use to soothe herself in times of stress. Instead, she needs the presence of others to reassure and comfort her. (In her journal Arleen wrote, "I feel I really couldn't be myself without another person to reflect on.") Just as an infant, in the initial months of life, cannot differentiate between the mother's temporary absence and her extinction, so Arleen did not have the assurance that Greg would eventually return home when he worked late hours. Out of sight was truly out of mind—and out of existence. "When you're not here, when I can't see you," she confessed to Greg one night, "you don't exist."

Solitude became intolerable for Arleen—when the borderline is alone, continuity and connectedness cease. Like sand falling through her fingers, her confidence—even her sense of reality—slip away.

Symbols of Connection

Stuck in this illusory abandonment scenario, Arleen tries to "hold on" to her partner by wearing his sweatshirt, hoping to recapture his essence through the smell and feel of his clothes. This use of transitional objects, a common coping mechanism for borderlines, serves the same purpose as a favored doll or blanket does for a toddler—a way to maintain the connection with the mother. Typically, borderlines will pack a bounty of transitional objects—letters, snapshots, stuffed animals, and other reminders of home—when they travel or are hospitalized. In one study of psychiatric inpatients, more than 50 percent of patients who had anxiety-relieving transitional objects (usually stuffed animals or blankets) with them in their hospital rooms satisfied criteria for BPD, as opposed to less than 25 percent of those who did not bring these objects. One borderline patient would constantly call her therapist's office after hours—not to reach him in person but rather just to hear his voice on the answering machine; in this way she could feel attached without risking his exasperation over her dependency.

When Teddy Bears Don't Work

Transitional objects, however, have only so much utility for the borderline. Sometimes she may seek other avenues to feel connected to another. As Theresa Dunn discovered in *Looking for Mr. Goodbar,* the other avenues may include singles bars and other spots for forging instantaneous affairs, a sometimes dangerous pursuit that can have disastrous consequences (see chapter 5).

The Twin Terrors

As is the case with several symptoms of BPD, the borderline is the rope in a monstrous tug-of-war, stretched between two opposing fears—on one side the fear of abandonment, on the other the fear of engulfment. Just as she feels her identity evaporating when she "loses" her loved one, she also fears losing her sense of self when the loved one threatens to overwhelm or control her. The desire to merge, for the purpose of creating an identity, is juxtaposed with the fear of being swallowed up and losing the individuality that she sought so long to find in the first place. As desperately as Arleen wished Greg to hold her, she simultaneously needed to flee the suffocating restrictions she experienced when in his embrace.

Often, the result of this struggle is a series of frustrating romantic relationships—for both partners (see chapter 3). The more desperately the borderline tries to cling to the relationship, the more vulnerable she is to its eventual demise by suffocating her partner with demands. For the borderline, the dread of being alone is one of the most frightening experiences. Anticipating the end of a liaison, the borderline instinctively reaches out for the next, traversing relationships as if swinging, Tarzan-like, from vine to vine. Frightened by her fading relationship with Greg, Arleen embarks on an affair with her boss; later, sensing that this liaison, too, might be over, she is on the lookout for a new one. For Arleen, sexual intimacy is primarily a survival instinct, a way to preserve her identity when confronted with emptiness.

Instant Intimacy

This extreme bonding impulse often carries over into other relationships and friendships, even casual ones. "Can I come over for a minute?" can evolve into an all-night marathon. "Oh, just one more thing . . ." at the end of a phone call can turn into ten more things. A casual hug may be perceived as a passionate embrace. The borderline desperately and continuously seeks a new best friend or perfect lover. Exhibiting what the French philosopher Michel de Montaigne called "an insatiate thirst of enjoying a greedily desired object," the borderline endows each new friendship with the burden of a grand intensity that it cannot possibly support.

It is easy to see how the need for speed and instant gratification in modern-day society can reinforce these tendencies: the fastest way to lose weight is not dieting or exercising—it's liposuction! The most expeditious way to financial wealth is not working hard but day-trading in the stock market or winning the lottery! The typewriter was not efficient enough, so we invented the computer. But this year's computer is never fast enough, so we continually come up with faster and faster chips. Regular mail service was not fast enough, so we came up with express mail, which still is not fast enough, so along comes the fax machine and the Internet. Even dial-up modems are no longer fast enough for some people, so now we have digital cable and high-speed connections. Even though there are no computer chips or DSL lines for personal relationships (not yet, anyway), that does not stop the borderline from seeking a kind of high-speed connection or "instant intimacy" that rarely exists in the real world without time and effort.

Neurological Correlates

As discussed in chapter 1, certain biological peculiarities, such as serotonin dysfunction, have been associated with the general diagnosis of BPD. One recent study utilized PET scanning to demonstrate correlations between the *specific* BPD criterion of abandonment anxiety and cerebral blood flow. In this investigation, women with the BPD diagnosis exhibited alterations of blood flow in particular areas of the brain when exposed to memories of abandonment.

Relating to the Borderline's Abandonment Fears

If these conflicting fears and emotions are difficult for the borderline to handle, they are almost as difficult for those closest to him. Because the borderline splits his feelings into extremes of black and white, he experiences others as providing either exhilarating satisfaction or devastating frustration and rejection. Contending with a borderline's dependency needs requires navigating between the twin icebergs of being perceived as uncaring on one side and as trying to manipulate on the other.

Arleen's self-esteem is directly related to maintaining a relationship with a man who she feels desires her. She is valuable only if a man values her. And the only admissible evidence is wanting to be with her. Yet, for the borderline, there is no happy medium. The lover will either be perceived as being around too much and therefore controlling and manipulative, or he is experienced as not being involved enough and therefore uncaring and abandoning. She disdains him for being too easily controlled and is enraged if he tries to dominate her. Thus the borderline becomes threatened if she feels she is not in control of the relationship. Love and hate are inextricably bound. The lover entering the borderline's world may feel marooned between the devil and the deep blue sea.

It is important to understand that these abandonment fears cannot easily be more than temporarily assuaged. No matter how much reassurance and time are spent, an individual cannot independently exorcise the borderline's anxieties. Only as the borderline understands the insatiability of his own needs and is able, over time, to develop and accept his individuality and existential aloneness within healthy relationships, can the borderline overcome these fears.

Relating to the borderline requires an acceptance that whatever one does may result in his disappointment. Just as the borderline must learn to compromise his desire to achieve immediate intimacy, the partner must temper her own grandiosity and abandon the unrealistic hope that she can fashion an instant fix for his turmoil by attempting to satisfy all of his needs. This does not mean, however, that the relationship cannot be sustained. It is important to adhere to consistent limitations, while communicating your caring and your acceptance of his frustration with you. Encouraging personal transitional objects, such as pictures or possessions, can ease the borderline's loneliness. (See chapter 11 for a thorough discussion on communication.)

The most important parameter to embrace when living with or loving someone with the abandonment anxieties of BPD is *consistency*. It is better to be consistent than it is to be right! If you can bring some predictability to the often chaotic borderline universe, you are beginning to participate in his growth and maturation.

ACTION STEPS: *Dealing with Borderline Fears of Abandonment*

1. *Understand and accept borderline anxieties.* For the borderline, living a life apart from her *is* abandonment: a husband who works late at the office (like Greg), a girlfriend who spends time with other friends, a therapist who sees other patients, all may be perceived by the borderline as abandoning. Such feelings are real and must be acknowledged.

Trying to use logic to convince the borderline that you are not abandoning her is usually fruitless.

2. *Respect your own limitations.* While accepting the borderline's need for constant reassurance, don't totally abandon your own interests. Establish compromises between the borderline's needs and your own, and stick to them.

3. *Don't try to play doctor.* Interpreting behaviors in a clinical way may be perceived as controlling and can result in anger and greater defensiveness. During a conflict, never ask, "Did you take your medicine today?" This will only reinforce an insulting implication that the borderline is "crazy."

4. *Prepare the borderline for separation.* For many borderlines the future, particularly an unpleasant future event, does not appear on the radar screen. The hope is that what hasn't yet happened perhaps never will. However, ignoring it will only precipitate more severe hurt and anger when it occurs. Don't mention a weekend fishing trip with the guys two months in advance and then avoid discussion until the night before. Instead, remind her about it and propose some compensatory activity: "Don't forget, honey, next weekend I'll be out of town with the guys. I know I'm really going to miss you. Let's go out to a really nice restaurant and show this weekend." Though you may be trespassing into self-serving strategy with this kind of reminder, it is better than intentional silence or avoidance of the issue altogether. Similarly, the therapist needs to periodically remind her patient about her upcoming vacation.

5. *Utilize transitional objects.* "Something to remember me by"—a picture, an audiotape, an article of clothing, or any possession that links the borderline to another person of importance—can lessen the pain of separation.

6. *Be consistent.* Work for a compromise and stick to it. Ambivalence will only result in more pleading and conflicts later.

3

Unstable Interpersonal Relationships

Mastery of others is a strength;
mastery of yourself is true power.

—CHINESE PHILOSOPHER LAO-TZU, SIXTH CENTURY B.C.

"There are two kinds of women: high maintenance and
low maintenance."
"Which one am I?"
"You're the worst kind. You're high maintenance, but you think
you're low maintenance."

—NORA EPHRON, *When Harry Met Sally*

The life of the borderline is strained by a continuing pattern of chaotic relationships in all important areas—family, romance, marriage, work. The parent, lover, or colleague of a borderline can be a hero one day, a villain the next, resulting in an emotional roller-coaster ride for all concerned. In this chapter you'll learn about Patty and her succession of turbulent romantic involvements and marriages that ultimately threaten the safety of her own child. The subsequent discussion focuses on "splitting," a primary psychological mechanism involved in this "worship to washup" dynamic, the possible physiological roots of splitting, and how people close to the borderline can better deal with the constant upheavals that threaten the relationship.

PATTY: PART ONE

When Didi sees the backup on 405, she flirts for an instant with the idea of taking Sepulveda all the way to Van Nuys. A busy surface street that stretches forty miles from Palos Verdes to the Valley, Sepulveda would be no cakewalk either, but at least it *moved,* and in her current frayed condition she dreads sitting on a freeway, knowing that her mind will start to wander to her baby niece and she'll start imagining all sorts of horrible things: tiny Laurie being drowned or dropped on her head by a baby-sitter barely capable of making a phone call. How old *is* this baby-sitter, anyway, this Angela—maybe twelve, thirteen tops? She's barely out of diapers *herself!* How could Patty leave her baby with a girl this young?

At first Didi thought the call was from one of her own daughter's friends, which immediately put her on alert, seeing as Danielle's friends rarely spoke to Didi, much less called her at the office. "Yes, this is Didi Rollins," she had replied impatiently to the nervous preteen voice on the other end. "Who is this? Is something wrong with Danielle?"

"Danielle? Is the baby's name Danielle? Patty told me it was Laurie —"

"Baby? What baby? *Patty's* baby?"

The voice became even weaker and more hesitant. "Yes . . . Patty's baby . . . I don't know what to do. She keeps crying and crying . . . Patty gave me your number. . . . She said you'd know what to do if I had trouble . . ."

It all became clear. The confirmation of her worst premonition. She knew her sister would do something like this sooner or later but not *this* sooner. After reassuring the girl (her name turned out to be Angela, a seventh-grader who lived upstairs from Patty), and reassuring *herself* that Angela could handle the situation until she got there, Didi grabbed her briefcase and practically flew out the door of the Harrison & Lambert Law Offices, leaving her fellow attorneys' mouths agape. What else could she do? She made a mental note to call her boss later and explain the situation.

Resisting her freeway dread, Didi turns her Mustang onto the San Diego cloverleaf, praying that a nearby stall is causing the gridlock but recognizing that she will somehow have to find a way to tame her tension and imagination if it's jammed up all the way to Van Nuys. Sighing, she slips in her Alicia Keys CD and gropes in the glove compartment for her Salem Ultralights—her last vice. For the past six New Year's, she has given up one harmful substance after another: last year pizza and ice cream (and anything else edible with more than two hundred calories per serving), the year before liquor, the year before that . . . was that the "Year of No More Couch Potato"? The cigarettes are all she has left (even now she keeps her packs hidden in the car, reserved for occasions precisely like this one), and after next New Year's, a mere three months away, even the Ultralights will have to go.

She suddenly marvels at how *different* they are, she and her sister. While Didi seems dedicated to eliminating bad habits from her life at every turn, Patty is heading in the opposite direction, collecting bad habits like Beanie Babies. On the other hand, they've *always* been polar opposites, Didi reflects grimly. Growing up, Didi was the smart, stable, older sister; Patty the younger, prettier, flightier starlet, breaking into whimsical dances at the drop of an encouraging smile. Twenty years ago, when their mother died and their father fell into a severe depression, Didi would try to console him with the straight A's on her report cards; Patty would dance circles around him in her ballet slippers, as if he were a Maypole. At the time, Didi was so sure she was adopted, she went to the Los Angeles Hall of Records to check her birth certificate.

As her Mustang rolls slowly by the Santa Monica Freeway exit, she sees the sign for Olympic Boulevard, reminding her of the small stucco house—just two blocks off Olympic—where the family lived for a year when their father remarried. "Wanda the Witch," they called her. Wanda was a piece of work, all right, a dual personality if there ever was one, all smiles and sweetness when their father was around, all sneers and snipes when he wasn't. Listen to Wanda long enough and you had to believe that Didi and Patty were the Satan Sisters, conniving conspirators who were ruining Wanda's life and making their father sick. One by one, photos of their real mother disappeared from the house or were somehow broken and never replaced. In his decrepit condition, their father deferred all childrearing responsibility to Wanda, and Wanda never relinquished an opportunity to use discipline. The girls had only each other. They were twin Cinderellas battling the evil stepmother but with no fairy godmother in sight.

To Didi's astonishment, she spots a gap in traffic a hundred yards up the road and realizes that it's not a stall causing the gridlock but an accident and that once she passes it she will have smooth sailing to Van Nuys.

"What am I *turning into*?" she says out loud, scolding herself for the gratitude she is feeling about seeing an accident. Trying to blot out the guilt, she takes a drag on her Salem and turns up the volume on the stereo, listening to "Fallin'." Boy, if those lyrics didn't fit Patty to a tee! (Was her sister moonlighting as a songwriter?) Patty fell in and out of love about as often as most people changed their socks. When Patty was a teenager, Monday's new boyfriend, wonderful in every conceivable way, was a jerk by Friday—a boy not remotely worth a moment of her time or attention.

The same for other people and things in her life. Didi would be allowed to sit at the side of Princess Patty's throne, only to be discarded for no apparent reason for months on end, banished from the kingdom, as it were, until Patty decided to reinstate her. On a whim Patty had tried out for her high school field hockey team; when she shocked herself and everyone else by making it, she lived and breathed hockey—for a month. She was even voted team captain. By the third game of the season, however, she was completely bored with hockey and quit.

"You *can't* quit, Patty—you're the captain!" Didi had blurted out.

"Oh, yeah? Watch me. I *hate* hockey! It's a *stupid* game."

Driving slowly past the accident now, Didi spies the two cars in the far right lane, a large black Buick and a smaller red car, the two male drivers standing on the shoulder, pointing and arguing. She steps on the accelerator and the Mustang responds, catapulting her up the slight grade toward Westwood. It suddenly dawns on her that the sisters' entire lives are connected to this 405 freeway—first growing up in Santa Monica, then Didi graduating from UCLA and UCLA Law, then working in Inglewood, and living now in Hermosa Beach, just twenty miles south. And Patty's many marriages and affairs, of course, dotting the 405 corridor like land mines along the way.

Patty wanted to go to college as well—to study fashion design—and she could have done just that if not for Larry. They had gotten married right out of Santa Monica High, right around the time their father died. Both girls had taken the death hard, but by then Didi was deeply involved in college life and probably did not spend enough time trying to talk her sister out of marrying so early. At first Larry (like all of Patty's men) was perfect. A mechanic in his father's Honda dealership, Larry was not too bright (when she was angry, Patty would say that if Larry were any dumber, he would have to be watered twice a week), but he was sweet and caring and a good provider, and for a while the marriage was almost idyllic. Larry had never felt particularly attractive and was amazed that a vibrant, beautiful woman such as Patty could find him irresistible. At times she seemed to worship him. It was the *other* times that were difficult. But he persevered despite Patty's rages and criticisms—or, perhaps, *because of* her tantrums. Maybe he deserved her wrath. After all, no other woman as exciting as Patty would ever want him.

But then things fell apart—quickly. They fought, mainly about money. Larry did not make nearly enough of it, according to Patty; Patty spent way too much of it, according to Larry. For two months Didi got an earful on the phone virtually every night. Mel, Didi's husband, nicknamed Didi's upstairs extension "the Patty Gauge" because it was a barometer of Patty's mental state: long periods of silence meant Patty was okay; incessant calls signaled trouble and a lot of it.

One day, Patty just left him. Packed an overnight bag, moved into an Encino apartment complex, hired a local moving company to get her clothes and boom box, and that was that. She called Didi the next day, bursting with pride about her achievement. She had gotten married too young, she said, she needed to be on her own, Larry would never amount to anything. . . . They were so different, she and Larry, she *needed* things in her life, a better car, more clothes. All Larry needed was a box of wrenches and a TV set.

It didn't take Patty long to find a new husband. With her vibrant good looks and flirtatious nature, she had no problem lining up beaus, and a month after her divorce with Larry was finalized—and barely out of her teens—Patty was saying "I do" again, this time to a rising junior executive in a downtown ad agency. Ten years older than his newlywed, Jack Wheeler was slick, confident, and earned $100,000 a year.

But six months later, the Patty Gauge was climbing rapidly. Under all that self-assurance Jack was turning out to be a control freak, Patty complained. Sure, she could go out and get a new car—as long as Jack chose the make and model. Sure, she now had a closet full of new clothes, but most of them were conservative business outfits so she could show properly on Jack's arm at his many receptions and dinners. Why couldn't she go to Rodeo Drive and pick up some cool stuff that she *really* wanted?

They argued continually. He left, then came back. She left, then came back. Patty accepted and quit a number of meaningless part-time office jobs. She volunteered as an aide in several hospitals, though she was unable to stick to any of her jobs for more than a few weeks. She began to see a shrink in Beverly Hills and then another and another; none of them understood what she was going through. One afternoon, Patty appeared in front of Didi's desk at H & L to make an announcement: *she was pregnant!* Exuberantly, Patty reported that Jack was equally delighted with the news. Didi, as usual, was more pragmatic: How would a baby survive the unraveling lives of these two people?

At first, the pregnancy was as contentious as the rest of the marriage. After Patty's amnio revealed a girl on the way, Patty wanted the nursery covered in a flashy wallpaper she had seen in a designer home-furnishings catalog; Jack wanted the room painted in a subdued pink. Didi did notice, however, that after a while both soon-to-be parents were a bit more willing to compromise than before: Jack insisted that there would be no nanny or any other form of outside childcare for his new daughter—Patty would stay home as a full-time mom, a role that Patty seemed to look forward to. Didi tried to be optimistic about the family's chances.

But again, things just didn't work out for Patty. When Laurie showed up, a tiny package of wailing dependency that needed attention 24/7, it was as if a live hand grenade had been dropped in their midst, and neither new parent had a clue as to how to disarm it.

The Patty Gauge threatened to blow totally off the charts. Relying on Didi's experience with Danielle, Patty phoned hysterically at all times of the day and night. Didi felt like a pinball, caroming among the office, her own house, and Patty's. She was putting in more time as Laurie's mother than Patty was, and Mel was becoming perturbed.

One night, the trio was watching *Law and Order* when the show was interrupted by a news bulletin about a fire sweeping through a ramshackle welfare hotel in East L.A. The camera showed the agony of the victims moaning in pain with third-degree burns, and Patty gasped in horror. Didi and Mel had never seen Patty react with such intensity to a news story. Even major tragedies evoked only a blasé or flippant response, which annoyed Didi to no end. The World Trade Center, Patty once said, "ruined the skyline anyway." But watching these poor L.A. burn victims, Patty lost it completely, and when the report moved into a segment explaining that the mere touch of a nurse or the application of a bandage could cause a burn victim to wail with pain, Patty's tears really started flowing. "I'm just like them," she kept saying over and over. "That's what I feel like all the time."

Zipping along at eighty miles per hour, Didi passes the Wilshire exit and glances in the rearview, praying she would not see the revolving beacon of a Highway Patrol car. Off to the right, the glass skyscrapers along Wilshire glint in the late-afternoon sun, and she does not need to be reminded that the plush offices of Scott Powell, Patty's divorce lawyer and the primary cause of her sister's current problems, sit on the twentieth floor of one of them. Making his reputation in the 1980s during the proliferation of Hollywood palimony cases, Powell had all but disappeared from the headlines by the time Didi met him at a family law conference in San Francisco in 1999. A gentle, soft-spoken widower in his late fifties, with a mane of white hair that he kept tied in a ponytail, Powell was not at all the shark that Didi expected. After listening to his presentation "The Multifaceted Role of the Divorce Attorney in Family Law Practice," she went up to the podium and asked for his card. Six months later, when Patty needed a lawyer for her second divorce, Didi suggested Powell. The Rollins sisters were well rewarded: Patty gushed with excitement about Powell's understanding and compassion. He spent hours with her in his office, and when 5:00 P.M. rolled around, they continued discussing the case over dinner.

Didi should have seen it coming—especially after Patty's court filings revealed that she was relinquishing her right to alimony! Even though she had been married to Jack for only a few years, judges were typically willing to award some alimony in a case like this. (In exchange, Patty was asking for a run-down sailboat that was now languishing in Marina del Rey virtually unused and unmaintained—not nearly the value of several years' alimony payments.) What about Patty's wardrobe, her chance to shop on Rodeo? Had Patty's brain circuits finally blown a fuse? To make things even more obvious, Patty was not asking for sole custody of Laurie. Even though Patty—with her spotty work history and frequent visits to shrinks—would be lucky to be awarded sole custody, judges usually were willing to preserve a central childraising role for the mother in all but the most extreme cases. But Powell's documents requested a joint custody time-share in which Patty would have responsibility for Laurie less than half the time. Poor Laurie was being bandied about like a bargaining chip in a business deal.

It all added up to one conclusion: The "Scott-Patty" duo was much more than attorney-client. At long last Patty had found her sugar daddy. And this particular sugar daddy—kind, sweet, lonely himself, and head-over-heels for his young client's beauty and vitality—had no interest in being a daddy to a sixteen-month-old baby girl. Laurie had become the most recent in a long line of field hockey pucks in Patty's chaotic life.

Didi emerges from her reverie to discover she has gone up and over the San Fernando grade, winging downhill at ninety now, just a couple of exits from Patty's house. But it's too late—the dreaded light show in Didi's rearview is not her imagination. As she stubs out the cigarette butt smoldering in the ashtray and pulls over, she prepares her story. She is on her way to rescue her niece, she will say, so would the officer *please, please* give her an escort? As a lawyer, she knows the chances of a cop believing *that* story, but the truth in this case is her best strategy.

Patty's story continues on page 151.

The Procrustean Bed

Continuous entanglement in chaotic interpersonal relationships is one of the most distinguishing features of BPD. One study found that turbulent relationships and impulsivity were the two most discriminating criteria for defining BPD. In depressed borderlines, a disturbed relationship is the primary predictor of self-destructive behavior, such as suicide attempts and self-mutilation. Anger and paranoia are lesser risk factors.

The borderline molds his close relationships like Procrustes molded the lodgers to their beds in his roadside inn. A scoundrel of ancient Greek mythology, Procrustes would coax passing strangers into his lair by offering them a pleasant meal and a night's rest in his special bed, which could "magically" adjust its length to whoever lay down upon it—or so he told his unsuspecting guests. As soon as the poor fellow went to sleep, Procrustes (whose name literally means "he who stretches") went about his dastardly deeds, stretching him on the rack if he was too short for the bed, or chopping off his legs if he was too long. Similarly, the borderline tries to force his relationships into a Procrustean bed, eventually destroying most of them in the process.

A borderline's significant other is apt to feel like an *in*significant other much of the time. After a while he feels like he is in a perpetual "no win" wonderland in which every response is wrong. He may feel he is constantly waiting for the next shoe to drop. It is not uncommon to hear the partner of a borderline claim that his lover has been taken over by aliens—or the devil.

While the borderline caroms between smothering and rejecting his close relationships, he expects just the opposite treatment *from* them—stability and balance. Rejection or smothering is likely to be met with rage or depression from the borderline.

Splitting

The borderline tends either to idealize or denigrate features of the external world and imposes this kind of black-or-white perception on his relationships. These perceptual extremes roll like marbles along a constantly tilting tabletop, first to one side, then the other, but never coming to rest, never balancing in the middle. This "polar perception" utilized by borderlines in relationships is called *splitting,* a coping mechanism that is normally expressed among eighteen-to-thirty-six-month-old infants and toddlers. Because babies at this age do not easily tolerate ambivalence or ambiguity, they split the world into all-good and all-bad compartments. When the mothering figure satisfies the child's basic needs, she is seen as all-good. When she frustrates these needs or is unavailable, the child transforms her into an all-bad persona. Only as the child develops can he integrate these opposing perceptions. Eventually he learns that someone he loves and admires can still disappoint or frustrate without transforming him or her into a hero or a villain. Heroes can be accepted with flaws. Villains can be perceived as having some worthwhile qualities.

The borderline, however, remains stuck in this childlike black-and-white topography because it protects her from the anxiety that accompanies attempts to reconcile contradictory feelings. Larry, Patty's first husband, was "perfect" for a short time—a pattern of temporary idealization that Patty had followed for years with her other boyfriends. Yet a borderline's idealization, or more closely *idolization,* can turn dramatically to exactly the opposite—disparagement and ultimately banishment—when she uncovers flaws in her mate and he loses the patina of perfection. Similarly, she may abruptly vilify the relationship if she senses that he is becoming dissatisfied with her, for the dissatisfaction can lead to abandonment, which, for the borderline, is intolerable.

"At the outset of close relationships, [Princess] Diana usually screened out negative characteristics in the other person," writes Sally Bedell Smith in *Diana in Search of Herself*. "But, inevitably, the object of her affection would let her down, perhaps by failing to praise her enough. Then she would see only the worst in that person. Virtually everyone was destined to fail her, because Diana couldn't accept the fact that every relationship has its ups and downs."

Ricocheting like a pinball from one extreme to the other often characterizes other aspects of the borderline's life. One month Patty was immersed in all the possibilities of excelling on her high school field hockey team; the next month she dismissed the sport as totally worthless. To some, these oscillations may seem like pure whimsy, or the height of fickleness, or even a way to rationalize a "fear of failure." But other issues may animate this behavior. The fear of failure is certainly real, of course, but with failure might come rejection, which is even more frightening. For Patty, the lure of succeeding on her hockey team is also the lure of *belonging,* of being accepted by her teammates, coaches, and classmates; if she fails, she may be exiled by those from whom she most wants acceptance.

The All-Consuming "Now"

For those not afflicted with BPD, this apparent flitting from one partner or activity to another might be the most difficult borderline trait to understand and tolerate, much less sympathize with, for it can easily be perceived as weakness or an inability to persevere—indeed, as abandonment in its own right! The first instinct of a boyfriend, girlfriend, or close relation, like Patty's sister, Didi, is to exclaim, "Can't you try to work it out? Surely there must be a middle ground." If it's an endeavor—a sport, job, or career—we feel like saying (or screaming), "Well, for God sakes, try harder! You wanted it so much *before*—why are you giving up *now*?!"

What Didi doesn't realize is that, for those with BPD, there is no middle ground, no room for compromise. Because the borderline's perceptual balance is always moving from one extreme to another, to expect stick-to-itiveness is to expect too much, for perseverance presupposes a significant level of past achievement: for the borderline there is no past, only the *now,* and a now that happens to include failure can erase even the most success-filled past in an instant. The borderline personality is not only an "emotional hemophiliac" but also in some ways an "emotional amnesiac." To get a feeling for the impact of emotional amnesia, imagine how your own workplace morale would suffer if you had no history of achievement on which to rely. Or how your motivation to "work things out" with your spouse might wane if you had no memories of the fun times in your lives together. The borderline often feels caught in a "Groudhog Day" kind of world, in which each morning she must awaken and start all over again—not only to prove once more her own worth and abilities to herself and others but also to recalibrate the value of those around her.

In a way, BPD is a kind of *sustained* attention deficit, where memory is lost not for the recent activity but for feelings and experiences from the distant past. Actually, there are many similarities between borderline personality disorder and attention-deficit hyperactivity disorder. Adult BPD is frequently associated with a history of childhood ADHD symptoms. Both are characterized by moodiness, irritability, impulsivity, unstable relationships, and a poor self-image. Frequently, compulsive, self-destructive behaviors are expressed, and drug or alcohol abuse also are common in both.

Splitting and Brain Physiology

Recent advances in brain research suggest a possible physiological basis for the borderline's abnormal retention of the splitting mechanism. Development of the brain begins at the fetal stage and continues through early adulthood. Connections between the brain's limbic system (where emotion and instinctive behaviors are believed to derive) and the prefrontal cortex (the front part of the brain) continue to mature through adolescence. However, substantial physical or emotional stress can interfere with natural brain cell development during this time by disrupting the brain's neurotransmitters—brain chemicals that facilitate the transmission of messages between connecting brain cells. Subtle abnormalities in electroencephalograms (EEGs), computed tomograms (CT), and magnetic resonance imaging (MRI) scans, and in neurological testing have been documented in borderline patients who have suffered emotional or physical trauma in childhood.

There also may be anatomical correlates with splitting: The brain is divided into right and left hemispheres, which are connected by a midline structure called the corpus callosum. Nerves connecting the two sides of the brain intersect at this structure. Further, it has been demonstrated that the two hemispheres serve somewhat different functions. Emotions, particularly negative emotions, are associated more with the right hemisphere. Logical cognitions and positive emotions may predominate on the left side of the brain. Under ideal circumstances, both hemispheres balance each other. However, when a stroke or other neurological injury occurs in one hemisphere, an asymmetry between emotional expression and self-control often develops. Perhaps stress in the borderline disrupts the laying down of the brain cable that connects and balances the two hemispheres. If so, it is possible that negative experiences are shuttled to the right hemisphere, where they are quarantined. Positive perceptions may be billeted on the left. The usual communication channels between hemispheres remain underdeveloped. In this model, it is proposed that stress disrupts normal brain development, especially the connections between the two parts of the brain, resulting literally in a partitioned brain. It is also conceivable, of course, that *congenital* malformation produces the developmental disconnection, producing a subtly handicapped child whose compromised coping skills frustrate caregivers. When parents are unable to soothe a perpetually crying infant or to calm a continuously volatile child, they may feel inadequate and thus be more prone to be abusive. In this paradigm, the childhood trauma is the result rather than the cause of the congenitally determined BPD elaboration.

Does psychological stress cause neurological dysfunction, which causes splitting, which heralds the development of BPD? Or does genetic predisposition cause the neurological abnormality, which defines splitting, which disrupts family relationships, which results in BPD? This is another "chicken or egg" question for which, at present, there is no definitive answer. Perhaps both pathways exist. In any event, borderline splitting may indeed be the result of literally perceiving the world with two disconnected brains.

Sex and the Pity

Patty's attachment to a succession of men is typical of borderline functioning. Impaired self-esteem and defective self-image left her with the perpetual feeling that "something is missing." (At one point, Patty confessed to Larry, "There's a hole inside of me that I cannot fill.") So she frequently turned to lovers in an attempt to fill this emotional void. However, after the initial idealization of her lovers inevitably swung to disappointment, the entire relationship was then contaminated and had to be discarded.

This process is painful for both the borderline and his partner. The borderline must now again deal with the omnipresent void, and the partner is whipsawed from worshipful attentiveness to sudden rejection. Such relationships are loud and dramatic. Borderline emotions flood and overflow the banks of reason, leaving both exhausted, much like George and Martha at the end of Edward Albee's *Who's Afraid of Virginia Woolf?* However, unlike that couple, whose connection was based on (perhaps even thrived on) the combat of intellectual equals and who would, presumably, return to fight another day, many couples mired in BPD are unable to sustain the relationship. Typically, the borderline seeks partners who are in a position of power. The most common scenario involves the younger, attractive, borderline woman and the older, narcissistic man: the secretary embarks on an affair with her older, married boss; a student becomes involved with her professor; a patient with her doctor; and so on. Aching to fill the emotional "hole" of self-doubt and insecurity, she attaches to someone who—on the surface, anyway—appears self-assured and powerful. The male, attracted to his young partner's idolization and deference, assumes the mantle of mentor, hoping to mold the woman into his ideal, like Henry Higgins and Eliza Dolittle in George Bernard Shaw's *Pygmalion*. In Patty's case, her second husband, Jack Wheeler, the slick, confident ad executive ten years her senior, saw Patty as unsculpted clay that he could mold into a Barbie doll for his career needs. Later, Scott Powell, her divorce attorney, fulfilled the same Henry Higgins role.

Not surprisingly, such relationships almost always end unhappily. As the borderline begins to recognize the flaws in her savior, she becomes disappointed and frightened, the hope of salvation from a lifetime of self-doubt suddenly lost. Disappointment and fear eventually mutate into rage at this imperfect person who has failed her. Whereas once Patty had sought Jack's protection, she later bristled at his "control." From the partner's perspective, the worshipful woman who had once dedicated herself to stoking his ego morphs unexpectedly into an angry, criticizing harridan who now resents his guidance.

Psychiatric patients with BPD are the most likely to report affairs with their doctors. Such patients frequently seek medical attention and often appeal to some doctors' needs to feel appreciated and valued. Borderline patients in intensive psychotherapy may be frustrated in their attempts to achieve greater intimacy with their therapist and act out this anger through destructive relationships with inappropriate partners. In such situations, borderlines may seek hurtful relationships to punish themselves and others. For example, the borderline adolescent may cling to an abusive or otherwise undesirable boyfriend not only to soothe her internal emptiness but also to punish her parents, who oppose the union. Or she may stay with a boyfriend who has many problems of his own, who obviously needs *her* and thus is not a threat to abandon her. Simultaneously, she might rage at her parents, whom she sees as overly controlling (although, paradoxically, her outrageous behavior may be unconsciously begging for direction and control). Thus she flaunts a kind of "pseudo-independence": She has convinced herself that she is choosing the relationship independently, on her own volition, but she is in fact *re*acting to her parents' disapproval. Ultimately, the threat of her boyfriend's inevitable mistreatment serves as exculpation of her unconscious guilt at defying her parents.

Tea and Empathy

Borderlines are exquisitely sensitive to others' plights. Many work in the helping professions as doctors, nurses, counselors, etc., as Patty worked for a time as a volunteer aide in several hospitals. Similarly, Princess Diana was well known for her tireless charitable efforts, which revolved mostly around health care, especially for children, including AIDS and cancer. Ultimately she was a patron of more than a hundred charities. This sensitivity, coupled with the need to be connected to other people, may accelerate the progress of a romantic or sexual relationship as the borderline seeks a kind of "instant intimacy." Once disappointment sets in, the dissolution of the relationship may proceed as rapidly as did the intimacy. Ironically, despite their sensitivity to others, borderlines may be less connected to their own feelings. Additionally, when they are hurt, their rage at those who have hurt them may be intense and cruel and devoid of concern or understanding for the other party. The borderline is capable of great sympathy and comforting but often may lack true empathy, the ability to put himself in the other person's shoes, in appreciating how others are impacted by his behavior.

The Borderline Relationship

A relationship with someone with BPD requires patience and understanding. The borderline's attractive qualities are typically evident, sometimes even striking, but the contradictions that define the borderline world must be understood. Borderline ambivalence is typified by fears of suffocation if another person gets too close, alternating with terror of abandonment if he strays too far. Thus a "damned if you do, and damned if you don't" situation emerges. Sometimes there is no "right" response to a borderline statement or question:

> BORDERLINE: "Do you love me more now than you did before?"
>
> PARTNER: "Of course."
>
> BORDERLINE: "Then you didn't love me before, did you?"

If the partner replies "No" to the first question, the borderline's reaction is likely to be: "Don't you love me anymore?"

The borderline will set up this kind of catch-22 as a subconscious protective preparation for disappointment. Because many borderlines are convinced that the realization of their greatest fear—abandonment—is inevitable, there is a kind of "hurry up and get it over with," waiting-for-the-other-shoe-to-drop anticipation, which can be maddening. Thus the borderline may aggressively probe for problems in the relationship. Such challenges also seek insatiable reassurance that the relationship can indeed be viable.

Needless to say, maintaining a relationship with someone with BPD can be challenging. Understanding this "no win" paradox is essential. Convincing the borderline that you are unconditionally accepting (since virtually no one else in his life has been) is almost impossible. Demonstrations will never be enough. So don't try. Giving advice, even—or, particularly—when solicited, is fraught with peril. In such situations it is usually better to help him understand and accept that he may be frustrated at *anything* you might say. You may be able to "walk him through" how he might respond to any potential response:

> BORDERLINE: *"Do you love me more now than you did before?"*

PARTNER: "Now, dear, you know I have loved you since we met and will always love you. But I think if I answer "Yes," you might get mad and think I didn't love you before, which isn't true. And if I answer "No," then you might think my love for you has diminished, which it hasn't. So I think I'd better be really careful here!"

An exchange like this is apt to elicit lighthearted laughter, which is the best outcome to be hoped for with a loaded question such as this.

Trust and intimacy are some of the most precious treasures of being human. Achieving stable relationships is difficult for all of us. For the borderline and his partner it requires much more work and endurance, since past pain must be assuaged and replaced with healthy associations. Both partners, however, can take heart in knowing it is attainable.

ACTION STEPS: *Dealing with Intense Relationships*

1. *Don't try to win the "no win." Instead, just "hang in."* The "damned if you do, and damned if you don't" dilemma haunts many borderline relationships. Beware of giving opinions, especially during times of conflict, because there may be no right answer. Instead, it is better to defer to the borderline for his opinion.

   Another technique is to explicate the "no win" flavor of the situation: "I know if I leave now, as you're demanding I do, you're just going to follow through on your threat to get drunk. But if I leave and you hurt yourself, you'll question my caring for you by allowing this to happen. And I know that if I stay, you'll be mad at me for not respecting your wishes. Since I think you'll be upset with me either way, I'm going to do what I think is best for you and stay here, so you won't be able to be as self-destructive."

   The therapist also must cope with vacillating demands. The borderline patient is constantly hiring and firing his doctor. (One psychiatrist's secretary quickly learned which patients were borderline by how often they made, canceled, and rescheduled appointments. She knew to make their appointments in the scheduling book with a pencil!) Hanging in with the borderline is the most therapeutic behavior a friend, lover, or therapist can show. Demonstrating unflagging constancy—no matter what—is the most important message to convey. The borderline often feels worthless and expects to be abandoned. Trust is a precious commodity. Much more valuable than what is said is the reassurance that you are going to be there.

2. *Predict the unpredictable.* The world of the borderline is immersed in confusion and impenetrability. As confusing as the behavior can be for significant others, it can be even more distressing for the borderline himself. Although reactions may not be easily foreseen by the borderline, they may be easily predicted by another. Predicting behaviors may better prepare all parties for upcoming events. It also demonstrates that what may seem chaotic to the borderline is not inscrutable to those around him. Finally (and ironically), predicting may discourage him from acting out in the way you predicted, just to show you:

"Dear, I know you said it didn't bother you that much if I go out with my girlfriends next weekend, but I suspect it bothers you more than you feel right now. I'm afraid that what may happen is what happened last year—that by around Wednesday or Thursday we may start to be more irritable with each other and pick fights, and your migraines might get worse from all the tension, so that by Saturday morning you'll be furious with me for all sorts of reasons, including leaving you with a bad migraine. Let's try to be prepared and not let that happen again this year."

3. *Detach occasionally.* At times, when his rages seem eternal and overwhelming, you simply need to *let go*—from your partner and the relationship. When the going gets tough, the tough must sometimes *just go.* No one should have to endure a continually abusive relationship. Take some time for yourself. Go out with friends and/or engage in activities or pursuits completely unrelated to your partner. You cannot be everything to him all the time; it's not only impossible, it wouldn't work even if it *were* possible: He may experience your constant attentiveness as controlling, even smothering, which will eventually lead to more anger and turbulence in your relationship. Always explain your behavior. Pulling back without explanation will be seen as abandonment. Reassure him of your *unconditional* commitment to him and to the relationship and remind him of your own need for space.

Despite the romance implicit in the concept, two lovers cannot exist in a "world apart." Just as you cannot be everything to him, the reverse is also true. You will find that your borderline partner can learn to live with—even appreciate—temporary detachment and that detachment does not mean divorce or a breakup. The time out might even result in a new perspective for both of you.

4. *Examine your own actions and motivations.* Support, but don't collude. You can be supportive without joining in a mutual denial of reality. Avoiding confrontation or anger by validating unrealistic views will only postpone conflict and sustain unrealistic perceptions (a pattern of behavior sometimes referred to as "codependency"). Empathizing with a disappointing situation is more helpful than blaming others. Denying your own feelings to "keep the peace" will eventually frustrate both of you. (The husband of a borderline woman once remarked that his tongue was bloody from biting it so often!)

Many partners of borderlines and even some therapists either arrive with or adopt a "savior complex." Don't fall into this trap. You can spend twenty-four hours a day feeling her pain and trying to solve problems for her, without any change. By trying to become her hero, you may only succeed in becoming her goat, resulting in frustration for both of you. Examine your need to be a "hero," which may more accurately reflect your own needs than hers. *You are with this person to love and help her, not to rescue her.* Miracles are part of God's repertoire; do not persuade yourself that you can pull off a burning bush. You did not create her BPD, and you or your love alone will not be able to cure it. Only the borderline herself can do that and usually with the aid of a mental health professional. But only when she is ready; constant prodding to seek professional help will often have the opposite effect.

Be sure to take care of yourself. After weeks of trying to cope, are you drinking too much? Eating too much? After achieving little or no success in changing your partner or your relationship, are you feeling inadequate? Examine the changes in your own psyche and adjust accordingly. (Professional counseling might now be in order for you as well as your partner.)

The emotional roller coaster you've been riding may be affecting you in more insidious ways. Episodes of anger and clinging, anticipation of the next outburst, the amount of time spent on constant "borderline vigil" can cause over time unconscious resentment, even among the most saintly of souls. Make sure you don't become a second victim.

From time to time, examine your own feelings for evidence of resentment and other negative reactions that may be making your relationship even worse.

5. *Challenge unrealistic characterizations only when they are negative.* In psychoanalysis, trainees are often advised not to oppose the patient's early idealization of the therapist. Only when it turns negative and threatens the therapy is confrontation sometimes necessary. Likewise, when the borderline idealizes a relationship, trying to respond with an "Aw, shucks—I'm really not that great" reply may precipitate frustration. Although unrealistic idealization should not be fostered (for the ultimate fall will be that much more disastrous), it need not be contradicted.

In personal relationships when the inevitable devaluation occurs, reality reminders that emphasize the difference between feelings and actuality should be proffered:

"Honey, I know you *feel* like I'm never home and don't want to spend time with you and the kids, but please don't forget that the special evening meeting the boss called was last Tuesday, and I've been home for supper every evening since. I know it *feels* like I'm gone a lot, but I really am home—and want to be home—with the family as much as I can."

6. *Learn how to effectively communicate with the borderline.* In chapter 11 we describe the SET system of communication, which is designed as a template model to aid in dealing with borderline dilemmas. This system proposes balancing all interactions with statements endorsing personal *S*upport and *E*mpathic acknowledgment of the person's stress with *T*ruthful confrontations of realistic issues.

4

Identity Disturbance

Sow an action, reap a habit;
Sow a habit, reap a character;
Sow a character, reap a destiny.

—WILLIAM JAMES

L ike Bobby, whom you will meet in this chapter, most borderlines never develop a separate sense of self. Only who he is, or what he does, *today* determines his worth, with little regard to past achievements or failures. He has no history on which to draw, no laurels on which to rest. The borderline is burdened with a constant sense of "faking it," and with the constant terror of sooner or later being "found out." This lingering sense of inauthenticity probably originates in childhood, when the "pre-borderline" is discouraged from maturing and separating from an overbearing parent, or when, at the other extreme, he is forced prematurely to adopt an adult's role (for example, to parent his own parents). After hearing Bobby's story (in his own words), you'll learn about Erikson's and Kernberg's work on identity diffusion, categories of identity problems, and techniques the borderline can utilize to help establish and maintain a sense of self.

BOBBY: PART ONE

Doc, you probably want to hear how awful my mom and dad were. That's what you shrinks like to do, isn't it—blame everything I do on my parents and how I was raised? Well, actually they weren't that bad. It's true I have a lot of emotional baggage, but it's mostly carry-on. Dad worked hard. Mom was home with me and Julie. Julie was the apple of her eye, my mom's pet. But that was okay. I really didn't mind that much. My sister was beautiful. A lot changed when she got sick. She had some kind of lymphoma. She went through all sorts of damn treatments, which, of course, only made her sicker. Yet through it all, she kept this calm, angelic smile.

I remember when Julie was dying, Mom was holding her in the hospital bed and I just stood there in the corner, afraid to get too close, afraid she would somehow infect me. She lay there, stroking my mom's hair, telling her not to worry, she would be okay. The poor kid was suffering so, but there she was—spending her dying energies trying to comfort *us*.

I guess that all affected me. I mean, I cried some, but I couldn't come close to my mom's wailing. I remember missing Julie and wishing she'd come back to play with me. But after a while I wasn't bothered that much. I knew I should have felt bad, but I didn't. After a while I just felt guilty because I didn't feel bad. Mom drank a lot after she died, and I had to take care of her sometimes, especially when a hangover kept her in bed all day. She and Dad argued more, but then it was like they'd look at me and figure, Oh, God, we still have to take care of *him!*

It was a pretty confusing time. Along with her booze, I became mother's little helper. After she and Dad would fight, I was assigned to comfort her. They both expected it. Dad would storm out and knew that by the time he returned, I'd quiet her down. I would explain Dad's argument to her a lot better than he did, and she became less hostile. Then I would sit Dad down and explain how he shouldn't go running out like that, hurting Mom's feelings and all. I remember him looking down as I talked, ashamed, like a chastised little boy.

The worst part of it was that they used my sister as the final wound. Each would blame the other for doing something or not doing something that might have made Julie better. I hated them using her memory like that. But she remained a ghost in our house the whole time I was growing up. Their fights were really stupid, too. It was like, I was the parent, and they were the kids! I had to miss school a few times, since I'd been up all night with the two of them, negotiating a new peace settlement. In some ways I had to grow up too fast. But in other ways I didn't get to grow up at all. I remember not going to the big dance in eighth grade because Dad, who was supposed to drive, stormed off again, and Mom was too plastered to get out of bed. I missed a lot of school things that way. Mostly they just yelled, then cried, and talked about Julie. Didn't they know I missed her, too?

•   •   •

I was pretty good in school. Mostly A's. I really didn't have to study that hard. Most of it came easy. The teachers told my parents I was gifted. What crap! I was just faking it, couldn't they see that? If you put on the old charm and make a teacher like you, it was easy to get a good grade. I guess I deserved something for the acting job, like an Oscar, but not the honor roll.

They tried to put me on an honors track, but I nipped that pretty quick. I didn't want to leave my friends, so I just screwed up some tests and acted up in class. They sent me back to regular classes pronto.

Anyway, when I started screwing around, that's when they sent me to my first shrink. Doc, you would've loved this guy. Very serious dude. He'd look at you with this stern frown. Then he'd get down on the floor with me and try to get me to play some games, which I thought was stupid and wouldn't do. So then he'd sit me up in a chair and talk to me, which I thought was also pretty stupid. Once I overheard my parents arguing over the therapy and how much it was costing, which really made me feel guilty. So I tried to take it more seriously, but I still didn't know what he wanted me to say.

•   •   •

In high school I hung out with the wrong crowd for a while. Actually, I hung out with a *lot* of different wrong crowds. One group, I guess people would call them "slackers," we started to smoke pot and cut classes. We'd go to this kid's basement and get stoned and listen to CDs all afternoon. It was fun for a while. But later on I felt it was all catching up with me. I knew I was destined to fail, so I figured, hurry up and get it over with already. I could always fake school, so actually I continued to do okay there. But I felt like a loser, so I hung out with losers.

It was like I was leading a double—no, triple—life. My teachers saw me as this brilliant, shy kid who didn't say much but gave great papers, man. When my English teacher learned they found pot in my locker and expelled me, she completely freaked! To my slacker friends I was kind of crazy, willing to do anything. I kept some straight friends to study and go to movies with, and I was pretty quiet around them. With my folks, I was like the referee in their World Wrestling Federation gig. It would get weird when the streams would cross. Once we were going to a grunge concert, all dressed up in black—you know, Goth? And I saw one of the straight girls from school, who I'd talk to every once in a while and even did a decorations committee with for some school dance. She did a kind of surprise double-take spasm. My friends just laughed, but, man, I was really uncomfortable. It was hard enough playing these different roles. I hated to be caught without my costume.

• • •

It was getting real tiring playing Mr. United Nations at home. So one day I just said to hell with it and started hanging out in my room, you know, the whole slamming doors, I didn't ask to be born, you don't understand me adolescent production. After a while they didn't even bother to try to talk to me. I can just imagine what they must've thought. Actually, I can't. Here I was, this angry, hostile dude, going off to school in my khakis and polo shirts—hell, I even went to the prom one year! Then coming home and changing into my Marilyn Manson threads and running out the door with an entirely different set of friends to some bangers concert.

So they sent me to another shrink. A sweet little old lady with this high-pitched, singsongy voice, which drove me nuts. And she had this way of talking, like if I cursed or acted up or something, she'd say, "You're behavior is *inappropriate.*" After a while I got so pissed off, I'd curse on purpose, you know, as a goof, just to hear her say "inappropriate." And then she'd say "okay" at the end of every sentence: "Let's talk about your parents, *okay*?" Like she was pretending that she needed to get my *agreement* on everything. "I'd like you to try some medicine, *okay*?" "It's time to end now, *okay*?" "I have to go take a crap, *okay*?" I begged my parents to let me stop seeing her, and they agreed, since by that time I had stopped hanging with the druggies and was spending more time with the smart geeks, which everyone agreed confirmed my progress. I was turning really *appropriate*!

• • •

Nothing ever felt right to me, you know what I mean, Doc? If I didn't get what I strived for, it was bad luck. If I *did* get what I worked for, I felt like I was just *fooling* everyone, and they would find me out sooner or later.

That's always been my biggest fear: that they would find me out someday. I could fake "smart" for my teachers, and "sincere" for my parents, and "interested" for my friends. But when it was two o'clock in the morning, all alone, in the dark, I wasn't sure who I needed to be, for me, I mean—who I really was. And in the meantime, I was always running scared, one step ahead of whomever I was trying to impress. I was sure that Toto would snatch the curtain, like in *The Wizard of Oz,* and expose me for who I am—whoever the hell that is supposed to be! It's like those TV shows about undercover agents; that's what I felt like—an undercover agent. It was just a matter of time until I blew my cover and the bad guys had me shot.

●　●　●

You still with me, Doc, or have I put you to sleep yet with my whining? Well, hang on, there's plenty more. So I graduate from high school and go away to college. When it comes to applying to big-name colleges, being from Birmingham, Alabama, has its benefits; they're curious to see what a southern hick looks like. I think they have a quota of so many hicks they have to accept every year, like blacks and lesbian trombonists. So I had no problem getting into a few big-name schools—Boston U, NYU, and Rutgers. I wanted to get as far away from home as possible. I probably would've applied to the University of Alaska at Anchorage, but I don't like cold all that much. So I wound up going to BU. Did you know that Boston has more colleges for a city of its size than anywhere else? It seemed that everyone there was going to college. And what a range of people! You had your Harvard snobs, the MIT geeks, the Tufts wanna-be Harvard dudes, the townie girls at BU and BC, scouting for Harvard husbands. No matter who you were, there was a niche out there in Boston somewhere for you, ready to swallow you up. It was liberating to go from an environment of wondering how to fit in, to a place where you had to fit in *somewhere.*

My folks thought that after college I should go to law school, so I toyed with that idea for a while. But I just couldn't see arguing passionately for some cause that I didn't believe in. I probably could argue either side and be damned convincing! But I'd never know for sure which side I was really on.

Like I say, I change my scenes often. First I joined a fraternity and did the weekend party boy shtick for a semester. Second term I went inactive and hung with the political crowd, a group called Committee Against

Organizational Stupidity, or CAOS, as we called it. We protested animal cruelty, ozone depletion, cafeteria food. You name it, we marched for it. Or against it, as the case might be. It wasn't hard to pick a target—there were so many to choose from. If somebody was hurting somebody else, we'd picket them. Pretty soon that got old, and I kind of dropped out of everything.

•   •   •

My social proclivities seemed to follow along with my changing political tastes. When I was dancing the fraternity fandango at Omega Chi, I dated Erica, a cute blond sorority girl. Then during the CAOS days came Jody, who was kind of bedraggled, not nearly as polished or as pretty as Erica but a helluva lot smarter. Then nobody. And then after nobody, I became aware that I was attracted to certain guys. I had this disastrous fling with Antonio. I don't know if I was a romantic or an idiot, but he was so kind and gentle and sweet—until he turned mean and ugly. Since then, I think the gender almost doesn't matter, if I find the person attractive. I don't know if that makes me gay or bi or tri or what.

•   •   •

My major? Make that plural, Doc. General studies, communications, psychology—let's see, I'm probably forgetting a few. But isn't that the idea—to become a well-rounded citizen of the community? As soon as I got bored with one, I'd hop on a different bandwagon. Actually, I took whatever means of transportation that would keep me from committing to a career. I just didn't know what I wanted to do. When I ran out of majors, I switched schools. My parents thought I would do better closer to home, and frankly, I thought maybe I was a little homesick. So, in the middle of junior year, I transferred back home, to the University of Alabama at Birmingham—sort of my junior year not abroad. Some credits didn't transfer, so I was now even farther from graduating, which, thankfully, seemed a long way off. But then I had a new dilemma: After a few years of disguising my southern accent, I now had to bring it back for the locals. I discovered I was, in fact, multilingual—I could speak Brahmin New Englandese for my Boston friends and Good Ole Boy for the Alabama townies. I had to be careful, though, that I didn't change in midsentence, as I sometimes did in Boston. My friends would laugh at me. "There he goes again. Old Bobby is pulling his humble, country cousin routine."

Well, it took me $5^1/_2$ years, but I finally got a degree—in sociology, I think. After that, Every Good Boy Goes to Work, as they say. I lived at home while I searched for a job. I started off doing temp work. Then I caught on as a teller at a bank. They liked me there. I made a good appearance and learned the routine quickly. But, like always, it didn't feel like me. I would stare at my nameplate on the counter, wondering, Is that really me there? Or am I just faking it again? And I was never good enough. If my boss criticized me for doing something wrong, I couldn't stand it. Like one time, after I'd been there a few months, I gave a customer $100 too much cash back and we didn't balance at the end of the day. My boss, a young guy like me, tried to be nice about it, but I could see in his eyes he thought I was an imbecile. And that's pretty much the story of my life. One day I'm a genius, the next I'm a moron. I wish I had some continuity in my life. My old girlfriend who I told you about, Jody, she told me once I'm like an amnesiac, I don't have any history, I don't give myself any *credit* for a history, for anything *good* I've done. I start every day without any context, like it's The First Day of the Rest of My Life. Is everyone like me, Doc? Are they just acting like I am, or are they really confident? What's wrong with me?

Maybe I'm too much of a perfectionist. That's what my dad told me once after I went on a crash diet. I was self-conscious about my weight and vowed that I'd lose ten pounds in a month. When I found I lost only eight lousy pounds after starving myself for four weeks, I went ballistic and started pounding walls. Maybe I was crazy from not eating, I don't know. Anyway, he heard me screaming and said, "Perfection is for God, and you're not Him. Learn to live with the gifts God gave you." That's the problem, Doc. I don't know what my gifts *are*.

● ● ●

Anyway, I quit the bank and moved to Colorado and got a job in a ski shop. I went skiing in Vermont a few times when I went to BU and I loved it, so I figured this would make me happy. Well, skiing is fun, but working in the shop sure isn't. All these weekend dilettantes, bitching about the gloves or the poles. The equipment wasn't right, the lift lines were too long, the snow was too slushy. I couldn't support myself, my skiing habit, or my sanity with these bimbos, so I came home.

After I got back from Colorado, I thought I would try to get spiritual, maybe figure out what religion I should be. So I went to a Buddhist temple. It was really interesting for a while, but I couldn't sit still long enough for the meditations. Every time I went down into myself, it was like a black, bottomless pit. To be honest, I'd get scared. I think you're supposed to reach a place of calm and peace and feel content. But for me it was anything but. It was empty and terrifying, like I was dead. I thought I'd never be able to get out. I guess you're supposed to find the core of your being, but I never found mine. Maybe I don't have one.

So I started going to the Universalist Life Church—you know, that modern Unitarian church over on Bryant that looks like Frank Lloyd Wright built it? Unitarianism should be the official religion of people like me. No strict rules, no teachings—you don't have to *be* anything, and since I don't know what I am, it's perfect! It was cool for a few months. But it was so loose I kind of lost interest after a while. Too many barbecues.

•   •   •

I found a job in this store where they actually made me a supervisor, at least for a week. Matt, this local high school kid, came onboard to work Inventory Week, and all he had to do was stick price labels on toys. Anyway, he was doing okay; after all, Doc, it's not rocket science. But one night I noticed that all the Monopoly games had the wrong price label, ten dollars less than it should've been, and I came down really hard on him. I mean, I took his label gun and threw it against the wall, told him he was dumber than dirt and that he was going to put Maxwell's out of business. Next day, in a meeting, I tried to make it up to him and told everyone that Matt was the best worker in the store. His eyes got bigger than the proverbial flying saucers. You should've seen his face! He was terrified. I was, too, kind of. It was like I was Dr. Jekyll and Mr. Hyde. I don't think I'm cut out to be a supervisor.

Lately I've been working in a clothing store. They want to make me a manager, maybe even a buyer. I've also been seeing this girl, Marie, who wants to get married. But I don't know if this is the career I want. I don't know if this is the woman, or even the person, I want. There's nothing wrong with my job or my girlfriend—I just don't know if I can play the roles expected of me. I don't know if you can help me, Doc. You see, I don't know where I've been, and I sure as hell don't know where I'm going. And all my sloshing through old events or your grand pontificating won't change that. But what worries me the most is, I don't know who I am! *Bobby's story is continued on page 117.*

Bobby's story is continued on page 117.

The Identity Spectrum

"I don't know who I am" is a plaint heard often from many borderlines. Just as their perception of others frequently whipsaws from glorification to vilification, their own self-image often caroms back and forth between extremes. Many become obsessed with physical appearance. For example, some borderlines develop an overly critical preoccupation with a body feature (such as the nose), which defines their self-esteem, a disorder classified in the *DSM* as body dysmorphic disorder. Others may develop a full-fledged eating disorder, such as anorexia nervosa, in which self-image varies wildly, dependent completely on the numbers on the weight scale. In addition to these dramatic fluctuations in self-perception, sometimes (especially when alone) the borderline may feel he does not exist at all. While the other eight criteria that define BPD are endorsed equally between men and women, only identity disturbance is reported significantly more often by women.

The *DSM-IV* definition for identity disturbance simplifies that described in *DSM-III*. The earlier version required "uncertainty about at least two of the following: self-image, sexual orientation, long-term goals or career choice, type of friends desired, preferred values." *DSM-IV* omits these specific areas of disturbance, which are suggestive of primary adolescent developmental issues, and instead requires only "unstable self-image or sense of self."

Identity disturbance is associated with varying degrees of impairment. At one extreme, some (particularly those who have suffered severe physical or sexual abuse in childhood) may experience dissociative episodes during which they lose contact with here-and-now reality (see chapter 10). At such times the borderline goes on a kind of "automatic pilot." In chapter 5 we relate the story of Liz, who would often feel herself slipping into a distant reverie when she visited her mother and abusive stepfather. She would mouth the usual platitudes to her mother while avoiding her stepfather but would wander through the day as if in a dream. Later she would retain only the haziest recollection of the visit.

For others, identity disturbance is the frustration of drifting without anchoring ideals, upon which they can establish a consistent sense of self. These individuals recognize that their attitudes, values, and behaviors mimic those of the people they are with at the moment and may change when they are with others. Thus they feel like chameleons, with no independent identity of their own.

Bobby often felt he was "borrowing" a "self" from someone else. He joined a fraternity in college after being wooed by Bruce, the rush chairman. Bruce was charismatic and self-assured, and Bobby was thrilled when Bruce agreed to be his sponsor. Only after his fraternity brothers began laughing at him and calling him "Mini-Bruce" did Bobby realize that he was unconsciously mimicking Bruce's mannerisms, his walk, even his New York accent. Initially flattered, Bruce eventually became annoyed with his protégé's adulation and began to distance himself from Bobby, who then felt more alone. For Bobby, each foray into a new, idealized identity ended in disappointment and frustration. For many borderlines, this failure to establish a consistently satisfactory self-view leads to feelings of nihilistic emptiness and meaninglessness (see chapter 8).

Identity and Splitting

The well-respected psychologist Erik Erikson was the first major theorist to focus on the significance of identity. Establishing a core sense of unique individuality, Erikson believed, was one of the major tasks of adolescence. During this time, as the adolescent identifies with the values of his parents, his peer groups, and others, he absorbs some ideals, overidentifies with others, and rebels against and rejects still others. From this conglomeration he forges a constant sense of self, which allows him to establish friendships, to embark on a career or educational path, and to develop a sense of belonging in the larger society. Role (or identity) confusion results when the teenager is unable to resolve this mission. Later, Otto Kernberg expanded this concept of inconsistent self-image referred to as "identity diffusion."

Splitting is the primary mechanism for coping with identity disturbance and other BPD struggles (see chapter 3). As previously noted, many theorists speculate that splitting emerges from disruptions in consistent

mothering. Healthy attachment and identification with the mothering figure, from which the sense of individual identity develops, is disturbed.
Deprived of the consistent, unconditional acceptance from the most
important figure in his life, the child perceives the world as unpredictable.

Impressions in the present do not reliably predict reactions in the
future. The developing individual, unable to connect past experiences to
future occurrences, develops ambivalence and confusion. The security of
feeling accepted by others is based solely on the present. To escape this
anxiety-provoking chaos, to simplify the incomprehensible, the child
splits the world into "all good" and "all bad," thereby instantaneously eras-
ing ambiguity. Certainty replaces ambivalence. There is no in-between.
The catch, however, is that approval remains conditional, spurring the borderline to constantly seek it, yet never trust it.

For Bobby, childhood was a collage of inconsistencies. Neither parent
was available to provide reliable standards to guide their son. Each day was
different. Each day required new coping capacities. Bobby could not define
from one day to the next what was "good," what was "bad," or what was
expected of him. Without context, he had to reinvent his behavior each day.
But as he matured, Bobby became proficient in discovering what role others
wanted him to play, and he learned how to play them all. As with some
actors who immerse themselves in their characters, he was in danger of losing the real "Bobby." Splitting all perceptions into good or bad simplified
his chaotic world. Yet it left him bereft of a consistent identity.

The Components of Identity Disturbance

Some researchers have subcategorized borderline identity disturbance into
four components. One grouping, called role absorption, refers to patients
whose identity is defined in terms of a specific role or cause. Some cult
members reflect this pathology. They literally change their identity by
changing their name and belief system, while rejecting family and friends.
They may blindly follow a charismatic leader, abandoning all sense of
individuality and becoming consumed with a specific role dictated by the
cult leader. Unfortunately, we have seen numerous examples of these
types of cults throughout the past fifty years—from Jonestown to Waco,
from Hezbollah to Al-Qaeda. And we have seen how individuals, starved
for an identity and a value system, can become attracted to, immersed in,
and eventually destroyed by the cult.

A second component of identity disturbance, painful incoherence, reflects the borderline's experience of feeling lost and empty. Such a person may feel "unreal" or describe a "false self" as she attempts vainly to fit in. Periods of dissociation may ensue. "Lacking any firm identity," Sally B. Smith writes in *Diana in Search of Herself,* "Diana frequently felt lonely, empty, and bored." Painful incoherence is the only factor highly correlated with a history of sexual abuse and is the component most closely associated with the BPD criterion of identity disturbance.

Inconsistency, the third subtype, causes less subjective distress. The individual transforms into a "chameleon," whose opinions and values depend on who is in his company at a particular moment, much like the title character in Woody Allen's *Zelig.* He may assume inconsistent, even contradictory, positions. There may be a strong attraction to a controlling, charismatic figure who offers the hope of consistency.

Lack of commitment, the fourth component, reflects the borderline's difficulty in sustaining goals and interests. Frequent alterations in educational interests, job changes, and multiple relationships (including serial divorces and remarriages) characterize this struggle. This is the weakest of the four factors in predicting BPD.

In some ways, role absorption is the opposite, compensatory experience for the other three subcategories. By engaging the individual in a rigidly defined system, role absorption may represent an attempt to avoid the pain of existential confusion endemic to the other three.

Bobby's identity problems, at one time or another, probably involved all four categories: his experiences with religious sects (role absorption); his need to "fit in" (painful incoherence); his attempt at becoming the fraternity leader (inconsistency); and his frequent job changes and (as you will see in chapter 7) multiple relationships (lack of commitment).

The Way Home

For Bobby, the journey of discovery of the self began with his relationship with his therapist. For much of his life, Bobby had kept people at arm's length, fearing that he would be engulfed by relationships, as he had experienced with his family. He also feared that a close relationship would reveal aspects of himself that he was not ready to understand and was unsure he could embrace. Seeking therapy was difficult, for it meant accepting his own weaknesses and allowing another person access to his self-doubts.

During his initial therapy sessions, Bobby parried the therapist's attempts to establish trust, using sardonic humor and weary cynicism to shield himself. He perceived the treatment as an invasion that would ultimately lead to his humiliation. He challenged his doctor's credentials, demanded guarantees that therapy would help him, and accused his therapist of exploiting him, extracting his fees without any promise of a cure.

His therapist endured the challenges with steadfastness and good humor. After several months Bobby began to trust that the doctor would not abandon him. As Bobby began to open up, he felt accepted, without criticism, for the first time. He could talk from the heart without needing to guard his words.

The more Bobby talked about his life, the more he felt that he *had* a life—and an identity. He became more at ease around others. He felt more comfortable about expressing his opinions. Ultimately Bobby embraced his career as a retail store manager. He broke off the engagement with his fiancée, convinced that he had to explore his sexuality further. Astonishingly, he discovered that she wished to remain close friends. Bobby was developing his own "self" and finding that he and others could value it.

The desperate need to establish a sense of identity is strongly related to other BPD behaviors. In turn, BPD behaviors are associated with genetic, biochemical, and anatomic factors. The task for future research is to discover how these various ingredients are stirred to color BPD presentation. The task for the borderline is to learn how to discover himself.

ACTION STEPS: *Establishing a Sense of Self*

1. *Join healthy groups.* Involvement in self-help groups and membership in church activities, charitable campaigns, community projects, political campaigns, and other group activities all promote social interactions and working toward worthwhile goals.

2. *Be part of a team.* Joining a softball league, participating in a bowling tournament, volunteering for an office project, and being part of a neighborhood watch committee are commitments to work with others on a continuous basis.

3. *See it through.* When borderlines are disappointed, they often become immediately discouraged and drop out. Scholastic, occupational, and romantic commitments are frequently changed without thoughtful

consideration. Exercise your emotional endurance muscles by continuing with your obligation to a logical end point. Finish the semester, complete the season, conclude the assignment, continue until your term expires. Even if your undertaking is ultimately regrettable, you will learn more about who you are by honoring the commitment to the end.

4. *Look for the "gray" within consistency.* Embrace, rather than flee from, inconsistencies and contradictions. Accept that you, like everyone else, can maintain consistent views while acknowledging incongruities. ("The mark of a first-rate mind," wrote F. Scott Fitzgerald, "is the ability to hold two opposing ideas at the same time.") Don't expect your boss, professor, political candidate, or lover to satisfy your ideals all the time. Unrealistic expectations of yourself and others leads to disappointment.

5. *Maintain perspective.* Don't automatically change your opinion over a minor point. Recognize that some elements are more important than others. A bad experience or failure on one specific project doesn't mean you should question your career choice. Put relative value on the pluses and minuses of your situation before you feel compelled to change it. If you can learn to accept disappointment yet maintain commitment, you are establishing an identity—because you are accepting yourself.

5

Destructive Impulsivity

Impulse has more effect than conscious purpose in molding men's lives.

—BERTRAND RUSSELL, *Autobiography,* 1967

When a prisoner sees the door of his dungeon open, he dashes for it without stopping to think where he shall get his dinner.

—GEORGE BERNARD SHAW, *Back to Methuselah,* 1922

Impulsivity, perhaps the most common symptom of BPD, can trigger related borderline behaviors—sudden outbursts of rage, volatile relationships—or emerge from others, such as mood swings and stormy relationships. To make things more complex, the borderline's impulsive actions are typically *self-destructive,* leading to substance abuse and sexual promiscuity (as was the case with Lizzie, the subject of this chapter's story) or other addictions, such as anorexia, bulimia, gambling, shoplifting, and excessive spending. This chapter distinguishes the impulsivity exhibited by borderlines from that exhibited by victims of other mental illnesses, explores the new research into the biophysiology of impulsive behavior, notes new psychotherapeutic and medical treatments, and provides ways for the borderline to manage this difficult trait.

LIZZIE: PART ONE

It is 7:00 P.M., and Lizzie Compton is almost positive that everyone else in the dental office has gone home. She had seen Dr. Vitale and Nan, the

71

receptionist, leave for sure, and the lights are out in the bookkeeper's office. Likewise for Vitale's new young partner, Dr. Bradford, and Marge, the X-ray tech.

As she finishes up sterilizing the instruments, Lizzie peers out the windows at Halstead Street. It is a cold, windy Chicago evening in late March 1998, and dusk has not quite settled into darkness. Her pulse begins to race as she contemplates what she is about to do. Even though the "happy cabinet" is locked, as it always is after hours, she knows that the key will be in the top drawer of Vitale's desk.

Outside, on Halstead, the streetlights come on, flooding the equipment room with halogen light and taking her back to her parents' house, where a similar streetlight outside her bedroom window would illuminate the picture of the Little Girl on her bedroom wall. Lizzie didn't know who painted the picture or where it came from, only that it had been hanging above her dresser for as long as she could remember. The Little Girl, maybe six or seven years old and wearing a bright yellow bathing suit, stood on a beach looking out over the ocean. Her hands were clasped behind her back, and her long brown hair flew to the side, as if blown by the wind. Lizzie remembered her father, before he died, standing by her crib, next to the picture of the Little Girl, singing to both of them, as the waves swept gently over the room. Late at night, after her parents had gone to bed, Lizzie would stare into the painting, imagining that she was standing next to the Little Girl. They were friends.

Sighing with the pleasant memory, Lizzie puts away the last of her instruments and treads silently into the corridor, listening again for any sign of human presence besides her own. Nothing. Only the muted tones of "Soft Jazz 93.7" on the office intercom speakers.

"Hello?" she calls plaintively. "Anyone still here?" Louder: *"Hell-lo-oh? Anyone?"*

Tall and slim, dressed in her white hygienist's uniform, she strolls into Dr. Vitale's office with the nonchalant walk of a runway model, figuring that if someone does catch her, she must appear natural—as if she is *supposed* to be here. She opens the top drawer of Vitale's desk and smiles: The key to the "happy cabinet" is right where it should be, in the wooden tray intended for paper clips. She takes it, closes the drawer, and leaves the office.

The white drug cabinet is in an alcove near the X-ray machine. A collage of little yellow happy faces (giving the cabinet its nickname years ago) smiles back at Lizzie. Once again she decides to test the silence: *"Hey! Anyone here...?"*

Still hearing nothing, she fits the key into the cabinet door and swings it open. The row of opaque plastic containers on the top shelf might be a problem for shorter women, but Lizzie is able to snatch the one she wants without even getting on tiptoes. The thrill of danger dances down her spine, the same tingle she felt years ago during her shoplifting period. "The Rush," her high school friends called it when they went to Caddell's Department Store—before the advent of electronic code detectors at every exit door, even before the era of security guards. The six of them would fan out in pairs, to the cosmetics counter, the jewelry case, the leather department—they were all fair game. While one girl occupied the counter lady with useless chatter, the other would pilfer lipsticks, bracelets, wallets—whatever was handy. An hour later they would meet in Sheila's bedroom to divvy up the booty, giddy with The Rush. Caddell's was *so-o-o-o snooty,* her friends argued, *they* deserved *to get ripped off! The prices they were charging,* they *were the ones ripping people off!* Not that Lizzie felt that the stealing was justified; on the contrary, she felt bad about stealing, which made it even more exciting. After a few heists, she ventured solo, going into Caddell's alone, knowing that what she was about to do was wrong, yet thrilled with the prospect of impulsively pocketing an item for which she had no earthly use and then plotting her escape. She didn't want or need any of the items she stole, and almost all ended up unopened in the bottom drawer of her bureau.

All that immature behavior transpired before she began drinking, of course. The liquor cabinet at home was stocked, and her mom never took inventory. Later came the drugs. *Thank God for narcotics,* she says with a sigh to herself, *they had saved her from a life of crime.*

The container opens easily, and Lizzie stares at her newest booty: a beautiful white hill of oval-shaped 5-mg Vicodins, intended for emergency surgeries and root canals. A veritable gold mine! With almost a full bottle, they'd never notice if a few were missing. Despite her nervousness, she smiles with satisfaction and relief.

"Have a toothache?"

She is so startled, her mind virtually jumps out of her body. The bottle squirts from her hands, scattering pills everywhere. Michael Bradford, Vitale's new young partner, stands behind her, grinning impishly.

"Dr. Bradford!"

"Here," he says, bending down to retrieve the pills, "let me give you a hand with those."

Scared out of her wits, she is in no mood for cooperation and is suddenly blinded by rage. "How could you *do* that? You could give someone a *heart attack* scaring them like that!" Only a tremendous effort of self-control prevents her from flailing out at him. Yet, peering up at her, his confident smirk forces her to adopt a more subservient tone. She exhales deeply. "My God, you scared the living daylights out of me! Where did you *come from,* anyway?"

Scooping up the last of the Vicodins, he funnels them into the bottle with his hand, and the clacking sound brings her back to reality, the trouble she's in. He twists the cap back on and hands her the bottle. "Here you go."

Tall like herself, Bradford is just a few years out of dental school. His dirty-blond hair, almost matching the color and length of her own, and back-country good looks give him the air of a young Robert Redford. His face is even slightly pockmarked like Redford's, prompting Marge to give him the nickname "Sundance" just that week. Even though his last patient left hours ago, Bradford is still wearing his white dentist's tunic, except that the two top buttons are undone, revealing a clump of reddish-blond chest hair. Despite the "Redford wanna-be" jokes, the women in the office had taken to wearing tighter jeans and more clinging blouses since he joined the practice.

"It's not a toothache," she says dolefully. "It's my head. I've been getting these migraines lately. I thought maybe one of these would help."

"Have you seen a doctor?"

"A doctor?"

"About the headaches."

"Oh . . . no, not really. Not yet. They just started. A few weeks ago."

"I see." A grimace replaces the grin, and his brow furrows. "Headaches can be pretty serious, you know. They can be signs of more serious conditions, I mean. And pain medications don't always work. Particularly if they're true migraines. My roommate in dental school used to get them all the time."

Standing there, she can't figure out what to do with the bottle of pills: Though Bradford really hasn't *accused* her of anything, placing them back in the cabinet would somehow be an admission of guilt, not to mention losing her any chance of scoring a few. She decides to play along with the charade a while longer.

"Well, what did *he* take?" she asks. "Your roommate, I mean, for the migraines."

"*She,*" he says, the grin once again turning at the corners of his mouth. "Can't really remember. Something like soma or zoma . . . it's a vascular constrictor, not a narcotic." Something in his smile tells her he *knows* her headache story is a lie, but he's willing to play along anyway, to give her a way out. "But you never know. Go ahead and take one," he says, pointing to the bottle of Vicodins. "Maybe it'll work."

With that, she is officially off the hook for her crime, and her gratitude for his mercy almost overtakes her desire for the drugs. For some reason she feels the need to reinforce a fact that they both know is fiction: "Well, maybe you're right, maybe I should wait until —"

"I have something else in my office that might help even more."

"Really?" Before she can ask what he's talking about, Bradford is heading toward his office. Leaving the pills on the counter, she doesn't move for an instant and then realizes that he wants her to follow him. Now that everything is out and aboveboard, she figures she can always come back later.

Up ahead, she can see him flicking on the light switch in his office. *So she had been right about his office being dark!* In that case, where was he all this time—sitting alone in a dark office? In the rest room, maybe?

"Have a seat," he invites her. "It might take a while to find it."

As she sits in one of two armchairs in front of his desk, it occurs to her that she has not been in this office for a while, not since Bradford started a few weeks ago. While he rummages in his desk drawers, apparently searching for the yet-to-be-determined medication for her nonexistent migraine, she surveys the room: framed portraits of two blond kids and a blond wife on the credenza behind his chair; diplomas from schools, one of them dental, no doubt, that she could not quite decipher from this distance; and tucked into the corner, almost unnoticeable, a portable electric keyboard on aluminum legs, with an old maple piano bench placed in front of it. She doesn't know exactly why, but her pulse starts to race, and she starts to feel uncomfortable.

"Ah, here you go," he says matter-of-factly, pulling out a small vial and flipping it to her. "This'll make you feel better."

"What is it?" she asks, though she is already reading the label: Percodan, 10 mg. Wow! She's hit the mother lode! Fearing that her eyes might give her away, she does not look up at him. "I've heard of these," she says innocently.

"It's okay," he says, almost laughing. "I'm a Dee-Dee-ESS. You have my permission. Hey, let me get you something to wash that down with." As she unwinds the childproof cap with the heel of her palm, he opens the door of the credenza. The vial, filled to the top with the small, round tablets, immediately takes her back to the eighth grade, when she swallowed a whole tin of aspirins that she kept in her book bag. She recalls now that she used to get headaches all the time in grade school—was that the origin of her excuse to Bradford? Expecting him to pull out a plastic bottle of water (Évian, maybe, or Crystal Geyser), she is amazed to see a bottle of J & B and two glasses materialize in front of her.

"You weren't expecting Coca-Cola, were you? Rot your teeth." He chuckles gleefully, while Lizzie can only stare at the bottle of liquor. "Don't be so surprised," he admonishes her, "nothing wrong with a drink now and then. Especially if you work late, like we do." With that, he pours the amber liquid into the two glasses and hands one to her. "Cheers," he toasts and takes a sip. But she is paralyzed. "Ah, you're worried about mixing pills and booze?"

Actually, that wasn't it at all; she had done it hundreds of times. After swallowing the aspirins she had spent the entire day hunched over the toilet, puking up her guts, while her mother pleaded with her to see a doctor. But when she weighed herself two days later, her eyes lit up— she had lost six pounds! Any fear she had of drugs vanished after that. In fact, if a drug binge led to a purging binge, so much the better; her safety valve had become its own reward.

As Bradford watches her, she feels part of a charade again, as if he can see right through her and is giving her every chance to play along. She suddenly feels deliciously wicked, as she has many times since she started working at the dental office. On Friday nights, when the office "girls" go to Marbury's for happy hour, Liz will stay long after they leave, as a mocking reproach to their straitlaced habits. "Don't worry, Liz—one pill won't hurt you."

Given the "all clear" sign, she pops one of the Percodans into her mouth. "Well, okay," she says with a shrug. "You're the doctor."

The pill and the scotch chaser go down easily, and she is already starting to feel light-headed, probably more the effect of the evening's strange events than the drugs. Bradford comes around to the front of the desk and leans against the front edge, his legs stretched out, only inches from hers.

"All right if I call you Liz, or do you prefer Elizabeth?"

She almost laughs; she had used so many names over the years it hardly mattered any longer. When she entered high school, after her sisters had moved out, she found she could change her identity at will. She insisted her new crowd call her "Elizabeth"—and amazingly, they did! By her junior year, after a brief flirtation with "Beth," she was "Betsy," more apropos for her hard-boiled, hard-drinking, secret-thief persona. When she was older, she reverted to "Elizabeth," which worked best for teachers and employers. At home, to her mother and older sisters, she was always "Little Lizzie," despite the fact that she was half a foot taller than any of them.

"Liz is fine," she says. Suddenly regretting her decision to wear a short skirt today, she feels the need to swerve the focus of the conversation from herself. "That's a nice-looking family," she adds, nodding to the portrait on the credenza.

"Thanks."

"How old are your kids?"

"Ten and eight."

She thinks back to her own family, when she was eight. Her father dead for three years, she was living with her mom and two older sisters. She recalls always trying to please her mother, in a futile attempt to compensate for her father dying. Colleen intimidated her; Liz's voice seemed half an octave higher in her own ear when she was with her, as if regressing to childhood. Liz did not even object when her mother began dating Mr. Lindsey, the organist at their church. She takes another sip of the J & B, a bigger sip than the first, the memory of Lindsey almost making her cringe in disgust.

"A penny for your thoughts," he says.

"Me? Oh, nothing . . . about kids, I guess."

"You have kids, Liz?"

"Oh—oh, no. No way. Someday maybe."

"Excuse me a minute, okay?" As he leaves the room, winking at her for some unearthly reason, she realizes that she is still holding the vial of Percodans. She could stuff a bunch more into her hygienist's jacket and he'd never know. The Rush returns but this time subsides just as quickly, diminished by the realization that Bradford probably wouldn't care—hell, he probably wouldn't care if she stole *all of them*. He could just write out another prescription to himself, right? Besides, she thinks, glancing around the office, this guy is so slick he might have some kind of hidden camera in the room, taping her every move. She is struck by the intuition that he *purposely* left her alone, that he *wants* her to steal more, that she is being led into some kind of trap but doesn't know what it is or why. Making as few movements as possible, she empties a few more pills into her palm, places them silently into her jacket, and closes the lid. Almost on cue, she hears Bradford enter the office doorway behind her.

But instead of returning to his chair or leaning against his desk, he sits on the piano bench in front of his keyboard. A flick of a switch, and the facing of the keyboard lights up like a car dashboard. "How old are you, Liz?"

"Young enough not to be insulted by the question," she says, using her mother's standard reply that Lizzie had long ago stored away for her own use. As Bradford pushes a few keys, releasing deep, organlike chords, the panic from years ago revisits her . . . Lindsey at the church organ again, his eyes staring blissfully off into the distance—the same vacant expression he had when he appeared so many times in her bedroom . . . Lizzie and her sisters sitting in the second row, next to their mother, fidgeting throughout the service, their mother smiling proudly. She tries to shake the memory out of her head. "Are you a frustrated musician or something?"

"Not so frustrated," he says. "I play in a band, you know. On weekends." After the service, Mr. Lindsey would stand on the steps outside the church, accepting the compliments of the congregation, the four Compton girls by his side. But when they returned home from the service, his face would harden and the spankings would begin. "You know, weddings, bar mitzvahs, that kind of thing. But we've got a few gigs coming up. Ever been to Saunders? The rock club over on Thirty-ninth? Nice place. You should check it out sometime." More chords, a simple C-D-G progression she had practiced so many times with Lindsey sitting next to her. When Lindsey moved in, he brought a piano and taught the girls how to play. Her hatred for practicing was exceeded only by her hatred for the lessons. "Remember this one?"

Bradford breaks into a revved-up version of the Beatles' "Yesterday," but he has changed the beat from slow ballad to Latin disco, and she has to strain to extract the melody. She prays he doesn't start singing, but he does nevertheless, and she detaches herself, a talent she had nurtured years ago to escape the pain of the spankings. After a while, it had worked. No matter how hard Lindsey hit her, she felt nothing.

After a few months, the punishments extended into the night. Mr. Lindsey came into her room, interrupting her communion with the Little Girl on the beach. "You've been very bad today," he told her. "I'm responsible for teaching you how to be a polite young lady, and I must fulfill this obligation from God. Spanking doesn't seem to turn you away from evil. What does it take for you to mind?"

Then he would pull up her nightgown. At first he pinched her thighs. Later he would massage her genitals, pinching and probing. "When will you learn to mind?" Lizzie would stare at the picture and gradually disappear into it. She would be with the Little Girl, standing on the sand, looking out on the waves. Surely she was a bad girl and would go to hell. That is what Mr. Lindsey kept telling her, and her destination was confirmed when she shuddered with spasms of shameful pleasure from all his rubbing. Sometimes in the dark, as she strolled the beach with her friend, she felt a force guide her hand against a bulge, until her palm became sticky. Even the cool ocean surf could not wash away the stickiness or the shame. The feeling of being a bad girl was always part of her.

By the time she was eleven, the nighttime intrusions concluded with Lindsey forcing himself into her mouth. At the culmination, she tasted the salty air of the ocean. When he left her room, she barely noticed. She and her friend continued to walk the misty beach.

"Do you play, Liz?"

"Four years of piano lessons," she says reflexively, bitterly. "Four *fucking* years."

"Really? Great! Sit here and play something for me."

She almost smacks her head with her palm. God, how could she be so stupid?! "Oh, no, it's been *years*."

"Oh, come on," he urges, turning to her. "Play me something. It's like riding a bicycle: you never forget."

She doesn't even have to look at him to know he's winking again. She takes a large sip from her drink and stands abruptly but almost topples over and must grab on to the arm of the chair to regain her balance. Taking a deep breath, the narcotic feeling of—what was it? contentment? confidence?—spreads though her. If painkillers could talk, she once told her friend Nelly, they would say, "Things aren't *that* bad."

Sliding in next to him on the bench, her stockings make a rasping sound, and she regrets again not wearing jeans today. She can feel Bradford staring at her now, feel his eyes dropping to her skirt, which has pulled up a few inches on her thighs as she sits at the keyboard. Is it her imagination, or is he licking his lips?

"Isn't that the way it should be?" he asks, placing his arm around her shoulders. "I play something for you, you play something for me?" And now it all becomes clear to her—the games at the "happy cabinet," the Percodans: Drugs, for Bradford, were simply a medium of exchange, a form of payment for services rendered, tailored perfectly for sickos like her. And now that he had made an advance payment, and dangled the bait of future bonuses, she is expected to render services. She can't, of course. If she was naked, he would see the cuts, and that would be the end of sex. The road map of scars that she had carved on her breasts and genitals over the years had been the undoing of men better than Bradford, and it would repulse him as well.

Despite her high—*magnified* by her high—a wave of nausea and depression almost overcomes her. She had spent years trying to get her life in order, and here she was right back where she started: on a piano bench, with a bastard beside her. She glances up, hoping to see the picture of the Little Girl on the beach, but there is no picture, only a diploma from a dental school that she's never heard of.

Lizzie's story is continued on page 90.

Distinguishing Borderline Impulsivity

Impulsivity, one of the core, consistent features of BPD, is related to other BPD symptoms, such as suicide attempts, self-mutilation, rage outbursts, and volatile relationships. This criterion has persisted over time without changes since it was rigorously defined as a core symptom of BPD in *DSM-III* in 1980.

Self-destructive impulsivity distinguishes BPD from the impulsive-ness seen in other conditions, such as intermittent explosive disorder (defined as aggressive impulsivity directed toward other people or property), antisocial personality disorder, attention deficit (hyperactivity) disorder (ADHD), bipolar (manic depressive) disorder, substance abuse disorder, post-traumatic stress disorder, and other such impulse disorders as kleptomania and pathological gambling. The borderline's self-destructive impulse behaviors usually are reactions to disappointments from someone close. For instance, Liz would frequently initiate humiliating sexual encounters with her neighbor (after which she invariably felt severe self-loathing) following an argument with her mother. Impulsivity is frequently associated with suicide attempts in borderline patients (see chapter 6).

Significant impulsivity sometimes is observed in childhood and may be suggestive of autism, attention deficit (hyperactivity) disorder, and/or conduct disorder (CD). Although it is difficult to make a confident diagnosis of BPD in childhood, many impulsive children fulfill BPD criteria by the time they reach adolescence or early adulthood.

Despite the common symptom of impulsivity, these other childhood disorders are distinct. Autistic children are detached from their world; their behaviors are responses to internal stimuli and usually are unpredictable. Children with ADHD and/or CD have difficulty coping with situational pressures, and they often express their impulses when frustrated and overwhelmed by them. Borderline impulsivity, on the other hand, frequently erupts as a manifestation of frustration with *people.* Liz's shoplifting as a teenager was more a reaction to her abuse from her stepfather at home than a result of external stimuli. Disruptions in serotonin metabolism may be common to all of these disorders.

Of all of the defining criteria, impulsivity is the most likely to persist over time and to be characteristic of unremitting borderline pathology. On the other hand, some researchers have reported that older borderline patients exhibit less impulsivity than younger patients—even when other less dramatic symptoms such as mood changes, identity disturbance, and interpersonal problems remain the same. This may be the basis of the often-observed "maturing out" of borderline patients over time (see chapter 11).

Coping Mechanisms

Anger, restlessness, guilt, and suicidal tendencies are specific elements of impulsivity associated with BPD. The borderline typically responds to frustration with mostly immature defense mechanisms, including:

- *Acting out: invoking behaviors—often self-destructive—to cope with uncomfortable feelings.* When frustrated with some of her coworkers, Liz would join them for "happy hour," but rather than leave with them, she would stay in the bar to get drunk and pick up a man for sex.

- *Regression: acting more childish when stressed.* When visiting her mother, Lizzie would find herself regressing to more childlike behavior.

- *Inhibition and withdrawal.* When feeling insecure among new acquaintances, Liz would withdraw and avoid interaction.

- *Passive-aggression: camouflaging rage indirectly.* When angry at one of her bosses, Liz would get even by showing up late for work or "forgetting" to carry out an assignment.

- *Splitting* (see chapter 3). Since all of Lizzie's friends would eventually disappoint her, she took it as proof of their disloyalty and banished them, leaving her frequently lonely.

- *Projection and projective identification: placing responsibility on others for behavior.* Liz's justification for shoplifting at Caddell's (the store's rip-off prices) transformed her from "thief" to "victim."

These mechanisms contrast with more advanced coping skills, such as:

- *Suppression: conscious, selective avoidance of uncomfortable material.* "Tomorrow, I'll think about that tomorrow," said Scarlett O'Hara.

- *Sublimation: redirecting unpleasant feelings into more acceptable directions.* For example, discharging anger by engaging in vigorous contact sports or rigorous exercise.

- *Humor,* which requires perspective and calm distancing.

The more mature coping style requires reflection, patience, control of emotions, and maintaining proportion, qualities that usually are inconsistent with borderline impulsiveness.

Comorbidity (Coexisting Illnesses) and Impulsivity

BPD coexists with several Axis I illnesses that also list impulsiveness as a core symptom. People with ADHD, like those with BPD, are often quickly bored and easily frustrated, and they frequently react with impulsive behaviors. A hallmark of both disorders is the blurting out of impulsive, immediately regrettable statements. Drug and alcohol abusers also are notoriously impulsive and possess other borderline features as well. Indeed, one study investigating BPD patients in the United States and Italy found that almost 50 percent of borderline patients abused alcohol and/or drugs. Impulsive drug use, eating, excessive spending, shoplifting, self-mutilation, sexual promiscuity, and other paraphilias (such as exhibitionism, voyeurism, and fetishism) often are associated with BPD. Axis I classification "Impulse-Control Disorders Not Elsewhere Classified" defines several diagnoses in which uncontrollable impulsivity is the primary feature. These include intermittent explosive disorder (rage outbursts), kleptomania, pyromania (fire-setting), pathological gambling, and trichotillomania (compulsive hair-pulling), all of which are often comorbid with BPD. Sometimes the borderline exchanges one impulsive behavior for another. Lizzie discontinued her stealing when she began using drugs, and sometimes a round of binging and purging would replace her self-cutting. Defects in serotonin utilization may be common to all of these disorders, in which self-control is a primary mechanism.

The most common comorbidity with BPD is depression. Some studies suggest that almost 90 percent of BPD patients also may suffer from major depressive disorder (MDD). Both illnesses reflect the victim's feelings of worthlessness, hopelessness, and poor self-esteem. However, swift, impulsive actions may be more characteristic of volatile borderlines, in contrast to depressed individuals, who more often experience slower thought and behavior processes.

The Role of the Brain

Modulation of impulsive aggression seems to reside in the prefrontal cortex—the front section of the brain encased behind the forehead. Some imaging studies further localize brain activity involved with aggression to the orbital frontal cortex, behind the eyes. Researchers believe that the prefrontal cortex is where reasoned decisions are made, where the brain balances instinctual impulses with social restrictions, intellectual reason, and moral judgment.

Brain Chemistry

Injuries to the prefrontal or orbital frontal cortex areas of the brain have resulted in uncharacteristically aggressive behavior, reflecting impaired social judgment and poor frustration tolerance. Positron emission tomography (PET), a specialized form of brain scanning, has demonstrated decreased metabolic activity in connected parts of the brain, especially the orbital frontal cortex, of BPD patients who exhibit impulsive aggression. Similar results have been reported in individuals who attempt suicide and who are impulsively homicidal.

Several brain chemicals have been associated with impulsivity and aggression. These include neurotransmitters linked to adrenaline, testosterone-related hormones, and endorphins. However, as noted in chapter 1, most research concentrates on the neurotransmitter serotonin, which is intimately involved with many emotions and is particularly prominent in the prefrontal cortex area of the brain. Low levels of serotonin, associated with depression and anxiety, also appear to be implicated in impulsive/aggressive behaviors. Several studies examining serotonin function in BPD patients confirm this association. Research measuring breakdown metabolites of serotonin in the spinal fluid reveals lower serotonin levels in impulsive BPD patients. Other experiments use PET to examine the effect of drugs that stimulate serotonin release. These studies indicate a blunting of serotonin discharge in BPD patients.

Animal experiments and human observations indicate that early life stressors affect serotonin function, which, in turn, correlates with impulsive/aggressive behavior. Like Lizzie, many borderlines have a history of severe childhood abuse, and some experts have hypothesized that childhood trauma may breed adult impulsivity. One study examined serotonin availability in impulsive borderline patients and control subjects. The BPD group exhibited a diminished response to artificial stimulation of serotonin. The researchers then further divided the BPD group into those who had experienced severe childhood physical and/or sexual abuse and those who had not. The abused group exhibited a statistically significant further decrease of serotonin response to the artifical stimulation, separating them from the nonabused borderlines. Those who suffered the most abuse displayed the greatest deficit. Perhaps, then, dysregulation of serotonin culminating in impulsive behavior may be more a stigma of past abuse than a specific marker of current BPD.

Can You Inherit Impulsiveness?

Family studies indicate that specific components of BPD, rather than the disorder itself, are transmitted through generations. Lizzie's mother, for example, exhibited some borderline traits (impaired relationships, destructive alcohol abuse, feelings of emptiness) that might have been transmitted to her daughter. The most prominent of these traits are aggressive impulsivity and mood instability. Impulsivity is a personality trait measured concordantly in identical twins (who share identical chromosomal material) much more often than in fraternal twins, other siblings, or other relatives. Some scientists have proposed that a specific gene, 5HT2A102, may play an important role in the regulation of impulses. This gene, which contributes to serotonin regulation, has been implicated in ADHD as well as in aggressive and suicidal behaviors. Individuals with two of these genes on paired chromosomes scored higher on personality tests of impulsivity than those with only one or no copies of this gene.

As discussed in chapter 1, one theoretical model proposes that personality is derived from a combination of heritable influences (temperament) combined with environmental forces (character). One of the primary dimensions of temperament is termed "novelty-seeking," which is characterized by frequent, impulsive decision changes; difficulty coping with frustration; and poor control of temper, all of which may be related to avoidance of boredom. This trait, which may be genetically transmitted, is prominent in BPD.

Social Influences and BPD

We, along with other authors, have suggested that rapid social changes in modern societies promote BPD by disrupting integrated social supports. Impulsive behaviors are especially unbridled when the harness of social constraints falls off (see chapter 11). Some have suggested that psychiatric patients in more traditional, structured societies are less likely to present for treatment with symptoms of impulsivity but rather seek help for anxiety conflicts. Joel Paris contends that "social factors interact with other risk factors and promote BPD by lowering thresholds of impulsive behaviors."

Treatment Approaches

Practice guidelines of the American Psychiatric Association for treatment of BPD recognize a dimension of impulsive symptoms. Initial pharmacotherapy recommendations endorse the use of SRI (serotonin reuptake inhibitor) antidepressants. These include Prozac, Zoloft, Paxil, Celexa, Luvox, and Effexor. Some observers have noted significant amelioration of symptoms of impulsivity within one week of treatment, much faster than antidepressant effects usually appear. Sometimes doses higher than those used for treatment of depression are necessary. Data also indicate that some patients will respond to a different SRI if the first one fails.

If an SRI provides only partial relief, addition of antipsychotic (psychotropic) medicine is indicated. Most research has evaluated older drugs such as Thorazine, Haldol, and Navane. However, emerging research endorses utilization of newer antipsychotic medications, including Risperdal, Zyprexa, Seroquel, Geodon, and Abilify. Another category of supplementary medicines shown to be helpful for impulsive/aggressive behaviors is the mood stabilizers, which include lithium and antiseizure drugs such as Tegretol and Depakote. When these combinations are ineffective, monoamine oxidase inhibitor (MAOI) antidepressants such as Nardil or Parnate are recommended. These medicines cannot be used in combination with SRIs because of the risk of severe interactions. They also require dietary restrictions, which render them less convenient for many patients.

Revia is an opiate antagonist, which blocks the release of endorphins and certain neurotransmitters that may be associated with compelling urges such as overeating, alcohol abuse, gambling, stealing, spending/shopping, and especially self-mutilation. The medicine appears to block the subjective experiences of pleasure and relief of tension, which these impulsive behaviors endow. Higher than usual doses may be necessary to effect improvement.

Traditional antidepressants—tricyclic antidepressants (TCA) such as Elavil and Tofranil—may decrease inhibitions, thus worsening impulsivity. The same has been observed in short-acting minor tranquilizers such as Xanax and Ativan. These medicines should be avoided in BPD. Longer-acting tranquilizers such as Klonopin may be useful for anxiety and are not as disinhibiting.

Psychotherapy approaches to impulsive behavior often employ cognitive/behavioral techniques. Insight-oriented, psychodynamic, or psycho-analytically oriented psychotherapy may not be well tolerated by an impulsive person. Behavioral approaches, particularly dialectical behavioral therapy (DBT), will be discussed in more detail in chapter 6.

ACTION STEPS: *Managing Impulsivity*

1. *Keep good company.* The more you are around others who are healthy, the easier it is to resist acting on destructive impulses. Calling your AA sponsor is wiser than calling your drinking buddy.

2. *Use healthy distractions.* When tempted to turn to self-damaging behavior, look for other diversions instead. Find something productive to do at home rather than visit the destructive girlfriend, or spend too much money at the mall, or drink too much at the bar.

3. *Postpone decisions.* Don't say no; don't say yes. Say *maybe.* Especially when tempted by another to become involved in potentially harmful activity, delay your response. Even if you think you really want to be with the abusive (or substance-abusive) boyfriend when he calls, don't decide at that moment. Tell him you'll call him back. *Try to ingrain a habit of contemplating your decisions.*

4. *Stay busy.* When you are engaged in healthy activities, it is easier to resist impulsive actions. Maintaining a regular exercise program is especially helpful in minimizing anxiety, which can lead to impulsive behaviors.

6

Suicidal Behaviors and Self-Mutilation

No neurotic harbors thoughts of suicide which are not murderous impulses against others redirected upon himself.
—SIGMUND FREUD, *Totem and Taboo*, 1918

What a child doesn't receive he can seldom later give.
—P. D. JAMES, *Time to Be in Earnest (autobiography)*, 2000

No BPD symptom is more difficult for family and therapists to comprehend and cope with than self-injurious behavior. The reasons for self-mutilation, which typically takes the form of self-inflicted cuts or burns to various parts of the body, are varied and complex. What may start as an impulsive action can, over time, become a ritual of relief from anxiety. Suicidal behavior is not always a wish to die but may be a mechanism to communicate pain and a plea for help. As you will recall from chapter 5, Lizzie was heading down a dark road of drug abuse and dead-end affairs, which in this chapter lead to self-mutilation and suicide attempts. Following this are alarming statistics on suicide; new research into genetic and bio-physiological influences, new psychotherapeutic and medical treatments; a special section on the role of the hospital; and finally ways those close to the borderline can deal with self-destructive behaviors and suicidal gestures.

LIZZIE: PART TWO

As Cable turns onto New Haven Drive, he is not surprised to see the large overhanging oak trees, just as Liz had described. "Doc, I bet if you saw New Haven Drive, you'd say *no way*," she told him in one session. "No way a family as fucked up as mine could live on a street *this* Middle America." But she was wrong. He knew all too well that bad things could happen on beautiful, tree-lined streets. After five years in practice, he was almost convinced that *more* bad things could happen here than on streets lined with slums. He did not have to search for the number of the house; he saw the red porch swing immediately ("That swing is my favorite thing about the house—figures, it's not even *in* the damn house") and knew he had the right place.

As with so many of Liz's phone calls, last night's call had come at 2:00 A.M. Liver cirrhosis had taken her mother, Colleen, there was the wake and the funeral today, and Liz was unraveling—would he please, *please* come, he was her only hope of getting through this. *No,* he thought. That would violate too many boundaries. And he was already way out of bounds here, having inadvertently ended up treating both Liz and then, one year later, briefly, her mother. Certainly he had come to the funerals of some patients before. But this was so much more complicated. Still, he had broken so many rules already in trying to care for this difficult patient, he decided to allow compassion to overrule professional protocol.

●   ●   ●

He had met Liz four years ago in the Mercy Hospital ER after her overdose. Just a year out of psychiatric residency, Jeff Cable was intelligent, self-assured, and enthusiastic. He had learned his values from a loving family. He had learned medicine from a top-notch medical school. He would learn psychiatry from Elizabeth Compton.

She sat on the exam table in her hospital gown, her mouth still outlined in the gray charcoal they had used to pump her stomach. Her hair was matted and hung over her eyes like the fronds of a weeping willow. A thick stream of caked mascara merged with the charcoal at her mouth. Tall, slim, her long, thin legs hanging off the table, she reminded him of a poor, helpless stork that had become mired in an oil slick and was fighting for survival.

Sitting on a chair next to her, his first question was one he would ask Liz repeatedly over the next two years: "Why?"

Her reply, still immersed in the swamp of the pills she had swallowed, rambled on about a dentist she worked for—a Dr. Bradford—with whom she had been having an affair. . . . Bradford's wife was visiting the office more often, glaring at her . . . the other women in the office winking at each other . . . Bradford saying it wouldn't be a good idea to keep seeing each other. . . . No, not really, she interrupted herself, that wasn't the reason, wasn't him or any of them in the office . . . it was the latest row with her mother . . . she couldn't stand it anymore. . . . No, that's not it. . . . Last night Rod—her neighbor, best friend, and occasional "fuck buddy"—announced that he would be moving to a new apartment. . . . Oh, she said, well, they could still visit each other, couldn't they? . . . Well, sure, he guessed so. . . .

Her garbled stream of consciousness focused entirely on recent events—the *now*—as if she expected him to somehow pick up these scrambled bits and pieces he was hearing about for the first time and fit them into her entire history, which he knew nothing about. The immediately preceding events were not what he was asking her about, of course, and something in her sad voice told him she understood that, but for the moment at least, she could not attempt to plumb the depths of the iceberg, only the tip.

She remembered opening a bottle of wine, she continued, to toast Rod's new place. . . . And then it came out that he was moving in with someone . . . and, well, that it just wouldn't be a good idea for them to stay friends. . . . He abruptly left the apartment. . . . Liz stared at the two poured wineglasses for a long time, wondering if *her life* was a good idea. Then she decided it was time to die.

Not just aspirin this time. After swallowing a tin of Bufferin, she started on the Sominex and then the allergy medicine. What the hell, she even finished her birth control pills! She cursed the world that she was out of Vicodin. . . . She thought of cutting herself, as she had been doing for years to cope with anxiety, but figured her sluggish blood would just loiter lazily in her limbs, so she didn't bother. By that time she felt dizzy and lay down.

After that, it all became fuzzy. She remembered the phone ringing and having trouble making her tongue move in response to her mother's questions. She remembered the paramedics and the bumpy ambulance ride. Mostly, she remembered retching in the ER. For someone who had gained some measure of comfort from vomiting, she was stunned at how bad it felt when it wasn't so carefully modulated.

•   •   •

The rickety porch steps creak under his weight, and one slat, he notices, is about to split altogether. With Lindsey the stepfather long gone and Colleen having been in ill health, Cable realizes, no one has been around to do the repair work. He stops on the porch landing to admire Liz's accurate reporting: the red swing, the two large multipaned windows, the old rusted screen door with the massive oak door now partially open behind it, revealing a knot of shadowy figures standing in the parlor.

"Jeff!" Before he can prepare himself, Liz bursts past the screen door and flings herself at him, almost knocking him over. She hugs him tightly. "You came! I was sure you wouldn't!"

He pulls away a bit, embarrassed by the hug and her use of his first name, to give her time to gather herself. "Sure, Liz, I told you I would try." He looks at her and something is slightly off-kilter; he realizes that it is her gaze, which is level with his. He is accustomed to talking with her while she wears flat hospital slippers or dental-tech shoes; standing now in heels, she is the same height as he is. "I'm so sorry about your mother, Liz."

She leads him inside, her hand tightly gripping his own, as though he would evaporate into thin air if she let go. "These are my sisters, Eleanor and Esther," she says to him. And then adds proudly: "And *this* is Dr. Cable." Shaking hands with each of them, he feels almost like a celebrity and prays that he is not blushing. Once again, he marvels at the precision of Liz's descriptive powers *("My sisters don't look like me at all, they're short, squat, and blond—they must've inherited my mom's genes, I got my dad's.")*. He makes a mental note to encourage Liz to investigate a career in writing or journalism when she is ready.

Having nothing more to say for the moment, they stand awkwardly in the empty parlor. He takes the time to peer into the living room, where the closed black casket holding Colleen's remains sits on a large oak table in front of the fireplace. Vases of various sizes holding bouquets of flowers surround the casket. Music fills the room, not the funereal organ music he expects but Mozart instead. No one else appears to have arrived yet, and he thinks that perhaps, in the panic of Liz's late-night call, he had written down the wrong time for the wake. "I must be early," he suggests.

The three sisters glance knowingly at each other. "No, you're right on time," says Eleanor politely. "We aren't expecting too many people. Just a few of Mom's friends from church. Most of her family passed away some time ago."

Cable and the three sisters go into the living room, drawn by the casket and the absence of other mourners in the parlor—it seems, simply, the prudent thing to do. That morning, dressing in front of the mirror, he realized he had never been to a wake before; his wife had to tell him that they weren't even called "wakes" nowadays but rather "visitations." What little knowledge he had of the ceremony was absorbed through movies and TV, and he had no time to make calls or do research. What did one do at a wake? Would the mood be mournful? Nostalgic? Celebrative (the deceased, now at peace, would have wanted it that way)? Did one bring anything—food, flowers, wine, a condolence card? He had decided against a gift of any kind, succumbing to the conceit that his simple presence was gift enough. Most of all, he worried if Liz would be able to get through it without caving in like the rickety steps outside. She had made great strides over the past few months, but a traumatic event such as this, coupled with seeing her sisters again in the house, could transport her back into depression. He wondered if he was destined to spend another evening in Mercy Hospital's ER.

The casket is made of hard metal (stainless steel, Cable guesses), and the sheer size of it surprises him. In his mind he can see tiny Colleen sitting in his office—*two* of her would fit in this chest. On top of the casket sit numerous snapshots of Colleen, Bill—the sisters' biological father—and the three daughters arranged in a semicircle around a much larger framed photo of the same family of Comptons huddled together on a dock, apparently, Cable guesses again, on Lake Michigan: Bill and Colleen, with the three grinning daughters kneeling in front. Liz, the youngest, couldn't be more than five. A light blue sailboat occupies the background.

"That was taken on July 4, 1975," states Esther, who passes for the unofficial "family chronicler," according to Liz, if there is such a thing in this family. "We still had the *Flying E's*."

"We were a real family then," says Eleanor, in a voice filled with longing.

By his side, he can sense Liz becoming agitated. Out of the corner of his eye he sees her staring intently at the photo; if her vision were laser beams, the photo would have two burn holes in it. Cable has seen that face in his office, right before she exploded in a rage, usually about her mother.

"Of course we were happy then, you moron," Liz blurts out in a short clip that could have snapped twigs if there were any around. "No *Lindsey* then. But you two wouldn't know about *that,* would you? You were older; you just left! I was the only one who had to take his shit!"

Watching the drooping heads of the two sisters, Cable notices that the light in both sisters' eyes (as well as Colleen's in the last year of her life) barely registers—a weak candle flame that a strong wind could instantly extinguish. Of the three "E's," only Elizabeth's eyes reflect the emotions boiling underneath. They all hear a hesitant knock on the screen door, but no one makes a move to answer it.

"You weren't," Esther murmurs finally, with a sidelong glance at Eleanor, "the *only* one."

• • •

Cable looked forward to their sessions in the hospital. Liz was attractive, expressive, and flirtatious. Though he secretly enjoyed her overtures, he parried them with a raised eyebrow and realigned the discussion to the seriousness of their work. She would never know, *could* never know, that over the years she also sometimes illuminated his fantasies.

After two days, her suicidal feelings had diminished, even though nothing in her life had changed. Liz complained of multiple side effects from the medicine and refused to continue it. Dr. Cable fought over the phone with Liz's insurance company, which questioned her continued stay in the hospital, since the nurses' notes now stated that she no longer felt suicidal and that she was refusing medication. Without insurance coverage, Liz worried that her hospital bill would be catastrophic, so she, too, lobbied for discharge. After five days, she got her wish. Her insurance allowed outpatient therapy with a social worker, but Liz didn't want a new therapist—she wanted Cable, and he agreed to continue the therapy.

After discharge, Liz returned to the dental offices of Vitale & Bradford but quickly learned that no one wanted her there. Vitale promised her a good reference if she resigned, and she took him up on it. Now unemployed, she couldn't afford to see Cable, but she did call him occasionally, especially when she was drunk or very lonely.

She was forced to move back in with her mother and stepfather on New Haven Drive. Her old bedroom was just as she had left it. The Little Girl in the picture still hung over her dresser.

Living in her old house, Liz was surprised at how easy it was for the occupants to avoid one another. No one said much. She and her parents ate dinner at different times and watched television or read in different rooms. Liz swayed on the porch swing, staring endlessly into the rustling leaves of the oak trees. Her parents displayed no reaction when she announced that she had a new job at the community dental clinic across town. Shortly thereafter, she moved out. It wasn't hard. It was like leaving a ghost town.

A couple of months later, Liz sat on the edge of the same exam table at Mercy with both wrists bandaged. David, the man who had dropped her off at the hospital, was long gone. She had tried to explain to him that she wasn't really trying to kill herself—not exactly. She was spending the night with him after they had gone to the South Side to score some coke. David had awakened to find Liz in the bathroom, cutting on her wrists. The bleeding was more than usual—the cocaine must have increased her blood pressure—and David just freaked! But she really wasn't trying to die, although, she supposed, that might have been all right. Anyway, she told Dr. Cable, there goes another boyfriend. And, by the way, aren't you looking spiffy!

After a few days in the hospital, Liz was discharged and agreed to keep up more regular appointments with Dr. Cable. She was now on different medications and tolerating them well, though psychotherapy was frustrating for both of them. Just when Liz felt she was making progress, he would be called out of town to attend a conference or leave for vacation. Dr. Cable would find himself extending the time of the session, thinking they were engaged in important issues, only to recognize that by the next week Liz had forgotten what they had discussed. Sometimes Liz had no recollection of what went on in therapy. Her thoughts would wander. She had a way of turning off her mind and imagining different shapes in the carpet patterns or conjuring up a different face for Cable. On other occasions she would take imaginary rides in a hot-air balloon in the painting hanging over his desk.

She gradually opened up about the cutting. When she was fourteen, she accidentally cut herself shaving her legs in the bathtub. But instead of grimacing with pain, she found herself staring dumbly at the oozing blood. There was no pain, only numbness, as the bathwater gradually filled with red clouds.

The invisible numbness enveloped her like a coat of insulation, and the curious scientist in her began to test its boundaries. She would bang her head or fist against the wall, seeking pain as if it were a mischievous playmate hiding from her. Once, styling her hair in front of a makeup mirror, she held a curling iron to her forearm to see if she could feel the burn. The smell of burning flesh reached her before the pain.

The razor, however, became her most comforting companion. Fondling it gently, she eventually carved a miniature road map of emotion into her flesh. Starting with her arms, she later moved to her legs, always at places where her clothes could cover the etchings. In later years, she would slice on her breasts and genitals. Over the years, her scars became a carefully maintained diary, documenting those times she was bad, or hurt, or dared to feel anger.

Sometimes Lizzie could actually experience pain, an exquisite burning that would snap her back into consciousness. If that didn't work, the streaming blood could awaken her from her reverie. Occasionally, however, her blood flow would dam up; she could not always maintain a consistent blood flow necessary to release the tension. She would cut deeper, pressing her flesh, milking the wound like a prostatic old man standing impatiently at a urinal.

But why, Cable again wanted to know, did she cut at all? Was it for relief from anxiety? Or from guilt? Was it a way of punishing herself? Did she experience pleasure from it?

After contemplating his questions for a moment, Liz shrugged offhandedly. "You can chalk that up to all of the above." Before cutting, she would often feel increasing pressure and tension. Then she would retreat to the bathroom, indulge her guilty pleasure, feel a transient flood of rapture as she watched the trickling red stream, and then be overwhelmed by guilt and disgust at her behavior as she vowed to herself to abstain from then on.

The cutting became a kind of masturbatory release. Unlike some of her girlfriends, Liz was uncomfortable touching her developing breasts or genitals and disdained her friends' interest in sex, but she experienced an orgasmic release when she cut herself.

When he focused on his concerns about her cutting, she would stop for a while but replace it with increased binging and purging. Then she would gain control of food, but replace it with alcohol and other drugs. At Cable's urging, she went to Alcoholics Anonymous but felt out of place and refused to return. When she thought the medicines were causing her to put on weight, she stopped them and increased her purging. When it came to her addictions and coping mechanisms, Liz could be very flexible.

•   •   •

Three hours later, the handful of mourners who did come to pay their respects have gone home, with the exception of Mrs. Marchand, apparently a parishioner at Colleen's church, who sits at the kitchen table with Cable and the three sisters. Wearing a fur coat, a strand of white pearls, and a black pillbox hat with net veil, she sits a few feet back from the table, her arms folded tightly over her purse. She said she was a good friend of Colleen, and none of the sisters has the heart to kick her out. Sadly, Cable recognizes, she probably has nowhere else to go. He had tried to extricate himself before the first bottle of wine but had failed miserably against Liz's pleadings and now they were uncorking the third bottle, a bottle of cheap Chablis from Colleen's bottomless liquor cabinet.

"She started after Dad died," reports Esther, ever the chronicler, to the group. "She'd take a bottle of burgundy and sneak off to her bedroom. She liked the red then. No one was supposed to know, but I would walk past her room at night and hear the glass tinkling. You guys were too young then, barely out of diapers. The next morning, I'd check the trash can and sure enough: empty bottles hidden under a pile of newspapers."

"You're joking!" exclaims Eleanor.

"After she married Lindsey, she changed to white, only God knows why. And then she went to the hard stuff—mainly vodka. Joey—you know, the kid who used to work at the 7-Eleven? He let it slip one day."

The name *Lindsey* falls like a live hand grenade on the kitchen table. Liz's jaw is jutting out, he sees, and she is having problems focusing, whether from inner emotional turmoil or the wine or both. Both Eleanor and Esther, recognizing that Esther has opened a can of worms, stare uneasily at the empty bottles of wine on the table.

"I couldn't tell anyone, not even Mom," Liz begins. "*Especially* Mom. She was enthralled with the bastard. The whole congregation was in love with him."

Four heads swivel as one to see the reaction of Mrs. Marchand, a long-time upstanding member of the aforesaid congregation. However, Mrs. Marchand only shudders, as if she had just swallowed a bottleful of castor oil. "Never liked the way Lindsey played," she says. "Too loud."

"Who'd believe an eight-year-old?" Liz says, more to herself than anyone around the table. "And if they did believe me, it would've been even worse. I thought, 'What if they put me in jail or electrocute me or whatever horrible things they do to bad girls like me?'"

"We all hated him, Lizzie," Eleanor says, putting her arm around Liz's shoulders. "You just didn't know why. Remember how we quit our piano lessons? Stopped going to church? That's why we got out of there— *here*—as soon as we could. We had to get away from him."

"I knew," says Liz, "deep down I knew. We just didn't talk about it. None of us talked about anything."

"We should have," Esther says. "It was our only hope. I've been meaning to say this to you for a long time, Lizzie. I'm sorry. I should have said something, done something. I was just so scared. I was the older sister. I should have protected you."

"Me, too," agrees Eleanor, on the verge of tears. "Me, too."

Mrs. Marchand, perhaps feeling that she had disappointed the group with her previous terseness, says: "It's always good to talk about things."

The sisters' confessions are barely registering with Liz, Cable sees. She is off in a reverie he has seen many times in his office. "I took it out on Mom. I blamed her for everything. How could she not know what was going on? She just didn't want to know. On the church steps she would just beam and pretend she had this nice little family, but back home she would just sink into the bottle. I think it's what she wanted to happen." Liz was shouting now. "I think she sacrificed us to him, so the prick would leave her alone!"

"Lizzie!" Esther admonishes reflexively, then looks down, ashamed. "Maybe you're right."

Cable is tempted to join the verbal autopsy but hesitates. For some months he had treated both Colleen and Liz without knowing they were mother and daughter. Called in by the ICU for a consult, he was met with an older woman who had been vomiting blood for a day before a neighbor brought her to the ER. Colleen's depression and self-destructive alcohol abuse were apparent. Dr. Cable agreed to follow her in the hospital and afterward. But it was several months before the converging stories hit him like a kick to the gut: Colleen Lindsey was Liz Compton's mother! A few months later, as Colleen got sicker, mother and daughter shared enough closeness to realize that they were seeing the same therapist. They were much less distressed about it than was Dr. Cable. Indeed, Liz was amused. But Dr. Cable's discomfort became moot as Colleen's deteriorating physical condition lessened her psychiatric visits. "Your mother was a sad, lonely woman who was scared most of her life," he interjects now. "That's why she needed the booze." Afraid he has said too much already and daring not to share the details he knew of Colleen's own abused past, Cable looks away, signaling that he will add no more.

"Do you know that I *cried* at Lindsey's funeral?" Liz says, "Can you believe that? Mom is sitting there at the service, saying absolutely nothing, drunk as a skunk, and here I am, crying a river. *Who* am I crying for? I kept asking myself, who . . ."

Liz drops her head to the table and begins to weep uncontrollably. "Funerals are for the living," states Mrs. Marchand, to no one in particular.

● ● ●

After Lizzie's first overdose at age fourteen, thoughts of suicide comforted her like an old friend. When she felt too much pressure that couldn't be relieved, she daydreamed about dying. Her second suicide attempt proved that drug overdoses were too uncertain, too messy. Maybe running the car in the garage was more efficient. She had written a will. She wanted to be cremated and scattered over the ocean near the beach. She could sleep forever. All would be still and peaceful. Time would no longer matter; it would no longer be something to be endured. She would just look out over the ocean, like the Little Girl in the picture. Liz could not understand why Dr. Cable was so adamantly opposed to her dying. Over time he became, more than anything else, another person to whom she felt responsible. She didn't want to disappoint him, as she had disappointed her mother and her old boss, Dr. Vitale.

Liz met and married Sebastian six months after she left the dental practice. Liz wasn't quite sure why she married him. Maybe because he asked. Maybe because she could not stand to be alone anymore. They had fun together. They drank together. He could be mean when he was drunk, but he always apologized afterward. Neither wanted children.

Cable was surprised when he met Sebastian. They did not look like they belonged together. He was a few inches shorter. While Liz was well dressed, he was slovenly. While Liz was insightful and sardonic, Sebastian seemed obtuse and absorbed no subtext in conversation. When he met with both of them just before the wedding, Sebastian seemed jealous of the special union Cable and Liz had established, leaving Sebastian on the outside. Dr. Cable felt compelled to explain Liz's inside jokes to Sebastian, who still seemed not to get them.

Liz became pregnant a few months later. No question that she would have an abortion, yet Dr. Cable noted an increasing, persistent melancholy after the operation. Adjusting the medicine didn't help. The self-inflicted wounds, which had been in abeyance for several months, returned. But now Liz began slashing her breasts—on the underside, where scars would not be noticed—and around her genitals. Within a year, Sebastian was gone.

Over the years, Cable frequently questioned his usefulness to Liz. One Monday morning, a few days following what he thought had been a productive session, Liz arrived for her appointment and took off her coat to reveal both her arms cut and bleeding. He could discern ragged muscle tissue where she had sliced deeply. As always, he maintained his surface equanimity, while his insides shook with helplessness and pain. He was able to take her to the emergency room and stayed with her for two hours while she awaited care. His day's schedule was in shambles, as he spent most of the morning guiding her through the ER maze and generating affidavits to hospitalize her involuntarily, since she was refusing admission.

It was all hopeless, she said. Shamefully, he was beginning to agree with her. He imagined how less complicated his life would be if Liz actually did kill herself. No more late-night phone calls. No more worrying about her safety. No more hospital visits. His guilt was compounded when he admitted to himself that two of his greatest fears were the embarrassment among his colleagues of losing a patient and the potential lawsuit from an angry family determined to blame someone else for Liz's death.

●   ●   ●

"Where's the bathroom?" Cable asks Esther. "I need to uh—you know—the wine."

Actually, he does not really need to relieve himself (he has had only a few sips of wine), but with Liz having left the kitchen five minutes ago, he wants to check up on her. Assuming the worst, he has learned the hard way, is probably the best course.

"Top of the stairs," replies Esther. "Make a left. Right next to Lizzie's old room."

Treading slowly up the stairs, he imagines the dire scene he will encounter when he opens the bathroom door—Liz lying on the floor in a pool of blood, empty canisters of pills scattered around her lifeless body. . . . Yet when he gets to the second-floor landing, the bathroom door is wide open and the room itself, he can see clearly, is empty. Her bedroom door, on the other hand, is closed shut, leading to a new dread set in a new location.

"Liz," he says, knocking softly on the bedroom door, "are you okay?" The silence that follows is endless, frightening. He knocks again. "Liz?"

The door swings open and she stands there, smiling weakly. "I'm okay, Doc. Thought I bit the big one, did you?"

He smiles back, trying mightily not to reveal the knot in his stomach. "The thought," he replies, "crossed my mind."

"Well, come on in, Doc. Nothing like visiting the scene of the crime to spark wonderful old memories." He walks in, surveying the furnishings, which in most respects resemble the room of a teenager: a cabinet holding a small hi-fi, speakers, and a turntable; a vinyl record collection underneath; posters of Madonna and Stevie Nicks and even one of Janis Joplin from way before her time—before *his* time. A white bookcase with a dozen Nancy Drew novels in perfect condition, standing in a neat row on the top shelf. And above her dresser the picture of the Little Girl on the beach. "Some things never change, do they, Doc?"

She's right about that, he thinks, but says instead: "Sometimes you're the only one who can make them change."

"I'm going back to school," she blurts out. "I applied to Loyola. I think I need to leave here for a while. They have a good nursing program there. Maybe I'll become a nurse or something."

He thinks that over for a moment and smiles. "Why not a doctor?"

She grins. "And become like you? On call twenty-four hours a day? Give me a break. I want a life, for Chrissakes." Despite his attempt to maintain his professional demeanor, he breaks up in laughter and recognizes that it is the first time they have so unabashedly enjoyed a laugh together. Something, he feels, is different about her today. A certain maturity? "I'm serious, you know. I talked to Eleanor this morning. She and Jake have plenty of money, no kids to support. She said she'd lend me the money for school. I'll pay her back, she knows that."

"Sounds like you've been doing a lot of thinking lately. We should talk about it."

"Of course. But I think I'm ready." Her voice suddenly gets softer, and her words come more hesitantly. "You know you saved my life, Dr. Cable."

For the second time that day, he hopes his face is not flushed red. "Liz, you're the one who's been doing the work. You —"

"Yeah, yeah, blah-blah-blah." But he wonders how much he really *had* contributed. In the end, it is up to her to change; she is making the journey, he is only a guide. And now she is pushing him away, saying she would make the rest of the trek without him, and oddly it feels comfortable. He has a sensation he does not often get to feel: pride. Naturally, her plans need to be discussed. Is she just running away again? Is school just a more respectable escape than a drug binge? But unlike some of her past impulses—like her misbegotten marriage to Sebastian—this sounds more hopeful. He marvels at the irony: a day that was supposed to be so bleak now holds such promise.

"I can give you a referral for a psychiatrist up there," he says blankly.

Suddenly she turns to him and grabs his arm. "You want to know what you did for me?" she says, as if reading his mind. "I'll tell you. You've been the only consistency, the only person I could count on who would be the same, unchanging. I always pictured you sitting in your office waiting for me, as if you didn't have any other life. It wasn't anything particular that you said or did. It was just your being there with me through all this craziness. I needed to connect with another human being, a healthy human being, someone who could remind me of what it was like to live. That's what you did for me."

"You know there's still a lot of work to do. There are still things to resolve," Cable remarks, sounding too stuffy to himself.

"I know," she says. "But you've been showing me how to do that work. I'm learning how to forgive—others and myself. And besides," she adds, "hate is just *so* exhausting," and walks out of the bedroom, leaving him behind, for a moment at least, to stare at the Little Girl above her dresser.

The Suicidal or Self-Mutilating Borderline

Stop by an emergency room in any large metropolitan hospital on a weekend night and you are likely to find at least one patient waiting to be admitted with self-inflicted wounds. Often, triage nurses are not overly gracious to "psychs" in the waiting room; they take up resources that should be used for people who are victims of injury or disease that is not of their own doing. Whether the suicide attempt or self-mutilation was done to die, to relieve anxiety, or to get attention doesn't matter. Someone who hurts herself intentionally is repellant and frightening.

BPD is the only psychiatric diagnosis that is partly defined by recurrent and deliberate attempts to self-inflict pain and/or commit suicide. This characteristic is one of the most difficult for others to understand. Although the motivations and the effects may differ, suicidal and self-harming behaviors are a distinguishing hallmark of BPD. Indeed, if psychosis or mental retardation is not the underlying pathology, recurrent self-mutilation virtually confirms the diagnosis of BPD. Further, a recent study indicated that patients with the most severe BPD symptoms exhibited the greatest potential for the highest number of—and most lethal—self-harming behaviors. And yet, many BPD patients with recurrent self-destructive episodes remain undiagnosed, in the United States and in other countries.

Suicide and BPD

Studies reveal that a diagnosis of a personality disorder accompanies completed suicides in almost 30 percent of cases. Personality disorder is the fourth most significant risk factor for suicide, following depression, schizophrenia, and alcoholism (all of which are frequently associated with a personality disorder). In the high-risk group comprised of adolescents and young adults (ages fifteen to twenty-nine), those who committed suicide had been diagnosed with BPD in a third of the cases. More than 70 percent of all BPD patients have a history of suicide attempts or self-mutilation, compared to only 17.5 percent of patients with other personality disorders.

The rate of suicide in borderlines approaches 10 percent, which is comparable to that seen in other high-risk populations, such as those suffering from affective or schizophrenic diseases. It is almost a thousand times the suicide rate in the general population. Although many BPD symptoms ameliorate over time (see chapter 12), the risk of suicide persists throughout the life cycle, even into the sixth decade. A number of factors further heighten the risk for suicide in borderlines. These include:

- Previous suicide attempts

- Prior hospitalizations

- History of persistent depression

- Hopelessness

- Impulsivity and aggression

- Comorbid antisocial characteristics (self-injury is often found in prison populations)

- Alcohol or drug abuse

- Substance abuse by a parent

- Unemployment and frequent job changes

- Higher education

- Young adulthood

- Older age

- History of severe childhood abuse (especially sexual) and/or early loss

- Financial instability

- Lack of stable residence

- Prison sentence

- Inadequate or inconsistent psychiatric care

Liz embraced the option of suicide like a comforting old friend. No matter how bad she felt, the awareness that she could terminate the pain by ending her life was soothing. Ironically, when she discovered how to inflict recurrent minideaths through cutting and burning, she felt, for the first time, in control of her life.

The Lure of Self-Injurious Behavior

Self-injurious behavior (SIB) can be expressed in many ways and may be independent of suicidal intent. It may take the form of overdosing, cutting, burning, head-banging, biting, hair-pulling, or severe recklessness. Its prevalence has been rising significantly over the past forty years. In a study of almost two thousand mostly male military recruits, approximately 4 percent reported a history of deliberate self-harm. Most of these individuals exhibited a higher proportion of borderline and other personality disorder symptoms. Although rare in the general population, self-mutilation occurs in the general psychiatric population at a rate estimated to be as much as 7 percent. In borderlines, the prevalence is about 75 percent. From 55 to 85 percent of self-mutilators have made at least one suicide attempt.

Other populations in which SIB occurs prominently include the mentally retarded and autistic, the psychotic, and incarcerated inmates. Self-harming in retarded or autistic individuals usually involves repetitive, compulsive, and stereotypical activity such as head-banging or finger-chewing. In the psychotic person, self-mutilation usually is a result of delusional thinking, often revolving around religious or sexual themes. One schizophrenic man, guilty over his compulsive interest in pornography, gouged out his eye after hearing voices telling him, "If thy right eye offends thee, pluck it out!" SIB is noted among prisoners but often is manipulative, designed to elicit transfer to another facility. Sometimes there is a contagion effect, in which several residents in an institution become self-mutilating. Self-mutilation also is often observed in patients with concurrent eating disorders. The recent trend of tattoos and body piercing may reflect an increasing fascination with this kind of behavior in our society.

Often the flirtation with death or injury is motivated by an attraction to danger. Unprotected sex or syringe-sharing with strangers, frequenting dangerous neighborhoods or seeking out dangerous situations or people, or mixing drugs and alcohol are some of the self-destructive behaviors that may result in harm but that are not specifically intended to cause death. One man, a wealthy businessman, was constantly attracted to danger. He avidly pursued bungee-jumping, skydiving, and white-water rafting during his leisure time. A cocaine abuser who easily could have arranged his purchases more safely would purposely cruise dangerous neighborhoods in his expensive car, looking to buy drugs. At one point, Liz's pursuit of self-punishment led to a punishing regimen of long-distance running despite (or indeed because of) severe knee pain and the discouragement of her doctors, who warned her of potential irreversible damage to her knees.

These actions are consistent with the frequent passive suicidal behavior of borderlines, who often espouse a kind of, "If it happens, it happens" attitude toward serious injury or death. Self-mutilators perceive their behavior as less life-threatening than those who attempt suicide. But suicide attempters with a past history of SIB tend to be more depressed, anxious, impulsive, and more likely to underestimate the lethal potential of their suicidal gestures. Therefore their risk of death is greater.

Self-mutilation usually begins in adolescence and may persist for decades. It may serve several different functions:

• *Feeling physical pain.* This is probably the most common reason for inflicting self-harm. As we have noted, many borderline patients describe feelings of dissociation, detachment from feelings; they may feel unreal and alienated. SIB may serve to snap the individual back to reality. Physical pain also may distract the person from her psychological pain, as with Liz, who would usually cut herself when she was feeling especially depressed and angry. In addition, the pain of SIB may be used to punish oneself. When the borderline becomes angry with herself, she may inflict pain as retribution and as expression of her self-disgust.

For many borderlines, especially after repeated SIB, the sensation of pain dissipates, similar to the way addicts build tolerance for certain drugs. They may then attempt to intensify the SIB. When they can no longer penetrate the insulation of self-imposed anesthesia, they may find some relief in merely observing their bleeding, bruises, and burns.

• *Relieving tension.* Liz's self-mutilation often was preceded by a buildup of anxiety and tension. During these times she was irritable and anxious. The sight of her blood allowed an almost orgasmic release. As she watched blood flow down her arm, she felt the tension ebb from her body and was finally able to relax and sleep peacefully.

• *Establishing control.* Many borderlines feel overwhelmed by a loss of autonomy in their lives. SIB allows some measure of control. They may carefully measure how deeply they cut, at times venturing deeper into the flesh, to determine how far they can go before bleeding or tissue damage divests them of that control. At such times they may feel a sense of pride in their ability to withstand pain while engaging in their unique ritual of self-mutilation.

Borderlines also may utilize pain as a way of controlling urges. One male patient, ruled by his religious doctrine forbidding masturbation, would cut on his penis in an attempt to eliminate his sexual feelings.

In addition, SIB may be a tool to manipulate others. It may serve as a plea for help, as an expression of anger, or as a way to maintain a relationship with a friend or a doctor.

• *Ensuring security.* Liz's SIB was a guilty pleasure, about which she would tell no one. It also served as her secret security, which she could rely on during times of intense frustration. When alcohol or drugs or stealing would no longer alleviate her pain, she could always depend on the relief afforded from her self-mutilation.

• *Searching for ecstasy.* Though most people find it difficult to understand, some borderlines find excitement in self-mutilation. They describe a feeling of living on the edge and experience a high when they inflict pain. For some, there is sexual excitement. Sometimes Liz would masturbate with scissors, reaching a stronger orgasm when she saw blood.

Characteristics of Self-Mutilators

Self-mutilation typically begins at an early age, often in adolescence, as was the case with Lizzie. A childhood history of severe deprivation or abuse is common. A borderline with a history of childhood sexual abuse is ten times more likely to attempt suicide than a borderline without this history.

The urge for SIB is persistent and chronic for years, but it eventually diminishes over time, although suicidality may persist for decades. A European study documented that within a year of an initial episode of self-harming, 15 percent of patients repeated the behavior, with a completed suicide occurring in up to 2 percent of individuals. A discouraging British investigation of self-mutilating patients found that active intervention by the primary care physician had little impact on diminishing future self-harming activity.

Depression, anxiety, irritability, feelings of emptiness, and chaotic relationships are frequently associated. Impulsivity is seen in both mutilating and nonmutilating borderlines and is therefore associated with, but not predictive of, SIB. Comorbid substance abuse and eating disorders often are present.

The beginning of the self-injury process is frequently marked by a feeling of dissociation. The individual feels numb and distant from others and his own feelings. Inflicting pain is sometimes an attempt, not always successful, to relieve this emotional anesthesia. Although most borderlines experience anger and aggression, self-mutilators appear to have less ability to express these affects directly and outwardly. For them, SIB may represent the traditional psychoanalytic model of "anger turned inward."

Genetic Influences

Family studies confirm that depression and suicidal behavior are more common among blood relatives. BPD and depression appear to have genetic links. However, no consistent studies have determined the heritability of SIB. One tantalizing case report from the Far East is suggestive. It describes a family in which six of nine siblings engaged in SIB. One of the siblings who engaged in SIB was adopted away at birth and maintained no contacts with the family of origin, thus eliminating any common environmental influences as a factor in the behavior.

Physiology of SIB: The Construction of Self-Destruction

As described briefly in chapter 1, neurotransmitters (NTs) may be implicated in a great deal of borderline behavior. Evidence from animal and human studies suggests that dysregulation of dopamine (DA), an NT related to adrenaline, results in increased SIB. When animal experiments are performed that increase the brain's sensitivity to DA, SIB increases. Agents that block DA activity reverse the destructive behavior.

Certain maladies in humans are also suggestive. Lesch-Nyhan syndrome is a genetic disease resulting in mental retardation and frequent SIB, a result of metabolic dysfunction. DA is very low in the brains of these patients, theoretically resulting in hypersensitivity to residual, ambient DA. DA-blockers decrease SIB in these individuals. The most common DA-blockers are the antipsychotic drugs.

The role of serotonin (ST) in depression and obsessive-compulsive disorder is well established. Since SIB is often related to depression, and since it assumes compulsive qualities similar to those in obsessive-compulsive disorder, its connection to ST is implied. Studies in animals and humans have correlated decreased ST levels in the central nervous system with increased aggressive and self-destructive behaviors. Suicide attempters and patients exhibiting SIB have lower levels of ST metabolites in their cerebrospinal fluid. Chemical manipulation of ST levels also affects SIB. Finally, studies have found higher levels of certain serotonin receptors (called 5HT2a) in the brains of adult and teenage suicide victims.

Other NTs, such as norepinephrine (which is chemically related to DA) and gamma-aminobutyric acid (GABA), also have been studied for their relationship to SIB. However, their connections to suicide and SIB are not as well established.

The body's own endorphin system is mobilized during SIB and may explain some of the ensuing analgesic, dissociative, anxiety-relieving, addictive, and euphoric effects of this action. Painful stimulation causes a release of endorphins, which are the body's internal opiates. These chemicals reduce pain and produce euphoria in some, just like the administration of opiate drugs. SIB patients who do not experience pain during self-mutilation often demonstrate generally higher pain thresholds. Some theorize that the SIB patient may become addicted to his own endorphins, thus compulsively repeating the self-administration of pain. Some studies revealed increased blood levels of endorphin-related substances in SIB patients.

Sustained stress has been known to affect a brain circuit that connects the hypothalamus, pituitary, and adrenal glands. This system controls cortisol secretion, which affects the emotional continuum from hyperarousal at one extreme, to dissociation at the other. Borderlines with a history of severe, sustained child abuse exhibit significant disruptions in cortisol levels. Self-mutilation and accompanying feelings of dissociation have been associated with fluctuations in cortisol levels. Medicines that modify ST levels (SRIs) correct these fluctuations.

Some have proposed an epileptic model for SIB. As noted in chapter 1, childhood trauma may interfere with development of the brain.

Some studies have shown brain wave electroencephalogram (EEG) abnormalities in some borderline patients. The experience of SIB mimics atypical, partial seizures, with feelings of dissociation and unreality, analgesia, visual distortions, and abrupt mood changes.

Treating SIB and Suicide

Treatment of suicidal and self-mutilating behaviors—keeping the patient alive—is the highest priority of any therapy approach. Choosing the setting for treatment is the first consideration. If the person cannot be managed safely at home, confinement in a hospital setting may be necessary, while allowing time for medication and psychotherapeutic interventions to be effective.

The Role of the Hospital

Actively suicidal patients should be hospitalized. Patients who continuously self-mutilate without suicidal intent also can present a danger, since they may underestimate the effects of their behavior. However, chronically suicidal patients gain less from hospitalization. In addition, frequent or prolonged hospitalizations can be countertherapeutic if they perpetuate dependency and postpone the patient taking active responsibility for treatment.

Thus, whether to hospitalize the patient is a complex decision. Over his years of treating Liz, Dr. Cable frequently wrestled with this concern. He feared she might get too comfortable in the hospital and avoid dealing with issues outside; yet not institutionalizing her during times of stress ran the risk of irreversible physical harm or even death. During crisis times, neither Liz nor Dr. Cable slept much.

A compromise solution is "day hospital," in which a patient attends hospital activities during the day but does not sleep there. This arrangement affords more flexibility and allows the patient to invoke more freedom in a less restrictive environment. Day hospital also can serve as a useful transition from inpatient care to outpatient visits in the office.

Riding herd over all of these difficult decisions is the specter of managed care. In today's political and economic climate, mental health care, to a great degree, has been removed from the hands of clinicians by insurance and managed care organizations. Although financial accountability and responsibility are clearly necessary, decisions about health care are too often made by those whose priorities favor profit over palliation. Research confirms that treatment for BPD, which may be life-threatening, requires intensive therapy for at least a year. Within that time, about 75 percent of BPD patients show improvement; almost 95 percent exhibit improvement after two years. Treatment may require several hospitalizations and at least weekly outpatient care. Some patients require extensive hospital stays lasting weeks or months, not days. With limits on the length of hospital confinement and the amount of care allowed, patients with BPD may not receive necessary treatment. Only a few facilities, which can be afforded only by the wealthy, are available today for patients who require lengthy hospitalization. Intensive out-patient programs such as dialectical behavioral therapy (see below) require extensive involvement of several professionals within the treatment team. Such programs are expensive and, though statistically proven to be beneficial, often are not supported by standard medical insurance coverage.

Pharmacological Treatments

Specific pharmacological treatments for suicidal behavior and SIB are based on the preceding understanding of physiological effects. Antipsychotic drugs (see chapters 1, 5, and 11) are powerful DA-blockers and are useful medicines for SIB. The newer, "atypical" antipsychotics are particularly promising.

Serotonin reuptake inhibitors (SRIs) have shown efficacy in treatment of destructive behaviors. Other agents that also affect the ST system and that may ameliorate suicidal fantasies and SIB include Buspar, a tranquilizing drug; lithium, a mood stabilizer; and certain beta-blockers (cardiac medicines that treat hypertension and angina) such as Inderal (propranolol) and pindolol. Lithium and beta-blockers also may impact self-destructive behaviors by their effects on the norepinephrine system.

Minor tranquilizers (benzodiazepines) such as Xanax, Valium, and Klonopin significantly affect GABA. Contradictory results have emerged from studies of these medications on suicidal feelings and SIB. Some have shown these medicines to decrease self-control, resulting in increased aggression and impulsivity. Other studies show some improvement in lowering impulsivity. Current recommendations avoid use of the shorter-acting medicines (such as Xanax) and advocate judicious use of the longer-acting drugs (such as Klonopin).

Drugs such as Revia, which block endorphin receptors, have had mixed results. In some patients these medicines may interfere with the analgesia and euphoric feelings resulting from SIB and thus extinguish the behavior. However, consistent improvement in large groups of patients has not been demonstrated thus far.

Anticonvulsants also have shown some efficacy for self-destructive symptoms. A comorbid history of epilepsy resulted in a better response. Most research has been done with Tegretol and Depakote.

Psychotherapeutic Interventions

Two psychotherapeutic approaches have submitted to rigorous controlled trials. One is a psychoanalytic/psychodynamic therapy, which has been explored in programs in England and Australia as well as in the United States. This technique reviews developmental history in attempting to make the individual more aware of underlying, unconscious patterns of behavior. By gaining this insight, the individual is better able to understand and control behaviors. Treatment takes place mostly in a day hospital setting. Individual and group therapy sessions explore events from the past, linking them to current functioning. Understanding is emphasized over short-term behavioral change.

The other therapeutic approach is dialectical behavioral therapy (DBT), specifically designed to diminish suicidal and self-destructive behaviors. DBT, developed by Marsha Linehan at the University of Washington, is a form of cognitive-behavioral therapy that focuses on correcting distorted thoughts and beliefs that are felt to generate maladaptive behaviors. Reviewing past history is not a priority; insight into underlying patterns is a less important goal. The primary objective is to alter dysfunctional thoughts, moods, and behaviors. Unlike most psychodynamic approaches, DBT usually is administered on an outpatient basis or within the context of a short-term hospital program.

As the most studied treatment of BPD, DBT directly confronts the "black or white" thinking of borderlines by emphasizing the paradoxes and contradictions of living. The goal, then, is to move away from the "black *or* white" borderline position to a "black *and* white" understanding. A primary issue in therapy is to address the contradiction (dialectic) that recognizes that the patient must both accept himself for who he is at the moment and simultaneously work toward changing himself for the future. The therapist must acknowledge that the patient is doing the best he can and yet also must strive to improve. For the borderline, who abhors ambiguity, these paradoxes are frustrating.

DBT consists of four components: (1) a skills training group, which focuses on improving social skills; (2) individual psychotherapy, which serves to maintain motivation and reinforce coping skills; (3) telephone consultations, which reinforce application of skills outside therapy; and (4) team consultation, which supports and motivates members of the therapy team.

DBT therapists (like all therapists who treat borderline patients) must possess certain characteristics. They must be able to balance warmth and nurturing acceptance with "benevolent demanding," which Linehan defines as "the ability to recognize a patient's existing capabilities, to reinforce the patient's adaptive behaviors and self-control, and to refuse to take care of the patient when he or she can care for themselves." She also recommends utilizing irreverence and humor in dealing with borderline patients, to maintain a sense of proportion as they confront problems. Therapy is conducted within a context that emphasizes the care and nurturing of the caregivers as well as of the patients. Team meetings that support the clinical staff are just as important as support for the patients. An integral part of DBT, supportive team meetings are important in any organized therapy system for borderlines, as we described in our St. Louis program for borderline patients.

As Linehan summarizes, "Stylistically, DBT blends a matter-of-fact, somewhat irreverent, and at times outrageous attitude about current and previous parasuicidal and other dysfunctional behaviors with therapist warmth, flexibility, responsiveness to the client, and strategic self-disclosure. The continuing efforts in DBT to 'reframe' suicidal and other dysfunctional behaviors as part of the client's learned problem-solving repertoire, and to focus therapy on active problem solving, are balanced by a corresponding emphasis on validating the client's current emotional, cognitive, and behavioral responses just as they are." This style is very similar to our SET technique (see chapter 12). Variations and modifications of DBT are being developed. One adapted model, manual-assisted cognitive therapy (MACT), specifically focuses on decreasing self-harming behavior in borderlines by adapting educational treatment booklets for patients.

There are more commonalities than differences among these two therapeutic strategies for BPD. Similar goals are emphasized. The top priority of DBT, like the psychodynamic and other therapies, is to prevent self-harming behavior. The second priority is to address behaviors that threaten to disrupt the therapy. After these goals are secured, attention is directed toward improving quality of life. Self-acceptance is an important issue for all therapeutic endeavors. Many treatment approaches employ individual and group therapies. A team approach, which emphasizes close collaboration and consultation among therapists, is an essential component of DBT and most hospital programs.

The volatility of impulsive, destructive behaviors is not only frightening to patients and their families but also invokes great anxiety in the clinician. Balancing several factors—consideration of safety for the patient, concerns of overdependence, restrictions of managed care, and caution to avoid litigation—can greatly complicate care. But as we continue to develop new strategies for the management of dangerous behavior, our success in helping borderline patients will continue to expand.

ACTION STEPS: *Dealing with Self-Destructive Behaviors*

1. *Offer other options.* Self-mutilation is often a source of tension relief and a form of escape. Suicidal fantasies, likewise, can be reassuring and soothing. It is not reasonable to expect someone to easily abandon a behavior that provides relief, but several substitutes have proven useful: (a) physical activity, such as running or vigorous exercise; (b) soothing behavior, such as relaxing in a bubble bath, sitting quietly in a peaceful setting, or masturbation; and (c) simulation of self-harming. In this latter case, some people find that holding ice cubes can provide physical stimulation, obviating the need for greater pain induction. Some who are soothed by the sight of their own blood find some release in painting their arms with a red Magic Marker.

2. *Arrange a support system.* Phoning friends, other members of a support group, or suicide hot lines can be life-saving at times of crisis. Help the borderline develop a phone bank in advance for difficult times.

3. *Make the environment as safe as possible.* All potential harmful elements, such as guns and other weapons, should be removed from the home or locked away. Unnecessary medicines should be discarded. In some cases, prescribed medications should be under the control of another person so that they will not be misused.

4. *Protect others in the home.* Other family members should have prearranged safe places to go if there is a crisis. Children, for example, should automatically go to a neighbor's house or apartment if parents become violent. Everyone in the home should be advised about protective and rescue services, including "911" access.

5. *Learn to respond to suicidal threats.* Suicidal threats should always be taken seriously. Professional help should always be sought. The borderline will often angrily demand that the doctor not be called, but it should calmly be explained that in view of the behavior, the doctor is in the best position to decide the course of action.

For the therapist, the plan of action is a complex dilemma. Hospitalization may be necessary (even if it threatens the alliance with the patient). But at the same time it may promote dependency in someone who relies too much on the facility to escape confronting issues in the home. By the same token, not institutionalizing a person who later harms himself may expose the practitioner to legal complications. In general, the better the therapist knows the patient, the better informed the decision can be. When in doubt, however, hospitalization, even if involuntary, usually is the safer course of action.

7

Mood Instability

*It is as if my life were magically run by two electric currents:
joyous positive and despairing negative—which ever is running
at the moment dominates my life, floods it.*

—SILVIA PLATH

Radical mood swings are symptomatic of many mental illnesses. Borderline mood swings can be veiled by other diagnoses, such as depression, bipolar, or impulse disorders, or they can coexist with them. Reading Bobby's story as he recounts his experiences to his therapist, the reader will see how hard it is to predict his moods, how rapidly they change, and how Bobby cannot grasp their origin. This chapter distinguishes the mood swings of BPD from those that signal other disorders, emphasizing the impediments to deriving an accurate diagnosis.

BOBBY: PART TWO

I'm back, Doc. Thanks for seeing me. I just didn't know where else to turn. I know it's been a while, maybe a year or two, so I'll try to catch you up. Frankly, the reason I didn't come back after our first visit was I just felt so depressed after our session. I know that's a lousy reason, but that's how I operate sometimes: when I get depressed, I just go off someplace and hide.

And well, I guess I was kind of pissed at you, too. You know, when you said you thought medication might help, I felt you really didn't give a damn and just wanted to drug me up. And then when I said I was

117

reluctant to take medicines, you just said that would be okay and we could talk about it some more the next time. You didn't insist or anything. So it was like you didn't really care enough to even try to talk me into it.

I know that sounds all fucked up, but that's how I am. Anyway, right after we met, I just felt hopeless and depressed. So I took off again. I don't know if you remember, but in our last exciting episode I think I was working at Maxwell's and was engaged to Marie. Yeah, I think so. Anyway, I just up and left. Quit my job. Broke it off with Marie and went back to Colorado. I just thought the mountains and the country would make me happy again.

And it did. For a while. I got a job at Hecht's, a classy department store outside Denver, and met some people. I felt free. There was something liberating about the altitude, I think. Maybe the lack of oxygen did my brain some good. You know how you can tell you're in Colorado, Doc? When you're driving down the road and see all these $2,000 mountain bikes hitched to the back of $500 cars. Well, that was me. I bought this raw mountain bike and whizzed around the Rockies like there was no tomorrow. It was great!

I also got into the gay scene around Larimer Square. Really did some partying, some drugs, nothing heavy, just some pot and ecstasy once in a while, and went out all the time. I was such a slut! I just tried to boogie as fast as I could, so nothing could catch up with me.

But after a while, it did. It started one awful drunken night with Patrick, a man I was seeing. Before him, I fucked some guys and a few girls, but I thought Patrick might be special. One night after we'd been together for a few weeks, we got really bombed and I suggested we bring another guy home with us. Boy, was that a blunder! His name was Bruce, a bartender at the nightclub where we hung out a lot. At first Patrick seemed kind of reluctant, but after a while it became obvious that he was really hot for Bruce, so thinking back, maybe Patrick was playing me, know what I mean?

Anyway, we went back to Patrick's place, and I was kind of, pardon the pun, odd man out. Watching them go at it really made me sick! I know—the whole thing was my idea—but I felt so disgusted, by them and myself. I can't explain it, how disgusted I felt. I know, Doc, one minute I'm flying high and the next I'm so low I'm looking up at roach dicks. It was like I could see my whole life around me, like I was in one of those 360-degree dioramas that my parents took me to once at Disneyland. But this one didn't have pretty scenes of mountains and lakes and Mount Rushmore swirling in a circle, like the one at Disneyland. These were scenes from my life, and they were ugly and stupid and worthless. And there was no "Exit" sign, like in Disneyland, either. I was trapped. And suddenly the pain was tremendous, overwhelming, worse than breaking your arm, which I did once and it hurt like hell, I'll tell you. But this was more like . . . being smothered. Like shrinking into nothingness. And nowhere to turn for air. There was no air at all. Only one way to escape.

So while they're bumping and humping in the bedroom, I quietly withdrew to the bathroom, where I proceeded to eat everything in the medicine cabinet. I mean *everything*. I knew Patrick's medicine cabinet and he must've gotten some new scrips, 'cause the thing was filled with Valium, Xanax, antidepressants, you name it.

Anyway, on top of all the booze I drank, it did the trick. Or almost. I'm pretty fuzzy on the details, but I do remember the nice paramedic boys, who seemed very serious on the way to the hospital. I don't remember what I said, but I thought some of it was pretty funny. In the ER, they stuck this hose down my nose and flooded me with ugly-tasting charcoal that's supposed to soak up the drugs. It was all over my face. I swear, when I was done, I looked like a performer in a minstrel show.

Some psych resident, she must've been about twelve, took care of me at Denver General. She seemed nice enough, but she looked at my chart for a few minutes, asked me about ten questions, told me I was "bipolar," and needed to be on lithium. Believe me, Doc, right about then I was really missing you.

• • •

They call Denver General DG for short, but the inmates call it the "Dungeon." I was still pretty depressed in there, but I went to the group sessions and talked a little. There were some sad people in the Dungeon, even sadder than me, if that's possible. I felt kind of close to this one girl who was there—Amy. Amy would do this thing, when she felt really bad, you know? She'd cut herself with a small Swiss army knife on her forearms and wrists. She had scars all over her arms. She called it a "monster grip of melancholy" that would come over her sometimes when she was sad. I could really relate to that. You're fine and then all of a sudden with some minor disappointment you feel devastated, like you want to die.

The lithium made me shake a little, but Dr. Minnie Mouse said I needed to live with it. She added some Paxil, and I must admit I did feel a little better—less moody, less annoyed with everything. She extracted blood for lithium levels and after a few days pronounced me chemically balanced and ready to leave.

As it turned out, Amy and I were discharged on the same day. We started seeing a lot of each other after we got out. I got another job. Amy's family had money, and they sent her some every week, so she didn't have to work. I think they did that just to keep her away from them.

Amy and I were together a lot. I practically moved in. She didn't tell her doctor about us, but I did. Dr. Minnie said Amy and me shacking up was a bad idea but didn't push me about it. Sometimes, though, I would leave for work in the morning and Amy would be in her bathrobe watching the tube, and when I got back home at dinnertime, she was in the same exact place I left her, lying on the couch in her bathrobe, staring at the TV, as if she were hypnotized or divining some grand plan. She hadn't moved all day. It was like time stood still in her apartment.

•   •   •

When we were together, I felt great. When we were apart, I got depressed. One time I got mad at her for not cleaning up the kitchen and was still pretty huffy when I left for work. When I got home that night, it was still as if she hadn't moved from the sofa—still in the bathrobe, parked in front of the television, but there was a trail of blood on the carpet. I tracked it back to the bathroom. She resisted at first, but she finally showed me her arms where she had cut herself. I kept asking her why, but she would only say she didn't know why, just that it made her feel better. The bathroom was all bloody, and the carpet looked like a scene from *Scream*. But by that time she wasn't bleeding anymore, and she wouldn't let me take her to the hospital anyway.

Sometimes with her cutting she would hit an artery, and the blood would really spurt all over the place, and I'd think her circulatory system was just like our relationship. I took biology in high school and did pretty good. I liked the way every part of the body has this role to play, as if it were a small city. She was the arteries, frantically pushing blood around her body, feeding her organs in volatile spasms; and I was the veins, desperately cleaning up her exhausted corpuscles and hauling them back to her heart, where she was only going to go spurting them around again. I'd think, "Why bother?" But then I'd get depressed wondering what I'd do if I left her. In a way, she kind of made me feel stronger. When she was depressed, I was able to call on some magical reserve, which made me feel calmly in control. My usual feelings of desperation would evaporate. And, somehow, she could do the same—jump in and take care of me when I was feeling hopeless.

I thought *I* was moody. Amy was the Cleopatra of moody. After a while I could see the changes coming even before she did. Just before she flew into a rage, for example, her eyes would kind of expand. And then they'd get this unbelievable hateful glare, like she was possessed by Satan. I didn't know if I should call a shrink or an exorcist.

After one of her crises I called her parents in California. They seemed concerned enough but didn't want to do anything, except ask if she needed money. They just kept reassuring me (and, I guess, themselves) that we could handle things. My parents, on the other hand, just wanted me to come home. I didn't know what to do. I was off the booze and working and taking care of Amy and riding my mountain bike. So sometimes I felt pretty good; and other times, not.

I stayed on the medicines and continued to see Dr. Minnie for a while. Then she was transferred out of the clinic, and I was assigned to some other resident, who didn't seem to be very interested in me. He just wanted to talk about my medications. After a while, though, he said he thought maybe I wasn't bipolar at all but had a form of schizophrenia. Then he changed his mind again and said I was just a recovering drug user who had destroyed half of my brain cells with drugs. He wanted me to go to AA and NA, which I did for a while. But I found that the more I went, the more I started to crave drugs again. So I figured I better quit before I really got into trouble.

During this time he kept changing the medicines. He had me on Depakote and Zoloft for a time, then tried some Prozac and Risperdal. I was like a barren field and he was a farmer experimenting with different crops to see what would grow. After a while, I think he was just throwing into the mix whatever samples the drug rep brought by that day. They all worked about the same—they helped settle me down and stabilized some of the ups and downs. But I didn't like getting blood tests every few months to measure the drug level. And sometimes sex was a problem—it would take forever to climax. Then Amy would blame herself and get upset. After a while the sex improved, but by that time sex, like the rest of life, was beginning to feel like too much trouble to be bothered with.

•   •   •

My moods were totally controlled by who was around me, which was mostly Amy. I could have a great day at work, get a raise, feel wonderful, but then come home, and if Amy was in a bad mood, it would all disappear, and I'd be flung into despair. The medicines didn't do anything then.

Finally, after one of her hospitalizations, Amy's parents came to Denver. They packed her up and took her back to California. She didn't want to go and looked to me to save her. But, truthfully, I was kind of relieved. We had become kind of Siamese Twins of the Soul—I would cry, and she would bleed tears; she would cut, and I would hurt.

With her gone, I suddenly realized I didn't have any friends. I had long avoided my old gay group. I was just doing time at my job. Before, I had crises to deal with. Now, when I came home, I was bored. I felt more and more isolated. So I sat and waited and hoped my parents would insist that I come home again, so I could surprise them and say yes.

I've been back now a few months. Looking for a job. Hanging at home. Watching TV. I don't hear from Amy anymore, which is probably good for both of us. I stopped taking the medicines and, so far, I feel okay. My mood swings are starting to come back a little, but I realize now that when everything was going crazy back in Denver, I might have been a little *too* numb. At least now I can feel, even if it is a little bit more feeling than I care for.

So, what do you think, Doc? Am I manic-depressive, or schizy, or drunk, or just crazy, or what? Will drugs help me without numbing me out? Will I ever be normal—whatever the hell *that* is?

BPD and Mood Instability

Affective instability (or mood change) is one of the most prominent characteristics of BPD. Emotions such as depression, self-reproach, elation, anger, or anxiety can change abruptly in reaction to external stimuli. Mood volatility is such a prominent part of BPD that in the past some have suggested that BPD should be classified as a subtype of mood disorders rather than as a personality disorder. To clarify the distinctions, the latest delineation of criteria for BPD in *DSM-IV* cites mood instability "due to a marked *reactivity* of mood, e.g., intense episodic dysphoria, irritability, or anxiety, *usually lasting a few hours and only rarely more than a few days* (authors' italics). These text changes from *DSM-III* emphasize the reactivity and transience of the mood changes, which distinguish them from those usually seen in Axis I mood disorders.

Studies have demonstrated that borderlines have more frequent and unpredictable changes in mood during a typical day than patients with other mental illnesses, including those suffering from depression, whose moods change less abruptly. Like Bobby, many borderlines experience these unpredictable and rapid changes in mood and feeling without understanding their origin. Such severe volatility is understandably frightening and frustrating for the borderline and those close to him.

Recent research has indicated that the moods associated with BPD do not involve all emotions. Specifically, BPD is strongly associated with greater lability of anger, anxiety, and severe oscillation from depression to anxiety. Surprisingly, however, oscillation between depression and elation does not correlate as significantly. The most discriminating emotion suggestive of the BPD diagnosis is anger lability, which predicts BPD versus another personality disorder with 72 percent accuracy. Both Bobby and Amy, throughout their tumultuous relationship, were trapped in a reverberating echo hall of reciprocal anger and mood changes.

Depression in Borderlines

Because depression is the most common diagnosis that accompanies BPD (see chapter 1), some studies have explored the relationship between the two. One investigation, examining several hundred patients, used objective rating scales to assess the severity of depression and anxiety in BPD patients with and without primary diagnoses of depression and/or anxiety. The BPD diagnosis consistently predicted both subjective and objective ratings of greater severity of depression and anxiety, regardless of the presence of an Axis I depressive disorder. BPD subjects, even *without* a concurrent diagnosis of major depression, rated themselves more depressed than nonborderline patients *with* the depression diagnosis. Although borderlines are often accused of being overly dramatic in describing symptoms, the congruence between ratings by both the patient and the clinician indicate that the borderline's pain is not an exaggeration but is measurably as severe as described. Compared to depressed patients, borderlines tend to be more self-critical. Bobby's constant, mocking self-deprecation ("I was such a slut") was more a function of his borderline self-hatred than a component of depression.

BPD is most often associated with a more chronic form of depression called dysthymia. Whereas major depression exhibits severe depressive symptoms for at least two weeks and then often fluctuates, the course of dysthymic disorder persists for at least two years, usually at a less severe intensity. Patients with dysthymic disorder are over three times more likely to have a concurrent personality disorder (most often BPD) than those with a diagnosis of major depression.

Borderlines and Close Relations: Familial Transmission

Studies of close (first-degree) relatives of borderlines reveal increased prevalence of affective and impulsive personality traits. Further, the likelihood of depression in a close relative is the same whether the borderline himself is depressed or not. Conversely, patients with a diagnosis of dysthymia, with or without comorbid BPD, have a higher-than-expected prevalence of BPD diagnosed in their first-degree relatives. Interestingly, both affective and impulsivity traits are not commonly observed in the same nonborderline relative, suggesting that BPD may be comprised of an aggregate of independent, separable, and distinct temperaments, which may be inherited separately. This concept is more consistent with a *dimensional* model of BPD (in which separate factors aggregate in various degrees) than a *categorical* view (in which the disorder is constructed by a list of features defining a discrete syndrome); for detailed discussion see chapter 1.

Comorbidity or Confusion

The intersection of BPD and other diagnoses often leads to confusion and misdiagnosis. BPD can be linked as the cause or effect of other illnesses. It can coexist with other disorders, and it can camouflage or be camouflaged by other syndromes. However, recognition of BPD is essential, since, when it exists concurrently with another syndrome, it significantly and negatively impacts the prognosis.

Part of the association with other illnesses may be a result of sloppy diagnostics and/or of pressure to avoid the stigma or problems of the diagnosis. Many psychiatrists, especially those whose orientation is more biological, are more comfortable with Axis I diagnoses, which imply a treatment regimen focusing on medications rather than psychotherapy. Another significant contributor is the pressure of managed care, which emphasizes short-term treatment for acute illnesses. Traditionally, insurance coverage does not extend to Axis II disorders, especially BPD, which are felt to be more ingrained and chronic. Therefore most clinicians reporting diagnoses must cite an Axis I label to attain full coverage.

BPD and Depression

Dysthymic disorder is the most common Axis I illness associated with BPD, followed by major depressive disorder. Uncomplicated depression has a response rate to treatment of about 70 to 80 percent. However, when it is accompanied by BPD, a favorable prognosis is cut in half. Complaints of depression can hide borderline symptoms if evaluation does not assess interpersonal relationships or look for evidence of impulsivity, anger, or other BPD characteristics. Conversely, depression may be overlooked if the focus remains only on outrageous behaviors.

Although both disorders overlap considerably, there are some general distinctions. Borderlines usually are more impulsive and engage in turbulent, unstable relationships. Depressives are more likely to be obsessive worriers who are self-conscious and less prone to mood changes. Relationships, though often unsatisfactory and based on dependency, are likely to be more lasting for those suffering from depression.

BPD and Bipolarity

BPD and bipolar disorder (BP) share several traits, including impulsivity, anger, and mood swings. BP, as developed in *DSM-IV,* has three types. BP I, traditionally referred to as manic-depressive disorder, describes periods of mania characterized by elation, hyperactivity, and grandiosity, alternating with periods of depression, with each period commonly lasting several days or weeks. BP II describes periods of alternating depression and hypomania, which is a less incapacitating form of mania, lasting at least four days but not interfering with the individual's routine as much as true mania. Cyclothymic disorder (CyD) describes frequent mood swings, over at least a two-year period, of hypomania and depressive symptoms that are not as debilitating as in major depression.

Mood changes in BP usually appear spontaneously and often are not related to environmental circumstances. The mood swings in BPD, on the other hand, are almost always related to external situations. Between mood swings, the bipolar individual functions well; the borderline individual experiences constant turmoil.

Bipolars tend to be less responsive to others. Especially when in a manic or hypomanic state, they are grandiose and often insensitive to those around them. Borderlines tend to be more sensitive and reactive to the nuances of others and are particularly fearful of rejection; their self-image is consistently more negative.

BPD and PTSD

Post-traumatic stress disorder (PTSD) also is observed frequently with BPD and can be confused with it. Both groups of patients may have a history of childhood abuse or trauma. The reckless, impulsive behavior often associated with BPD makes such individuals more vulnerable to dangerous situations, which might ultimately result in trauma.

The PTSD victim suffers symptoms revolving around a *specific* trauma. Reexperiencing the situation again and again and enduring recurrent nightmares typify this syndrome. Symptoms of BPD usually are more diverse and less preoccupied with one trauma. One recent study confirmed the differences between these two syndromes by exposing patients with either diagnosis (all of whom had experienced childhood trauma) to scripts describing situations of trauma and of abandonment. PTSD patients showed more profound physiological reactions (changes in pulse, blood pressure, and skin conductance) to the trauma script, while BPD subjects exhibited significantly greater response to the abandonment scenario.

BPD and Substance Abuse

These disorders frequently coexist, and the risk of suicide is greatly increased when either is complicated by the other. Depressant drugs, especially alcohol, are the ones most misused by borderlines. Borderlines may abuse drugs as a kind of self-medicating. For example, alcohol may be used to tranquilize rage or to decrease inhibitions. Unlike the regular routine of other drug users, BPD substance abuse may be impulsive and episodic. Rather than seeking a specific drug, the borderline may indulge in whatever is available (see Liz's story in chapter 5) or, as with Bobby, may be part of a social connection, rather than a result of craving.

BPD and Eating Disorders

Bulimia (compulsive binge eating) is the most common of the eating disorders associated with BPD. When linked to anorexia nervosa, it usually also involves purging, through self-induced vomiting or abuse of laxatives. Bulimia also can be associated with obesity.

The binge-purge dynamic may result when a person feels a need to relieve tension by self-indulgence with food. This is followed by a sense of shame and self-disgust, which prompts the purging. Binge eating leading to obesity is often associated with people who have been sexually abused and may function as an insulation from sexual involvement.

Bulimics usually are more impulsive than anorexics, who are typically more obsessive and perfectionistic. Bulimia, sometimes followed by purging, is often a self-soothing, tension-relieving activity, like self-mutilation, which explains its greater "popularity" among borderlines. Anorexia nervosa patients tend to exhibit borderline black-or-white thinking. The self-denying discomfort of starving is *good,* while the indulgence of satiation, which represents a loss of control, is repulsively *bad.* Just as the borderline never feels unconditional acceptance, the anorexic—constantly striving for perfection—never feels thin enough or good enough.

BPD and Hypochondriasis and Somatic Disorders

As noted in previous chapters, many borderlines are on a continuous quest for a nurturer or "caregiver"—someone they never had or *perceived* they never had—in childhood. This quest sometimes brings them to the attention of primary care physicians, from whom they may seek attention by focusing on their physical symptoms. One survey, of more than two hundred patients in a primary care practice, revealed a prevalence of BPD of almost 7 percent, considerably higher than estimates in the general population. Only half of these patients were receiving mental health treatment, and only 55 percent were recognized by the physician as even having a psychiatric problem.

In addition to seeking medical care as a result of dependency needs, individuals with persistent BPD symptoms also tend to lead an unhealthier lifestyle that necessitates more medical treatment. Compared to borderline patients who were no longer significantly symptomatic, unremitting borderlines were more likely to drink alcohol, smoke cigarettes, exercise less, suffer more household accidents, and be hospitalized. These patients also were more likely to require treatment for related diseases, including diabetes, arthritis, hypertension, obesity, and back pain, some of which are probably associated with these unhealthy habits.

BPD and Schizophrenia

Patients suffering from schizophrenia or BPD can experience hallucinations, delusions, paranoia, and other psychotic symptoms (see chapter 10). Both groups can be self-mutilating and suicidal. Psychosis in BPD, however, unlike in schizophrenia, usually is transient. Self-mutilation in schizophrenia usually is related to a psychotic experience, whereas in the borderline it is most often an intentional act designed to punish oneself or relieve tension (see chapter 6). Also unlike borderlines, schizophrenics usually maintain a flat, unemotional countenance and avoid social contacts. Both diagnoses do not generally co-occur.

BPD and Dissociative Disorders

Many borderlines experience fuguelike states or feelings of unreality (see chapter 10). Most patients with a diagnosis of dissociative identity disorder (DID), formerly multiple personality disorder, have a history of severe childhood trauma and a concurrent diagnosis of BPD. Most individuals with the BPD diagnosis, however, do not fulfill criteria for DID. Although many borderlines are aware of different parts of their personalities, there is usually not complete separation and unawareness of discrete, separate personality fragments, which is the hallmark of DID.

BPD and Impulsive/Compulsive Behaviors

Borderlines frequently engage in impulsive and compulsive activities (see chapter 5). Bobby's compulsive promiscuity and Liz's shoplifting and stealing (see chapter 5) are just two examples of how people with borderline traits may feel compelled to discharge internal anxiety through physical action. Outbursts of rage, compulsive gambling, binge eating, and compulsive hair-pulling or skin-picking are other methods used to alleviate the inner tension. Some borderlines feel that they will literally explode if they cannot in some way discharge this agitation.

BPD and Other Personality Disorders (PDs)

It is easy to understand why BPD, the most common of the ten defined personality disorders, is often comorbid with another PD or is misdiagnosed, since so many criteria overlap. Many borderlines share symptoms of paranoid personality disorder, including a tendency to read "hidden demeaning or threatening meanings into benign remarks or events" and a quickness "to react angrily or to counterattack." Schizotypal personality disorder also exhibits features of BPD, such as "unusual perceptual experiences, including bodily illusions" and "odd beliefs or magical thinking." Borderlines, unlike people with these PD characteristics, are less eccentric and more social.

An individual with a diagnosis of avoidant personality disorder, like many borderlines, "is preoccupied with being criticized or rejected in social situations," but, unlike borderlines, evades social interactions. Someone with dependent personality disorder "goes to excessive lengths to obtain nurturance and support from others," "feels uncomfortable or helpless when alone because of exaggerated fears of being unable to care for himself or herself," "urgently seeks another relationship as a source of care and support when a close relationship ends," and "is unrealistically preoccupied with fears of being left to take care of himself or herself." People with BPD, however, exhibit more mood changes, anger outbursts, and self-destructiveness.

BPD is more often associated with the other "Cluster B" PDs— histrionic personality disorder (HPD), narcissistic personality disorder (NPD), and antisocial personality disorder (ASPD). HPD is characterized by excessive emotionality, self-dramatization, seductiveness, attention to physical appearance, and "rapidly shifting and shallow expression of emotions." Anger and self-destructiveness distinguish BPD from this PD.

NPD and BPD share characteristics of excessive rage, feelings of entitlement, and exquisite sensitivity to criticism. However, the narcissistic personality exhibits a grandiosity and sense of superiority and entitlement that is absent in the borderline.

ASPD and NPD are more commonly diagnosed in men, while BPD and HPD are more commonly seen in women. Perhaps genetic differences contribute to these distinctions. The diagnoses may also be influenced by societal or cultural factors. Consider this example: A person has a fight with the spouse and storms out of the house to the local bar, where the individual becomes intoxicated, picks a fight with another patron, throws chairs around the bar, and flees in a car. Speeding down the highway, the person is stopped by a police officer, toward whom there is a tearful outburst punctuated by self-demeaning statements, and finalized with a pronounced wish to be dead. If such an individual is a woman, a likely outcome is transport to a hospital emergency room, where diagnoses of BPD and depression would likely be made. On the other hand, if the offender is a male, the more probable result is arrest and classification as an alcoholic with antisocial personality.

Both ASPD and BPD are characterized by anger, impulsiveness, and recklessness. The backgrounds of most people with these diagnoses are similar in the frequency of childhood mistreatment, poor relationships, and substance abuse. The primary distinction is that in ASPD there usually is a lack of conscience or emotion. People with ASPD are usually more aggressive and manipulate to gain profit or power rather than to seek nurturance. However, one can question whether cultural (or genetic) influences color assessments of male versus female behavior.

The Serpent or the Little Girl: Can the Treatment Be Right if the Diagnosis Is Wrong?

The surprising answer is "Sometimes, yes." Consider this dialogue from *Alice in Wonderland*:

> At one point during her travails in Wonderland, Alice encounters the Pigeon, who mistakes her for a serpent.
>
> "But I'm *not* a serpent, I tell you!" said Alice. "I'm a . . . little girl."
>
> "I don't believe it," said the Pigeon. "What does it matter to me whether you're a little girl or a serpent?"
>
> "It matters a good deal to *me*," said Alice.

In medicine, diagnosis is the key to treatment. However, the diagnosis of BPD can be as chameleonlike as the people who inhabit it. As we have observed, BPD can be veiled by other diagnoses. It can hide behind labels such as depression, bipolar disease, and impulse disorder. Fortunately, even if the clinician, like Alice's Pigeon, misidentifies the patient, the prescribed treatment may still be beneficial (which, of course, only reinforces the clinician's misjudgment). Thus, treatment with an SRI for putative depression, with a psychotropic for supposed bipolar disease, or with lithium or other mood stabilizer for presumed impulse problems, may greatly benefit the misdiagnosed borderline patient. In any event, the patient improves. Still, like Alice, he probably would have preferred the correct diagnosis.

8

Emptiness

We are rarely proud when we are alone.
—VOLTAIRE, *The Philosophical Dictionary*, 1764

By now the reader will perceive how the various symptoms of BPD form an organic constellation of interacting emotions: to a borderline, "emptiness" is an all-consuming sense of meaninglessness—a powerful, bottomless emotional void that can lead to identity crises, mood swings, anger, and even suicide. This chapter differentiates between depression and emptiness, and a special section provides "exercises" for dealing with consuming feelings of emptiness. When we left Arleen in chapter 2, she was living in Indiana, trying to juggle a dead-end affair with her boss, a career going nowhere, and a husband who was never home. We now catch up with her a few months later: She has left her midwestern roots to begin a new life in New York. Her first lonely weeks there are the backdrop of the following story.

ARLEEN: PART TWO

The heat that pummels her as she emerges from the Fifty-seventh Street subway is like nothing she experienced in Indiana. Breathing is almost impossible, as if the air has been sucked totally of oxygen. Sure, she had felt humidity before, growing up in Ohio close to Lake Erie, but these August afternoons in Manhattan were suffocating, like the steam bath she used a few times in Owens Rec Center waiting for Greg to finish his workout. On only her sixth day in New York, she has gone through nine or ten changes of clothes and makes a mental note to look for a pay laundry when she gets done with this job interview at Barasoni.

Confused for a second, trying to decide which way is downtown, she sees the smoggy outline of theater marquees a dozen blocks to her right and so heads in that direction, figuring that she'll cross over to Avenue of the Americas in a block or two. Her clothes are already sticking to her, and she has to look good for Barasoni. She can last only a few more weeks on the money she has. The two interviews yesterday went poorly, which was probably just as well, since she wasn't much interested in secretarial jobs anyway, but she has to get *something* soon.

Besides, this one holds promise. "Executive Administrative Assistant Liaison, Security Task Force, sought by property management firm of large midtown office building" said the want ad—and she had been assistant manager at Red Oak Realty, hadn't she? Sure, Red Oak employed only seven people, and Barasoni had more than two hundred in six cities, but offices were offices and property was property, right? Yesterday, after e-mailing her résumé to the address in the ad, "K. Crowley," human resources manager, replied an hour later, asking if she could come in to Barasoni headquarters at 1:00 P.M. today.

Walking down Seventh Avenue, passing the Carnegie Deli and then the Stage Deli a block farther, she thinks of stopping for a sandwich and a cold drink. She glances at her watch: twelve-fifteen—not quite enough time for lunch. Instead, she reaches in her purse and pulls out a cigarette. She had started smoking soon after Greg left; he never would have tolerated it while they were together. The night he walked out, swearing not to return until she got help, she felt as if her internal organs had been ripped out with a pair of pliers. Only a void remained, vast and threatening.

Her first thought was to drink herself into oblivion. Already gone a month from Red Oak, she had nothing to do but sleep and so took full opportunity, passing out drunk on the couch at seven or eight in the evening and often not waking until noon the next day. She watched hours and hours of daytime TV while she drank, hoping she could hypnotize herself into oblivion. But she couldn't focus on the cases in the courtrooms of Judge Judy or Judge Joe Brown or any other TV magistrate; *All My Children* made no sense to her, and *The Young and the Restless* made her think of Greg, which was intolerable; even the cable talk shows, blathering on about terrorist acts in the Middle East, did nothing to keep her mind off losing Greg. The only escapes were the commercials, which often were more distracting than the shows. Yet these, too, had their downside—she found herself running constantly to the refrigerator. Eventually she ran out of frozen dinners and began calling out for a pizza or Chinese food.

Anything to fill the hole.

One night, after two weeks of this regimen, she stepped on the bathroom scale and was astounded to see she had put on eighteen pounds! Nauseated with self-disgust, she thought of going on a diet or popping diet pills or even barfing after she ate—a skill she had learned from her college roommate and practiced with great dexterity for a time in her sophomore year. But the easiest route seemed to be cigarettes. Though she hadn't smoked a cigarette since a few experimental drags in high school— an experiment that made her gag and almost vomit—her aunt Tilda had taken off twenty pounds one week after she started!

Anything to fill the hole.

Now, crossing Seventh onto Fifty-third, she takes a last hit on the cigarette and flicks the butt into the gutter. The idea of moving to New York had come to her almost by accident. Surfing the Net, she had seen a link on Yahoo for cheap summer airfares, and the same travel site also had a category called "Summer Sublets." In the summer, Manhattanites were so anxious to flee to Long Island or Cape Cod, she could get a decent place for the same rent she was paying in Middleton! And why *not* New York?! No way she could be lonely there! Screw these one-horse towns. Screw Greg, screw Eddie, screw all of them. Within a day or two she had a $99 one-way ticket to JFK and a studio on the Upper West Side for two months at $600 a month.

"Hey, you! Lady! You got another one of those?"

The voice, more of a barking command than a question, comes out of an old gnarled black woman sitting cross-legged in a doorway. Next to her is a rolled-up sleeping bag and a small cocker spaniel, hardly bigger than a doll, its brooding face resting on its front paws. The woman is missing most of her front teeth, and her right arm is raised in the air, in a limp wave.

"Me? Oh, sure," says Arleen, and rummages in her purse for the pack. "Here you go." As she hands a Salem to the woman, she notices that the woman's right hand is not waving to her at all but inexplicably is *handcuffed* to a door handle! Instinctively, Arleen looks around for any sign of police, but no cops or police cars are in sight. "Why—why are you in handcuffs?"

Busy searching her sleeping bag, the woman somehow locates a pack of matches and deftly lights one of them and her cigarette with one hand. "I am Edmond Dantes," she proclaims proudly through a cloud of blue smoke, "the Count of Monte Cristo." Arleen can't help but wince and move backward, as if bouncing off the woman's insane statement. "You think you some hotshot, honey? You're in jail, too, ain'tcha! You a prisoner, too, honey, you just too stupid to know it."

•   •   •

"Nine-eleven, Ms. Petersen, changed *everything* about commercial property management," Ms. K. Crowley is telling her and then adds with a wry grin: "From top to bottom, you might say." They sit in a large, window-wrapped office on the Thirty-eighth floor of 1655 Avenue of the Americas. The head of Barasoni Human Resources is a full-bodied woman with a round, pretty face, red hair, and a sardonic New York sense of humor. Behind her, blanketed in a yellow haze, stretches the southern skyline of Manhattan—the top of the MetLife Building, the United Nations to the left, and the Empire State Building. Beyond that the smog looms so thick, Arleen can see nothing, but she knows that the massive hole that once was the World Trade Center is out there somewhere. After summarizing the job description, which had taken all of two minutes ("Essentially you'll be holding the hand of the director of building services, making sure he makes it to meetings on time"), Ms. Crowley is now giving her the inside poop on what is *really* going on at Barasoni.

"The name of the game now is *security,*" Ms. Crowley goes on. "Fire safety, evacuation procedures, bomb detection, surveillance, emergency power generation, you name it. We've had more fire drills in the past six months than we had in the past six years! As you must've noticed in the lobby, we have a complex set of sign-in procedures and a full staff of security guards. Most of them are in plainclothes, by the way, so you didn't see *nearly* as many as we actually have. This building has more video cameras—most of them hidden, by the way—than CNN and all three networks combined. Just a matter of time before we have electronic fingerprinting and video facial recognition systems. Last month, four of the larger tenants here formed a consortium to investigate *retinal scans*! By the way, you're being observed *right now* by two of our people on the sixty-second floor. It's still lunch hour, so they're probably eating tuna fish sandwiches watching their monitors, trying to get a little peek up your skirt. Want to say hi to them?"

"Huh?"

"See that little fixture on the ceiling? Go ahead, wave." Arleen glanced upward. Sure enough, on the ceiling above Ms. Crowley was a small circular object that could easily have passed for a smoke detector. "In case you didn't know it, Arleen—by the way, can I call you 'Arleen'? You never know anymore, the laws are so strict these days. You never know when some whacked-out job candidate is going to freak on you." Ms. Crowley shakes her head in ostensible disgust and sighs. "Anyway, companies are leaving New York in droves. Moving to Hoboken, Newark, White Plains, Des Moines, you name it. Why do you think that is, Arleen?"

Arleen reflects for an instant, wanting desperately to provide the correct answer, and then says brightly: "They're scared of another terrorist attack?"

"Nope," says Crowley, "but that's a good try. That's what most people think. And you're right to some extent. I've got this friend who works in the Empire State. She quit last week—she was seeing a shrink for months, scared out of her wits that a 747 was going to fly into her desk." Again, Ms. Crowley sighs in apparent disbelief at such an incredulous notion. "But that's not the real reason. The real reason is the bottom line. Fear just gives them an excuse. It's the almighty bottom line that really counts, always. Sad to say, nine-eleven was the best thing that ever happened to some of these companies. Now they can get office space at fifteen bucks a square foot in Jersey City or Omaha instead of paying seventy here, lay off ten thousand people in the process, and don't have to explain a damn thing to the employees or the board of directors. Sick world, huh?"

Yes, Arleen agrees to herself, it is, but what does this have to do with *anything*? Though Ms. Crowley seems to like her, she worries that she will not have enough time to explain to her how hard she would work and why she should get the job. And how desperately she needs it.

"In any case, those who stay don't give a hoot anymore about what the offices look like. Used to be, the higher the better, you know? Now it's almost the opposite. 'Got five thousand feet on the second floor? *Sold!*' It's crazy. Name of the game now is vertical conveyance."

Looking for a place to say something—*anything*—Arleen jumps in with: "'Vertical conveyance'?"

For the first time in the interview, Ms. Crowley regards Arleen with concern and glances down at Arleen's résumé. "You don't have much experience with commercial property, do you, Arleen?"

"Well, I —"

"Do you realize that more people *work* in this building than *live* in—where is it you're from, again—Middleton, Indiana?"

"Well, I haven't thought about it, but I guess —"

"*Vertical*, Arleen. You must start thinking vertical if you're going to make it here. In New York, it's all about getting people and things up and down—with speed and efficiency. Water pipes, sewage pipes, heating ducts, wiring, video cable, elevators, escalators. Horizontal, I suppose, still exists somewhere in the good old U-S-of-A but not here."

"Oh, *that*," Arleen says knowingly, as if she had been working with the principle of vertical conveyance her whole life.

Ms. Crowley sits back in her chair. "Well, thank you for coming in today, Arleen. We'll be in touch."

Arleen is stunned into silence. She had rehearsed her pitch for an hour the night before. "But I haven't told you my—my qualifications."

"I have your résumé. Your work experience is all in there, I presume? You haven't left anything out?"

"Well, sure," Arleen says uncertainly.

"Then that's it. You will be given every consideration. We want to hire someone by the end of the week. Any questions?"

Arleen picks up her purse and rises. "Ms. Crowley?"

"Yes?"

"Do I have a shot at being hired?"

"Let's put it this way, Arleen, and no disrespect intended, of course: if you have a night job, don't give it up."

●　　　●　　　●

As Arleen exits the air-conditioned fortress of 1655 Avenue of the Americas, the heat once again threatens to overcome her. Heading uptown to the subway, she can see it rising from the asphalt in shimmering waves, like a mirage in the desert. Her clothes are drenched with sweat, weighing on her shoulders like a backpack. Six days earlier, she had arrived in New York with only her clothes and her laptop, and now her vital fluids are being sucked dry as well. In a few hours she would be a mere pile of wet clothes, the Wicked Witch of the Upper West Side, melted into nothingness.

It was no use; she had to call Greg. She'd call him as soon as she got back to her apartment and tell him that she was leaving New York and coming back to Middleton. She'd beg him to come back home. She'd do anything he asked—see a shrink, go back to Red Oak, whatever he wanted. She still loved him, she would say, and always would. Life was not worth living without him; he *was* her life. He still loved her, didn't he realize that? If that didn't work, she'd make something up—yes, she was hit by a taxi and was dying from internal injuries—he had to come to New York and rescue her.

The full impact of her situation suddenly hits her, and only forward momentum keeps her plodding up the sidewalk. What was she *doing* here, banished to this godforsaken land? *Land? What* land? Except for bouquets of white roses shoved in her face by pushy street vendors, she hadn't seen a real tree or grass or flowers in six days! *How could Greg do this to her after all these years, after all the support she had given him?* Ten years of standing by him, and he jettisons her like excess baggage! Despite their years together, he turned out to be no different from all the other men in her life—her father, her boyfriends, Eddie, the list was endless. In the end, she was just a boat that men hopped on for a ride when they pleased and hopped off when they spotted a better one sailing by. And now, cut from its moorings, the boat had lost its bearings and had drifted into this godforsaken harbor called New York, another immigrant freighter swallowed by the maw of the Big Apple. How could she possibly think she could survive here? She'd wind up on welfare, handcuffed to a doorway begging for cigarettes, like Edmond Dantes.

You a prisoner, too, honey, you just too stupid to know it.

As she often had when she was younger, she feels a powerful sensation of insignificance, as though she would disappear if she closed her eyes. *What is it,* she wondered, *that people see when they look at her?* The streets are teeming with people who flaunt their own existence and ignore hers—she could be a ghost, for all they cared. Yet *they* all seem filled with such *purpose.* Dressed in business suits and summer dresses, carrying briefcases and handbags and holding cell phones next to their ears, they seem suddenly so—so *motivated,* composed of flesh and bone and propelled by some inner fuel she did not possess. They hurry. They have departure points and destinations. They have families and careers and passions and hobbies. Is it all an act? Yes, that's it, they're all extras, sent by Central Casting in an elaborate hoax to humiliate her. Or robots! The cell phones are really remote control devices connecting them to a tower, which at this very moment is transmitting instructions on how to act, what to do, where to go next. She had no cell phone, no instructions. What was she *thinking* when she left Indiana? *What was she doing here?*

Feeling faint, she needs to sit down and compose herself, but there are no benches anywhere—park, bus stop, or otherwise—as there are in Indiana.

"Hey, babe—you need a place to sit down? Sit on this!"

At first, in all the clatter of midtown Manhattan, Arleen can't identify who is speaking—or even *if* someone is talking to *her.* She turns to her right—half a dozen men of various sizes and ages, all in white shirts rolled up to the elbow, are leaning against the side of an office building, smoking cigarettes and smirking. None gives any sign of being the speaker, though it is now obvious that one of them was. Staring at them, she is surprised that she does not feel fear or anger or even irritation. On the contrary, what she is feeling is . . . *gratitude*! Someone is calling to her. *Her!* She is real after all: a living, breathing *person.* Doesn't matter a damn bit that they are jeering her—it's proof positive that her blip is back on the radar screen! Doesn't matter that these guys are probably all sexist pigs; not at all—she knows what *they're* all about! As their smirks begin to fall into puzzled, uneasy glances, and a few even avert their eyes, she realizes that she is grinning at them.

"Fuck you, assholes!" she yells at them happily, flinging her purse over her shoulder like a scarf. A slight breeze that she hasn't noticed before cools the back of her blouse, propelling her toward the subway.

•   •   •

Back home in her sublet studio, after sitting in a bubble bath for an hour and changing into shorts and Greg's "Go Buckeyes" T-shirt, which still exudes the unique Greg scent, Arleen boots up her laptop and feels almost human. The studio, on the second floor of a brownstone on West 107th Street, turned out to be better than she imagined: though the space (twenty by thirty feet) is much less than she is accustomed to, the longer wall boasts a regal fireplace, and the front has a large bay window and a narrow balcony, where she can sit and watch the street and even see a sliver of the Hudson River and the rolling hills of New Jersey on the other side. Undoubtedly it was once the living room of a larger apartment, before the apartment was chopped and sectioned into multi-living units, to increase the rental income. James Ellenbach, the regular tenant, went to Cape Cod for a couple of months, the agency told her, and he put most of his personal belongings in storage, but what he did leave behind—the furniture, plates, silverware, pots and pans, and an empty walk-in closet—were Arleen's to use if she saw fit.

Waiting for her connection to AOL to kick in, she unpeels a banana that she bought at a small fruit-and-vegetable stand on the walk back from the subway. The outdoor stand, the front part of a grocery store on Broadway, suited her just fine. She had no idea where to find a supermarket and didn't care. Years ago, the world had become a vast array of meaningless, superfluous options, and the world of food was no exception. Thinking about supermarkets somehow sparks the memory of the Ohio State Library, to that infamous day in 1992, the second week of her freshman year, when she went looking for a book on the American Revolution. In the library stacks she was met with *hundreds* of books on the topic. She pulled one out, a dusty red hardcover titled *Revolution for the Ages,* written by someone named Henry Dozier in 1953. Why read *this* book? she wondered. What made *this* book worthy and another not? Despite the book's six hundred pages, Dozier couldn't possibly have covered *everything* about the American Revolution. Sliding to the floor in the narrow aisle between the bookshelves, Arleen was suddenly overwhelmed by the sheer *enormity* of accumulated knowledge. She could see ahead to the same task of learning about chemistry, physics, biology, psychology, sociology—you name it! The library overflowed with thousands—*millions!*—of books about every subject under the sun. And that didn't include the decades of journals, magazines, and newspapers available on microfilm in the Reference Room! And this was only a *college* library—what about larger public libraries that dotted the globe from here to Timbuktu?

Well, if she couldn't read *every* book about the American Revolution, she resolved that day in the stacks, she would read *none* of them. What was the *point*? She'd let Greg handle the learning "thing"; she'd become a hair stylist or a clothes shop owner, some definable skill *with finite boundaries*. Greg had no hangups about knowledge. He could go into the Ohio State Library, find the right book, and be out in ten minutes. If there was something she needed to know, Greg would teach her.

Smiling over the memory, her AOL home page finally flashes on the screen, punctuated by the AOL man's baritone "Welcome, you've got mail." She clicks the "Read" button, hoping to see an e-mail from k.crowley but knowing in her heart that it won't be there. And it isn't. Only two junk e-mails, one offering a surefire way to reduce her mortgage debt and the other hyping a machine to enlarge her penis.

She is suddenly struck by the irony of her plight: here she is, exiled in the biggest city in the world, and she knows not a soul. People literally piled up on every side of her—horizontally and *vertically,* as Ms. Crowley made her painfully aware—and the only way to connect with any of them was through a tiny plug in a wall! Two nights ago, she had entered a chat room called "30s Women's Club" and bantered for two hours with a group of New York women—or women who *claimed* to be women—commiserating over their cheating husbands and their miserable marriages, just as she had done through the long, lonely nights when Greg worked late at Eastland. For all Arleen knew, these *supposed* women could actually be wrinkled old men living in Miami Beach! One could even be living next door, on the other side of the wall—a few feet from where she sits! Impulsively, she reaches for the phone, suddenly overwhelmed with a desire to talk to Greg, to hear him say that he wants her back.

As if on cue, Arleen is startled by a loud *thunk!* that shakes the dishes in the kitchenette area behind her. Staring wide-eyed, straining to listen, she can hear muffled, angry voices but can't decipher what they are saying. Finally, her curiosity becomes too much: sneaking on tiptoe, she pulls a glass out of the sink and places it carefully on the wall . . . definitely a man and a woman . . . and they are arguing . . . their words, however, are no more distinct than they were without the glass.

Disappointed, she is resigned to returning to her laptop when she sees a row of boxes on the floor, sitting in a shallow alcove that in a previous era was probably a much deeper pantry. She had noticed these cardboard boxes when she first moved in, but they hadn't registered then; she just assumed that James Ellenbach forgot to store them and thought no more about it. Now, after she has come up empty on her eavesdropping mission, they suddenly attract her attention. The boxes are sealed shut, she sees, though only with a thin strip of masking tape, the kind that can be easily purchased at any Rite Aid. Some of the tape, in fact, is already starting to peel off from the humidity. . . .

Anything to fill the hole.

•   •   •

An hour later, the three boxes rest at the foot of the bed. She has gone through two of them and replaced the contents just as she had found them. For the most part, the contents had proved less than revealing: a few pieces of china and two silver-plated serving trays (which, she surmised, Ellenbach had wanted to keep safe from the slippery hands of his anonymous sublessee), a golf trophy, and a framed portrait of a handsome gray-haired couple, whom she assumed were Grandma and Grandpa Ellenbach, living or dying peacefully in Podunk, Iowa. No love letters or documents linking Ellenbach to the assassination of JFK. Nothing really personal, nothing she can sink her teeth into. *Who are you, James Ellenbach?*

Opening the last box, she is immediately spurred on by the discovery of another framed photo, this one of a young man and a pretty blonde, both about her own age, giggling and holding ice cream cones high in the air in mock salute to the Statue of Liberty, which appears out of focus in the background. *Ah, is this you, James? And is this your sweetheart? Are you living together—here in this apartment, perhaps— in matrimonial bliss? In common-law sin?* Rummaging quickly through the remainder of the contents, however, she can see only more platters, plates, and other knickknacks. Everything really personal must be locked away, she deduces forlornly, probably in the basement or in some seedy storage container downtown. Disappointed, about to give up, she notices a light blue envelope leaning against the side of the box, as if hurriedly slipped in at the last minute. It is addressed—in a feminine handwriting—to "Jamie Ellenbach" but carries no address, stamp, or postmark. *Which means she must've delivered it herself,* Arleen thinks, *she slipped it in his mailbox or under the door.* Hesitating only a second, she opens it, and two pages of matching light blue stationery fall into her lap. The letter is dated June 12, just about the time James listed his studio for sublet.

Dear Jamie:

Please, please don't be angry with me for writing this letter. I simply have no other way of reaching you. You won't answer the phone or return my calls or my e-mails. I guess you know that was me downstairs last night, ringing the buzzer over and over. I could tell by the shadows on the ceiling that you were home. You're probably going to crumple this letter into a ball and burn it, and I don't blame you a bit. But please read it first, please, Jamie, after four months you owe me that much.

Last night, when I got home, I had kind of a revelation—an "epiphany," James Joyce called it, if I still remember English 101. I see now how out of control I've been and hope you will eventually forgive me. I am so, so sorry for all the trouble I've caused you. I'm probably the reason you decided to go to the Cape this summer. The pressure I put on you must've been unbearable. When I get carried away (you know that you are "my whole life," "I am nothing without you," and things like that), I see now how unfair and stupid it is. For months I've been clinging to you like a leech, and then, when you ask for a little breathing room, like going away for a weekend, I scream like a lunatic that you are leaving me, abandoning me. . . .

Please try to understand. From the time I was a little girl, my mother told me that my one mission in life was to find the right man and raise a family, that a family would be my only true source of happiness. It was carved into me like a commandment on the tablets. I grew up with no aspirations or ambitions. Some of my friends wanted to be lawyers or writers, but not me. Oh, yes, I went through all the motions, college and grad school and a good job and all that, but underneath I never really wanted to <u>be</u> anything or <u>do</u> anything, except to find the right guy.

So a part of me has always been missing—I could feel it, it was like a gaping wound, I just didn't know what it was. Then I met you and thought I'd finally accomplished my mission. (God help me, I even called Mom and told her that!) Everything was all right when we were together, I felt good, everything fell into place, like tumblers clicking in a lock. But my mother was wrong and my shrink was right—there's more to life than finding a man. And I was wrong—the missing piece is not out there somewhere, it's in me. I see now what is probably so obvious to you and everyone else. Another person can't give you your dignity or self-respect, no matter how much he loves you. I have to do that myself. Since I was a teenager, I've *followed my mother's orders like a good little soldier and allowed myself—my whole life!—to be defined by men. It wasn't fair to them, and especially to you. Most important, it's not fair <u>to me!</u> As long as I continue to let that happen, I'm shortchanging myself and whoever I'm with.*

Maybe sometime, a few months from now, we can get together again for a drink or something. Meanwhile, good luck to you, Jamie. I won't bother you anymore. You're right—it's best if we don't see each other for a while. I realize now I have so much work to do. I need to find this missing thing inside me before it ruins the rest of my life, and I don't have a clue where to start looking. I love you and will always cherish the times we had together.

Alicia

When Arleen puts down the letter, she feels moisture on her cheeks and knows it is not perspiration. What a sad, wonderful, horrible world it was! This studio, so wiped clean of history and people—so *anonymous*—just a few moments ago, had been throbbing with emotion before she arrived and would throb again after she left. People much like her, with much the same problems and the same joys. We are all interconnected, she thinks, in ways we can't begin to understand. *By the way, you're being observed* right now *by two of our people on the sixty-second floor. . . . Want to say hi to them?*

The sounds of the tempestuous couple next door, whose argument seemed to be in remission (or had she blocked them out while reading Alicia's letter?), start to heat up again.

"Hey, you two!" Arleen yells at the wall. "There's someone *living* here, you know!"

In the abrupt silence that follows, she can picture the stunned couple on the other side, staring wide-eyed at the wall. Arleen grins, gets up from her bed, and goes to the window seat. The sun is setting over the New Jersey hills, lending a silver glean to the Hudson River that she hadn't seen before. *This New York,* she thinks, *maybe this isn't such a bad place after all.*

Defining Emptiness

"I have of late—but wherefore I know not—lost all my mirth, forgone all custom of exercises; and indeed it goes so heavily with my disposition, that this goodly frame the earth seems to me a sterile promontory," Shakespeare's Hamlet laments as he describes an emptiness that nothing in the world can penetrate. This symptom is one of the most difficult to confront, not only for the borderline but for his intimates and therapists as well.

Feelings of emptiness have been associated with the concept of BPD since the diagnosis's reification in *DSM-III* (1980). Gunderson has suggested that compared to impulsivity, depression, and anger, emptiness is the emotion most resistant to alteration. He finds that many borderline patients tend to accommodate to such feelings rather than actually eliminate them. Until *DSM-IV,* emptiness also was connected to boredom as part of the defining constellation. *DSM-IV* deleted boredom as an appendage to the emptiness criterion, because more specific research did not support its inclusion as a primary borderline symptom. Indeed, boredom (defined as a weariness or loss of interest) is more consistent with the lack of empathy and detachment of narcissistic personality disorder.

The concept of emptiness is difficult to define. Usually it is described as a sense of meaninglessness or emotional void. Emptiness is a feeling that subsumes the sense of alienation that many borderlines experience. In turn, this connects to the BPD symptom of identity disturbance. Similarly, the inability to feel connected to the rest of the world may evolve into a desperate fear of abandonment and, ultimately, into feelings of dissociation. Arleen's sensation of emptiness often came on as an all-consuming helplessness, akin to being overwhelmed by an unexpectedly huge wave while swimming in the ocean. She would thrash around "underwater," unable to breathe, powerless to do anything, even to figure out which way was up. Worse, the emptiness would lead to physical pain—nausea and stomach pangs that would spread to other parts of her body. During these episodes, she would feel bombarded by ordinary stimuli that most people take for granted—the number of volumes in a library or brand names or sizes in a supermarket—culminating in the terror of losing her "self" in all this chaos and an inability to act, a kind of "mental paralysis" in which she would not be able to leave her room for hours or days.

Emptiness and Depression

People who are depressed may also experience feelings of emptiness. Indeed, some researchers have previously proposed that BPD is really a subdivision of affective disorders. Current research, however, confirms that the phenomenon of borderline depression is distinctive from Axis I major depression. Emptiness and loneliness are the most significant distinguishing features. Other subjective feelings characteristic of depression in BPD include anger and destructive impulsiveness, self-condemnation, desperation toward relationships, and dissociation. In contrast, people suffering from major depression more often experience guilt, remorse, self-consciousness, and withdrawal.

Psychological Theories of Emptiness

Freud and the early psychoanalysts described the stages of psychosexual development beginning with the oral phase. They postulated that frustrations in satisfying the primary needs of an infant during this period would result in an adult prone to depression, with an insatiable hunger for relationships, culminating in a perpetual feeling state of emptiness. Later theorists who emphasized object relations development (how the infant relates to his environment, rather than how he responds to internal stimuli) stressed that failures in early caretaking resulted in an inability to internalize soothing feelings of safety and contentment. As an adult, the individual is unable to evoke remembered images or feelings of soothing and is unable to self-soothe, resulting in the subjective sensation of emptiness.

The Role of the Doctor

This characteristic of BPD, more than any other, illuminates the dichotomy in the psychiatric profession's understanding and treatment of mental illness. Many psychiatrists perceive psychopathology as a function of biological/chemical/physiological/anatomic/genetic disruption. In this perspective, mental illness is defined by a defect in functioning human protoplasm, much like tuberculosis is a distinctive medical illness caused by a specific microbe, not just a really bad cough. Symptoms of tuberculosis such as cough, fever, sweats, and fatigue result from the spread of the bacilli and the body's immune system combating the bacterial marauders. Environmental components such as inadequate nutrition, poor hygiene, and contact with others infected with the disease are all risk factors for contracting via contagion. Further, genetic variabilities such as lung tissue changes or defects in the immune system may permit greater vulnerability to the illness. The doctor's goal is to eradicate the infection with medicine, minimize the environmental dangers, and educate the patient about his illness and its impact on himself and others. Ideally, the pathology is erased and health is regained.

Similarly, some psychiatrists perceive psychiatric symptoms as primarily a disruption in normal biochemical processes and explore ways to restore equilibrium. Doctors with this biological orientation use medications, electroconvulsive therapy, and, rarely, psychosurgery to alter psychopathology, which, like tuberculosis, transpires on a submicroscopic, cellular level. For these doctors, the subjective experience of *emptiness* is caused by a flaw in the human *physiological* mechanism. The symptom is perceived to be part of the syndrome constellation of depression and is treated as such. In this medical model, symptoms are pathological—by definition, "bad"—and must be eradicated by treatment. Treatment includes medication and education about environmental and genetic risk factors.

At the other extreme in psychiatric thought are those who focus on the mind instead of the brain. They perceive mental illness as the result of an individual's internal struggle, which has diverted from the path but remains tethered, however tenuously, to normality. Treatment for this group focuses not on microscopic manipulations but on person-to-person communication, with a goal of understanding the whole person's past and present experience within a social context. In this paradigm, healthy change results not from passive introduction of chemical compounds, but through the afflicted's active, willful participation in the process.

If the struggle inside is unconscious, psychoanalytically oriented psychotherapy may, by making these conflicts conscious, move the person back within the boundaries of what we accept as "normal." If pathology is a result of erroneous thinking, cognitive techniques can cleanse the psychic wounds. If the struggle results in habitual behaviors, behavioral modification can convert pathology. Symptoms are not seen as particularly "bad," so much as representative of the person's pain caused by a wound as opposed to an invading organism or breakdown in biological function; thus treatment means healing, not excision. In this model, emptiness may be perceived to be the result of past disappointments and traumas, resulting in a fear of caring or of commitment, or as a failure to develop values for one's world or oneself. Whatever the etiology, active talk therapy is the primary treatment approach.

Obviously both models are valid, and most practitioners accept that a biopsychosocial confluence is optimal in treatment. Thus, when this symptom is prominent, antidepressant medication usually is indicated. Therapy centers around helping the borderline derive a sense of purpose. When an individual begins to feel that her existence in some way truly makes a difference, emptiness begins to be sated.

The Role of Intimates

Friends and family can help the borderline achieve a sense of purpose by emphasizing how vital he is in their lives. Just as important, they can help him derive a sense of fun. Emptiness always is accompanied by extreme seriousness, which often is out of proportion. Leading the borderline to fun activities distracts him from existential worries and physical complaints.

Humor also can be a useful tool. (Indeed, it is an acknowledged device in Linehan's DBT model.) A sense of humor implies a sense of proportion. Laughter rescues the borderline from her impalement on hopeless emptiness. However, the borderline can be very sensitive to certain types of humor, such as sarcasm, perceiving them as ridicule. Therefore it is important that levity be more generic than personal, more silly than dark—for example, a slapstick comedy is more appropriate than a black comedy.

ACTION STEPS: Filling the Emptiness

Emptiness is an all-consuming feeling. The borderline is tempted to withdraw, as Arleen did on several occasions. With isolation, the muscles of existence atrophy. Thus, "exercising" all areas of experience is vitally important.

1. *Physical exercise:* Physical action such as sports, aerobics, jogging, and so on enhances well-being. The endorphin release accompanying vigorous activity has antidepressant components. Self-soothing activities such as a relaxing bubble bath, practicing yoga, watching a beautiful sunset, or sexual self-stimulation also can be helpful.

2. *Intellectual exercise:* The brain muscles also need exercise. Challenging the mind by reading, debating, following current events, pursuing interests, or even working puzzles can develop a sense of purpose.

3. *Social exercise:* Connecting with others helps fill the inner loneliness and challenges the borderline to venture outside her barren domain and interact.

4. *Spiritual exercise:* Contemplating forces outside oneself, long a part of Alcoholics Anonymous and other twelve-step groups, allows a flow of greater meaning to fill inner recesses. Other examples: church involvement, group meditation, or private reflection. Spiritual exercise does not necessarily mandate religious belief or involvement; atheists who reject the notion of a Supreme Being can be engaged in intense philosophical exploration and discourse. Even a serene walk in the woods allows contemplation of the world's joys.

9

Anger

Anger is a brief lunacy.

—HORACE, *Epistles*

A s opposed to other expressions of anger, borderline rage is marked by a suddenness and unpredictability that could be described as emotional spontaneous combustion. Even though borderlines may seem to explode for no ostensible reason, the anger is always present, lying hidden under the surface, suppressed by the fear of abandonment, or turned inward and transformed into self-destructive behavior. This chapter explores the psychological dynamics of intense anger as well as possible neurobiological contributors. Through the continuation of Patty's story, you will understand how borderlines experience and express anger and how it is connected to other BPD symptoms. Finally, we offer several strategies for coping with borderline rage.

PATTY: PART TWO

With Laurie finally asleep in her crib, the baby-sitter sent home, and the mess cleaned up as much as possible for now, Didi has her first chance to relax. She flops down on Patty's sofa and surveys the living room. Not bad, considering that two hours ago it was a disaster area. Crawling around in the living room, Laurie had burst through her diaper in a big way, not only splashing her own chubby little legs but also leaving a trail of brown stains across the rug. By the time Angela had pulled off her Walkman and realized what had happened, Laurie was in the kitchen,

151

knocking over a metal wastebasket and frightening herself into a crying frenzy in the process.

Angela had done her best, but no twelve-year-old could comfort a screaming baby, change a diaper, and clean up a condo all at the same time. By the time Didi arrived, Laurie was bleeding from a small cut on her pinky, probably the result of her encounter with the wastebasket; Angela was in tears; and crumpled diapers were strewn everywhere. Half the pages of the day's *L.A. Times* were spread over the carpet—a twelve-year-old's naive presumption that a baby could somehow be handled like an untrained puppy.

Once calmed down, Angela was able to tell Didi the whole story. Patty had left a few hours ago with "this older guy with a ponytail." No, they didn't say where they were going, but they'd be home by five. Laurie was asleep when Patty left but woke up and started crying, and Angela figured it was okay if she took Laurie out of her crib. When Laurie "is, like, crying like crazy," and "I'm, like, saying, 'Oh my God,'" Angela had tried to call Patty's cell phone, but there was no answer. She was supposed to call Didi's number if she had any problems. Didi knew the rest.

It was a miracle, Didi knows, that nothing worse had happened. And it certainly might have if the Highway Patrol cop had not given her a free pass when she explained the situation and showed him her ABA card. She makes a mental note to find out his name and recommend that he be awarded a Congressional Medal of Honor.

Didi hasn't been here for a few weeks, and the condo shows the results of a whopper of a shopping spree, courtesy, no doubt, of Mr. Scott Powell. The sofa is made of soft black leather and has a matching armchair, which faces a big-screen TV that occupies most of the far wall. Against the adjoining wall sits a dark oak entertainment unit that displays all sorts of high-tech audiophile equipment. At this point Didi can only guess if Powell bought all this stuff for her sister or has already moved in. Judging by the quick look she had of Patty's bedroom, with its unmade bed and clothes scattered about, she wagers that they have not yet reached the live-together stage, thank goodness.

For lack of anything better to do, Didi starts to fish through the *Times* to see if the business section has made it through the ordeal unscathed, when she hears laughter in the hallway. As the giggling becomes louder and a key is fitted into the door lock, Didi glances at her watch: five thirty-seven.

"Didi!" Patty exclaims. "What are you doing here?"

"Stop it, Patty. You knew damn well I was here as soon as you drove up."

"No, I —"

"My car's parked right outside, Patty. You *know* my car."

Though vowing to keep calm, especially if Powell is with her, Didi cannot keep disdain out of her tone. As Patty places her keys on the TV, Didi sees she is dressed in a white miniskirt and white stockings that reach just above the knee, leaving a long expanse of tanned thigh. Her streaked blond hair is tied in two pigtails. Didi hasn't seen Powell since the day of his seminar three years ago, but he seems younger now than her image of him, probably attributable to the exuberance with which he entered the apartment. He wears a tailored navy blue suit and a light blue shirt open one button too far, revealing a full matte of gray-blond chest hair.

"Hello, Counselor," Didi says. "How are you?"

"Uh-fine," he replies awkwardly. "And you?"

"We *could've* come in the back way, you know," Patty blurts out suddenly, "through the parking garage."

"'*Could've*,'" Didi repeats contemptuously. "Meaning you *didn't*."

"What is this, Didi—the third degree? Are you cross-examining me? Two damn lawyers in the room is too much for *any* human to tolerate."

Sprawling on the leather armchair, Patty looks to Powell to acknowledge her wit, but none, to her consternation, is forthcoming. Perhaps his attorney's intuition, sensing an imminent confrontation, is kicking in; until he learns more his initial exhilaration is turning into cautious observation. He can't even bring himself to sit on the sofa next to Didi or stand near Patty, thinking either action might be interpreted as taking sides, and instead leans on the Switzerland afforded by the big-screen TV.

"I'm okay," Didi says to Powell, "or *was* until a few hours ago."

"Tell me about it!" Patty interjects. "What a day! First the rude waiter in Spago and then that awful salesgirl in Valentino's." Patty shakes her head in disgust. "You know what it is? I'll tell you: people just don't *care* anymore, that's what it is. Just do your job and get it done. There's no pride anymore. Scotty, am I right or am I right?"

Powell hesitates, like a witness on the stand recognizing that the wrong answer could be disastrous. Throughout Patty's harangue, Didi can feel the fillings in her teeth being ground into the enamel. "She's obviously a new employee," he replies quietly, turning his gaze to the floor.

Didi turns to Patty. "Haven't you forgotten something?"

"Forgotten? No, I don't think so. A store has a responsibility—"

"*Your daughter, damn it!* Remember Laurie? You haven't even asked about her!"

Patty's smile has the rigidity of steel. "I don't need to, Didi, you're here. It's simple logic: if you're here, Laurie is fine. You're the perfect mother, therefore Laurie must be fine. QED."

Didi can hardly form syllables, much less words or coherent sentences. "Two hours ago, your baby was running wild through this place. Your prepubescent baby-sitter called me, hysterical. She didn't have a clue—"

"*Okay, that's it! Get out of here! Get out now!*" Patty jumps to her feet so abruptly, it's as if the armchair is an ejection seat, catapulting her into the air.

"What?!"

"*Get out of my house!*" The sheer ferocity of Patty's command is so explosive, so intense, Powell's head jolts back as if hit by a brick. "I'm so tired of your bullshit, Didi! Telling me how to run my life, how to raise my kid. 'You're not doing *this* right, you're not doing *that* right.' Big sister knows all! It's always been that way. Well, I've got news for you, Didi: *you don't know shit!*"

While Powell stands open-mouthed and speechless, Didi is more prepared. From long experience, she knows that the length of Patty's fuse is microscopic. Unlike most other people's anger, Patty's rage does not start as dark storm clouds that roll in and then burst into thunder and rain. Instead it erupts from out of nowhere, with no warning. No one builds a fire under Patty; she ignites. Spontaneous combustion.

"I tell you what, Ms. Know-Everything Perfect-Mother," Patty screams. "*You* take her."

"Get a grip, Patty. You don't realize what you're saying."

"I don't? You think you can do a better job? *Prove it! Adopt her!* We got two fucking lawyers in the room, we can draw up the papers and be done with the whole thing *in five fucking minutes!*" Wakened by her mother's harangue, Laurie begins to stir in her bedroom. All three adults freeze in suspended animation, hoping futilely that she will go back to sleep if they don't say a thing. Of course, that doesn't happen, and Laurie's sobs are almost as sudden as her mother's outburst. Patty's glare at Didi could cut through diamonds: *"Now look what you've done!"*

As Patty runs out of the living room, the echo of her words becomes mere background noise to the wails now coming from Laurie's bedroom. Powell takes a breath, seems about to say something but thinks better of it, or, more likely, can't think of anything to say. Didi has seen this look many times before—on the face of her own husband after hearing Patty's hysterical messages on the answering machine at two o'clock in the morning.

"Welcome to Bedlam," Didi says. She is suddenly dying for a cigarette, but she left her pack in the car in all the turmoil.

"Maybe I should leave," Powell says softly.

"That's your decision, Counselor, but if you want my opinion, that would be the worst thing you could do—that is, if you still want a girlfiend when you leave here."

Resigned to his lot, Powell sits down in the armchair that had ejected Patty a few moments ago. He fidgets unsteadily, as if worried that it was a defect in the chair itself that had caused his girlfriend to act so outrageously.

"She's been under a lot of duress lately," he says.

"Yes," Didi agrees halfheartedly.

"Not only today. The divorce in general, I mean."

"I know. I've got many friends who've been through it."

"And trying to rear a baby at the same time."

A baby that you probably wish would disappear, she thinks. "Nope, a baby certainly doesn't make it any easier."

Now that they've run through the gamut of excuses for her sister, there's little left to say in her defense. Except the obvious: that she might be a raving lunatic who should be stuck in a cage and the key thrown into the La Brea tar pits.

On the other hand, she wonders if Powell has seen Patty detonate like this before. Only dating her a few months, it is perfectly reasonable to assume that he hasn't, in which case he might be seeing Didi through Patty's eyes—a meddling, overbearing, condescending pest. She wonders also what Patty has told him about their sibling relationship and their parents. Oh, well, she did not have time to set him straight now; an explanation would take hours, back through thirty years of family history. He'd learn in time—if he stayed around that long.

"Isn't she a doll?" Patty declares, reentering the living room, staring at her daughter who is now cradled peacefully in her arms, sucking from a bottle. "Yes, you are. You're my little poopie-butt, aren't you?" Instead of occupying the vacant part of the sofa next to Didi, Patty slides onto Powell's lap. "See what a little doll she is, Scotty? Not a speck of trouble, are you, honey-bunch."

Didi does not know if Powell has any kids of his own, but judging by his reaction, the answer is no. Powell seems more entranced by the sight of Patty's miniskirt riding up her thighs than of the esthetic qualities of her baby. He inspects Laurie as a dog-lover might examine a tiny but potentially snippy Pekinese, tickling her cautiously under the chin with his forefinger. Representing women in their divorce settlements, Didi realizes, did not include the prerequisite of relating to their children. She is just relieved he does not say "coochie-coo" or something equally lame.

A knock on the door swerves the focus of the room from baby admiration to more practical matters. Like a cool quarterback handing off a football, Patty deftly places Laurie in Powell's astonished hands and goes to the door. Instead of swinging it open in typical impulsive Patty fashion, however, she stops abruptly just in front of it.

"Yes?" Patty asks. "Who is it?"

"It's me," says a young, unsteady, and barely discernible voice, "Angela."

Patty turns back to the room, looking first at Didi and then at Powell. For a reason Didi cannot figure out in that instant, Patty is nervously biting her lower lip, as if the devil himself might be standing behind that door rather than a twelve-year-old girl.

"What do you want?"

"I . . . I . . ." The rest of the response is too muffled to understand, and for one terrible moment Didi thinks that Patty might not let her in. Powell is staring at Patty as well, with an incomprehensible expression that is probably the deciding factor. Patty pulls opens the door, and Angela stands in the doorway, looking shyly at the floor. "I—I just wanted to see how Laurie was doing."

"Fine," Patty bites off, impatiently shifting her weight to one hip. "Anything else?"

"Yes."

As Angela hesitates, apparently unable to form the words, Didi cannot tolerate her sister's rudeness any longer: "Hi, Angela, why don't you come in for a sec?"

"Well, okay." Angela walks in uncertainly and Patty shuts the door behind her. The glare that Didi absorbs from her sister could incinerate lead, but Didi is not to be deterred. Angela has changed her clothes since the afternoon's incident. Dressed in a miniskirt and high white stockings just like Patty, the pair could be members of the same high school clique. The sight of them standing together in the middle of the living room is shocking—a fully grown thirty-year-old woman and a twelve-year-old girl both trying to be seventeen. "I just wanted to say I'm sorry. Like, for what happened today. Laurie crying and everything and, like, messing up the rug."

Powell shifts uneasily in his armchair. He has been holding Laurie awkwardly under the armpits while she sits on his knee. For all intents and purposes, he is stuck alone in the room, the only male surrounded by four females of all shapes and sizes, and he doesn't know which one is going to erupt next. His eyes dart from one to another, searching for a clue.

"And, like, Laurie hurting her finger." Angela grimaces and knits her eyebrows, as if struggling to remember the last big line of her part in the school play—a play perhaps for which her mother rehearsed her. "Oh, and for, like, making you come all the way out here, Mrs. Rollins." Now that her lines are spoken and her final sin is out in the open, she looks expectantly at Didi, waiting for absolution. Didi cannot disappoint her.

"You did fine," Didi says with a smile. "You did the right thing."

Throughout Angela's apology, Patty's face has been a blank slate on which anything could be written. Now, with Didi's last remark, Patty appears drained and exhausted and Didi, despite her extreme irritation, feels sorry for her. The rage that had filled the room just minutes before seems part of a different era. Patty goes over to Powell and much to his relief removes Laurie from his knee and takes her into the unoccupied space next to Didi on the sofa.

"I promise I'll do better next time," Angela says, this time to Patty. "Please let me see Laurie again."

A stream of tears is now falling from Patty's left eye, taking tiny chunks of mascara with it. "You can always see Laurie, Angela. Only maybe next time I'll be here with you, okay? She's a handful, isn't she?" Whatever bond the sisters forged as children is stronger than Didi imagined. Even though Patty is looking at Angela, Didi is the only one in the room who knows Patty is really addressing her. "You'll always be a part of Laurie's life."

This is the closest that Patty will ever get to an apology, Didi knows, but in a way it is much more than that. While Angela grins with relief, Powell slumps in his armchair, looking like a man who has just caught sight of Everest and is not at all convinced he is up to the task of climbing it.

"Here," Didi says, reaching out for Laurie, "give your old meddling aunt a chance to screw up your life."

The Dynamics of Anger

Anger, a universal emotion, is prominent in several psychiatric syndromes. Among the personality disorders it is distinctive in borderline, antisocial, and narcissistic personality disorders. As a symptom of impulse control disorders it defines intermittent explosive disorder and is commonly exhibited by individuals struggling with substance abuse disorders and bulimia. Anger is often observed in those with attention-deficit/hyperactivity disorder. It also is a common component of mood disorders, especially mania.

Though the reader might presume that "a rage is a rage is a rage," borderline anger can come in several different varieties, be delivered in different ways, and be aimed at different targets. What sometimes distinguishes borderline rage is its concealment and its unpredictability. Some borderlines routinely suppress anger, fearing that its expression will result in retaliation and, ultimately and most feared, abandonment. Such individuals deflect their rage back on themselves and become self-destructive, as Lizzie did (see chapters 5 and 6). For others, such as Patty, anger is a startling, unplanned explosion, shocking the borderline herself as much as those around her. Often there is no buildup or observable progression. Calm may be shattered by a violent eruption spurred on by a minor incident.

Unlike the episodic anger observed in other pathological and non-pathological behaviors, most borderlines feel angry much of the time, even if the anger is not expressed. Frustration and self-reproach can unleash rage, which often is directed at those closest to the borderline. A study of domestic violence by men demonstrated that batterers had a greater likelihood of exhibiting borderline and/or antisocial characteristics than control subjects. Abusers scored higher on active hostility and self-criticism scales and were more likely to have been abused as children.

Another investigation confirmed that rage and hostility were significantly greater in borderline patients than in nonpatient participants in the study. Further, there was a trend for anger to be less intense in those borderlines who were depressed. This inverse relationship between hostility and depression suggests that perhaps depression diminishes the experience of anger in borderlines or possibly that expressed anger is a defense against depression. In any event, this observation may be unique to borderlines, since other studies of depressed psychiatric patients note that increased depression is correlated with *increased* anger and violence. The relationship between anger and depression remains unclear, but it is significant since both emotions are felt to be associated with serotonin irregularities. If, as some have suggested, depression is anger turned inward, then perhaps anger is depression splayed in all directions.

The Relationship between Anger and Other BPD Criteria

Anger is one of the most enduring characteristics of BPD—that is, no alterations have been made to the wording of this criterion since the BPD diagnosis was first included in *DSM-III* in 1980. It also is one of the symptoms most resistant to change. One study monitored persistence of specific defining criteria of BPD over a two-year period. Intense anger was the most enduring symptom, remitting in only 7 percent of subjects. In contrast, suicidal behavior resolved in 54 percent of cases over the two-year span.

Anger is intertwined with other DSM criteria that define BPD. Mood instability (see chapter 7) includes episodes of anger. Destructive impulsivity and suicidal or self-harming behaviors (see chapters 5 and 6) are often accompanied by feelings of hostility. Anger and frustration usually travel with the frenzied attempts to avoid feeling abandoned and persistent sensations of emptiness (see chapters 2 and 8). Anger and disappointment are prominent in unstable relationships, as the formerly idealized individual sinks to the level of being abhorred (see chapter 3). Fury can become so overpowering that it may distort reality (see chapter 10).

The Incubators of Anger, or How a Firecracker Becomes an Atomic Bomb

Early psychoanalytic writers viewed the newborn as a *tabula rasa,* literally a "blank slate." Behavior was felt to result exclusively from environmental influences. The angry adult was the harvest of the frustrated child, whose needs were not met. Literally and figuratively, early theorists blamed inadequate breast-feeding. The developing child, hungry for consistent nurturing, transformed frustration to aggression. Otto Kernberg, in his seminal work on borderline personality organization, was one of the first psychoanalysts in this field to acknowledge the potential contribution of genetics (what many current writers refer to as temperament) to the development of the borderline disposition. Kernberg suggested that an "excessive nature of primary aggression" may participate in the development of the angry adult.

Behavioral theories such as Linehan's DBT (see chapter 12) attribute aggression to the failure of an emotionally withholding environment to respond to the individual's inborn emotional needs. Probably the greatest failure occurs with severe physical or sexual abuse. Cognitive theorists emphasize that anger is a learned defensive maneuver that serves to protect the borderline from perceived exploitation. Interestingly, although all of these theorists approach the individual from different perspectives, their conceptualizations are not that disparate; all emphasize the failure of the environment to satisfy needs.

Neurobiologists correlate borderline emotions such as anger with alterations in the brain's internal chemistry through a cascade of interconnected and reciprocal nerve centers. The limbic system, a collection of structures located and connected deep within the brain, is significantly involved in emotional reactions. Animal experiments have determined that one area, the hypothalamus, modulates hormonal correlations with anger. The amygdala, another member of the limbic brotherhood, regulates the hypothalamus, activating and/or suppressing its activity. In turn, the prefrontal cortex, in the front of the brain, modulates activity in the limbic system. The prefrontal cortex, which developed at a later stage in the evolutionary process, applies rational and social inhibitions to the primarily instinctive responses in the limbic system. Positron emission tomography (PET), a specialized process of brain scan, has demonstrated abnormalities in these regions of the brain among individuals with a history of aggressiveness. Numerous studies have demonstrated that decreased serotonin activity is associated with impulsive aggressiveness and depression in individuals with BPD. Patients who prominently exhibit these characteristics respond most positively to serotonin reuptake inhibitors (SRIs). Interestingly, one study demonstrated that even in normal subjects, administration of an SRI reduced feelings of hostility and negativity.

How Borderlines Experience Anger

For many borderlines, anger derives from frustration. Continuous disappointment simmers undetected and eventually boils into a fury directed blindly at a hostile world. Anger may be displayed prominently and in many cases preemptively: "I *know* you're going to hurt and abandon me soon, so hurry up and get it over with. Waiting for the inevitable is making me so anxious, in fact, I'll hurry it along by being angry and spiteful, just to speed up the process." Patty's experiences with relationships and projects, such as quitting her high school hockey team (see chapter 3), reflect this underlying expectation of disappointment disguised as ridicule and hostility *("It's a stupid sport!")*.

In other cases, the anger may be camouflaged by ostensibly opposite behavior, such as trying to please everyone, regardless of the price. The borderline might freely lend money to almost anyone, despite personal poverty, or engage in meaningless sex with casual acquaintances. A permanent smile is plastered over suppressed anger. In these situations the borderline tries to avoid his anger by covering it over; yet, ironically, his fruitless quest for reciprocal nurturing only increases the frustration.

Often the borderline harbors a sense that mistreatment is deserved, thus replicating abuses from childhood. Anger is unacceptable because punishment feels appropriate. This may partially describe the plight of the abused wife who keeps returning to her punishing husband "because I love him." Anger also may be diluted when the borderline provokes abuse to reenact old scenarios from the past, a phenomenon known as "repetition compulsion." Psychoanalytic theory suggests that this behavior is an attempt to reconstruct past experiences with a more favorable outcome—that is, "to get it right this time around." Such provocation also may allow the borderline to feel more in control of the relationship by creating a situation in which the partner loses his temper, becomes rageful, then remorseful, finally begging for forgiveness from the victimized but now empowered borderline.

For some borderlines, expressed anger provides a sense of control, transforming her vulnerable masochistic fears into an imperious sadistic rage. Most borderlines have endured severe childhood abuse or neglect, often by a parenting figure. This betrayal is a terrifying experience, which presents to the child a sadistic, unpredictable world in which no one can be trusted, where affection can mutate into rape, and where abandonment is a constant threat. In recounting their abuse, many adult borderlines blame themselves. Although this distorted perception arouses much guilt and depression, it serves the purpose of allowing a sense of control. In other words, the borderline's horrific experiences can either be viewed as a situation in which she is a *victim* in a frightening, chaotic, and violent world, or a perpetrator of her own punishment. She can either be a helpless victim or a malevolent, aggressive manipulator. Given this choice, the borderline would often rather cling to the self-image of someone who has retained control in her life.

Some borderlines recapitulate the dynamics of childhood abuses in adulthood. An example is a sophisticated prostitute, with borderline characteristics and a history of childhood sexual abuse. Her customer views her as a pathetic, degraded victim who submits to his dominance. In her own perception, however, she is the controlling manipulator, earning her living by fulfilling her insecure client's fantasies. The hurt and anger she experienced from her father's abuse has been sublimated into a smug contempt for his proxy.

The *Kobayashi* Paradigm

In *Star Trek* mythology, the *Kobayashi Maru* test was a combat simulation specifically programmed so that the player could not win. Every Starfleet candidate failed the test (except, of course, Captain Kirk) because they did not realize that they were in a "no win" situation. The most important component in confronting anger in the borderline is recognizing that you are in a *Kobayashi* process.

Borderline rage is one of the most difficult predicaments confronted by a loved one or therapist. Crisis situations in which the borderline is actively self-destructive or psychotic are probably easier to confront, since the irrational behavior or physical danger trumps discussion and requires immediate response, such as hospitalization. However, when not imminently dangerous, borderline anger often invites debate.

The first instinct is to dispel the anger through logical argument. However, for the borderline, overpowering anger is the "prime directive" (in *Star Trekkie* terms) and the underlying presumption is, to paraphrase the Tina Turner classic, "What's logic got to do with it?" Regardless of the surface issue, rational attempts to dispute the issue typically result in a "damned if you do and damned if you don't" morass. In fact, the borderline may even "switch sides" as the argument proceeds.

During a marriage counseling session, forty-five-year-old Annette was discussing her frustration at losing her job and her concern that the family's financial health would now be jeopardized. She suddenly began shouting at her husband of twenty years, John, who she felt was no longer showing affection. She reminded him that he had recently been impotent on one occasion and accused him of being homosexual. John pointed out that Annette had recently become more withdrawn and had begun sleeping in another room. He acknowledged that the stress since she had lost her job may have affected them. Both responses only served to escalate Annette's fury: She shot back that John never hugged her and that she especially needed hugs of reassurance since her layoff. As she cried, John moved closer and hugged her. Annette then abruptly pulled away and yelled, "You hug me too tight!"

It is essential to understand that in some situations the borderline *needs* to be angry. This anger may be a deflection from disappointment in another, more "untouchable" person, such as a boss or a parent, or in himself. It may be a way of coping with depression. In any event, the circumstances justifying the anger at you may not seem to make sense. Accepting and tolerating the anger is what is important. Using SET principles (see chapter 12), one should acknowledge and absorb nonviolent anger. After some time devoted to venting, the anger will run its course and the underlying factors may be accessible for discussion.

ACTION STEPS: *Strategies for Coping with Borderline Rage*

1. *Understand: as it is with most everyone, intense anger usually is the outward expression of fear and pain.* To oversimplify, it is easier to be angry than scared. In Shakespeare's famous soliloquy, Hamlet asks if it is nobler "to take arms against a sea of troubles" than "to suffer the slings and arrows of outrageous fortune." Most borderlines would answer yes. In the military it is called a "preemptive strike"; in sports, "the best defense is a good offense." Similarly, the pain of past child abuse or an absent parent or a lost love can be salved by the heat of battle. Any way you look at it, try to understand that the anger of your loved one is almost always a reaction to—or intended to avoid—emotional hurt.

   But you must be aware that borderline rage is like no other in its intensity, irrationality, and apparent whimsy. "Fear is the mind killer," wrote Frank Herbert in *Dune,* and with fear and pain as her constant companions, the borderline can erupt at any time with no apparent rhyme or reason; the destruction, in an emotional sense, can be as swift and rampant as a midwestern tornado. Yet strangely, after a while, the borderline's anger can become remarkably predictable in its unpredictability. Greg would start to brace himself against an explosion of rage from Arleen after a tender moment (see chapter 2), for it was in that moment that Arleen would become most afraid of Greg abandoning or smothering her—equally terrifying prospects.

2. *Prepare.* Though you cannot accurately predict the precise moment of a borderline explosion, you can prepare for it when it does happen. Growing up with Patty, Didi knew that Patty's explosions could happen at any time and so had built a "bomb shelter" where she could automatically retreat when Patty detonated. What she and Patty had never done, however, was to talk about the reasons. Once you both understand the "triggers" of her rage, you will be able to plan for it together.

3. *Communicate!* If location, location, location are the three major factors in real estate, then communication-times-3 are the major factors in dealing with borderline rage. Communicating with a furious borderline is a delicate balancing act and can take weeks of practice (for a detailed discussion see chapter 12). On the one hand, you must convey support and empathy for the person's situation and draw upon your reserves of

self-control; on the other, she must be made aware that her unbridled, irrational outbursts are unacceptable.

4. *Reacting with rage is not part of the plan.* Fighting fire with fire might work in some contexts but not this one. John Lennon used to say "War begets war," and his insight also can apply on the personal level. Borderline rage feeds upon itself and off others'.

5. *Tolerating it also is unproductive.* You signed on as a partner, not a piñata. If you show via your own behavior that his rage is acceptable, it will only serve to reinforce it.

6. *Leave the scene of the crash.* If all else fails, if you are unable to settle her through calm reasoning of your own, you have no choice but to "hop on a bus, Gus," as Paul Simon sang in "Twenty Ways to Leave Your Lover." But we are not talking forever, just for a brief respite while she calms down. Accept the fact that change will take time, and return for another day.

10

Reality Distortions: Paranoia and Dissociation

> *All that we see or seem*
> *Is but a dream within a dream.*
> —EDGAR ALLAN POE, *"A Dream within a Dream"*

> *Billy Pilgrim has come unstuck in time.*
> —KURT VONNEGUT, *Slaughterhouse 5*

Unlike psychotic symptoms observed in other severe illnesses, such as schizophrenia and bipolar disorder, borderline dissociation usually emerges and resolves *suddenly*—much like borderline rage and mood shifts—and often is precipitated by stress. Such was the case with Todd, who typically functioned at a high level, until the Christmas holidays unearthed memories that sparked his break with reality. This chapter describes the different manifestations of borderline dissociation, such as illusions, hallucinations, confused thinking, paranoia, and feelings of unreality. A special section offers guidance for family members confronting this frightening symptom.

TODD

This was a hell of a way to spend Christmas! Brad sat in the uncomfortable vinyl chair in the North Shore Hospital emergency room. He rubbed his hands on the cold metal armrests as he looked around the room. A miniature Christmas tree with weak flashing lights sat mournfully on a table in a corner. Flanking the tree were two tattered signs: one said "Happy Hanukah"; the other, "Happy Kwanzaa." The glaring fluorescent lights belied the darkness outside and the wall clock, which signaled the approach of midnight. Like a Vegas gambling casino, the hospital was insulated from the night, sheltering patrons from the time and deterring them from any inclinations to leave.

But Brad couldn't go home. He had been sitting in the chair next to Todd for the past three hours, waiting to see a doctor. Todd was quieter now, less agitated, but Brad was still afraid to leave him unattended for even a few moments. No good deed goes unpunished, Cindy had once told him, and Brad was learning the wisdom of the aphorism firsthand.

A few weeks ago it seemed the Christian thing to do—to invite Todd over for Christmas Eve, since he was going to be alone. Todd had joined the insurance agency just a few months ago, moving to Quincy from Chicago "to start fresh." Todd didn't know anyone in town but liked the smaller community. And Quincy was close enough to Chicago that he could visit his two kids whenever his shrewish ex-wife would allow, which wasn't often. This brief history Brad had learned over the preceding months, after being assigned to mentor Todd through the orientation period. Their offices were close to each other, and they developed an easy and comfortable rapport over coffee and an occasional after-work beer.

Although Todd conceded that he was new to the field, he was a quick study. He attributed his chaotic work history to the demands of his ex-wife, who had constantly demanded that he make more money, spend more time at home, and move closer to—then farther from—her family. He had tried to keep the marriage together for the children's sake, but after six years she demanded that he leave. She hired a slick lawyer, who got her a nice divorce settlement, including virtual control over his life. That's why he just had to get away.

"After all, it's Christmas," Brad had explained to Cindy. Todd's kids were away for vacation; he had no other family. Brad had noticed that Todd was becoming friendly with the cute young secretary in the office, but Kim was taking time off around the holidays to visit her family in Kansas City. Brad felt sorry for him. No one should be alone on Christmas. Besides, it would be good for their seven-year-old daughter, Julie, to learn about charity and kindness to others.

At first, Todd resisted. "No, that's very kind of you, Brad, but I wouldn't think of imposing on you and your family."

"Don't be silly, Todd. Cindy and Julie will be glad to have someone over to share our Christmas. I can't bear thinking of you sitting in your underwear with a frozen dinner, watching Jimmy Stewart running through the snow on TV. Please. It will be fine. I really want you to meet my family. And after dinner we can go to Mass."

Todd didn't say much at dinner. Brad and the girls did all the talking. But Todd could be like that at work, too. At times friendly and gregarious, he could suddenly turn quiet and withdraw. Brad attributed this moodiness to Todd's evolving adjustment to his new home, new job, and new life. He just missed his kids, Brad thought.

After dinner, a group of carolers came to the front door, singing songs of baby Jesus and peace on Earth. Cindy and Julie sang along. But after "Silent Night," Todd became abruptly silent. He backed out of the hallway and ran into Brad's darkened den. A few minutes later, Brad followed him.

He was met by the sight of Todd rocking back and forth in Brad's desk chair. "They're following me," Todd proclaimed, peering down at the floor. "No matter where I go, they come after me."

"What?! Who?! *Who* is following you?"

"Can't you see?" Todd responded without looking up. "They're robots, and they follow me everywhere." He looked up at Brad. "You're real, aren't you? Or are you trying to kill me, too?"

Brad's first instinct was that Todd was kidding. But when he saw Todd's look of desperation, Brad knew that this was not a joke. "Todd, no one is going to hurt you. We're your friends. There's nothing to be frightened of."

"Oh, yes, there is. They came to kill Jesus, and now they're coming for me, too. They molested him first, you know. They sodomized him and then they killed him."

"What are you talking about? No one's hurting anyone. It's Christmas."

"Is it?!" Todd yelled. "Just because there's a tree and decorations? That doesn't make it Christmas! How do I know if you're real, or if I'm real, or if Jesus is real? All I know for sure is they want to kill me."

"*Who* wants to kill you?" Brad asked again.

"All of you!" Todd screamed, abruptly rising and pacing the room.

Brad looked up to see Cindy and Julie watching them. Julie was crying, clinging to her mother. He motioned to his wife to take Julie and leave.

"Todd," he said, "you're not well. We need to get you help."

"Yes!" Todd answered. "I've been poisoned. I'm dying. I'm dying for your sins. I can feel the poison circulating in my body." He held up his hands before his face. "See, there! My hands are dying!" he yelled, rotating his arms. "They're shriveling. They're falling off. It's my punishment."

"I'm taking you to the hospital," Brad said, ushering him to the front hall closet, where he grabbed their coats. "We'll get a doctor to examine you."

Cindy signaled to him from the kitchen. "I'll be all right," he silently mouthed to her and shuttled Todd out the door.

• • •

Todd was quiet during the ride to the emergency room, but in the reception area he became more agitated. After giving his name and address to a clerk, Todd produced his insurance card. When the clerk asked why he was there, Todd burst into tears. "He's been under a lot of stress and is acting very strangely," Brad answered for him. The clerk, wide-eyed and now fully attentive, directed them to the waiting area.

As the hours passed, Brad became more and more perturbed. He was not a novice to hospital emergency rooms, having been in for a few nasty ankle sprains suffered in his weekly pickup basketball game, and once for Julie's broken arm when she fell off the school jungle gym. Two years ago, he had volunteered as an aide for two weeks, to fulfill his company's community outreach program, but discovered that he could tolerate neither the giving, the extracting, nor the very sight of blood.

Through the swinging steel doors to the exam area, he watched the nurses jot notations on a white grease board—initials of patients and their check-in times down one column; the assigned doctor—"Dr. G," "Dr. B," and "Dr. P"—in the next. Apparently only three were on duty tonight, which he supposed was understandable considering it was Christmas Eve. The letters in the last column, he knew, were the presumptive diagnosis, and Brad tried to remember what the abbreviations stood for: "CHF" meant congestive heart failure; "COPD" signified chronic obstructive pulmonary disease, such as emphysema. Next to Todd's initials they had scribbled the Greek letter ψ, which meant psych case.

Next to him Todd began to mumble incoherently, but since he was calm, Brad felt it best not to interrupt his reverie. Finally Brad spotted a nurse and got out of his chair to stop her. "We've been here for three—"

"I know," she said, cutting him off. "I'm sorry, but we're very busy. It's Christmas, we're short staffed, and we've got some very sick people here."

"Yes, but we've been here longer than anyone."

"Okay, let me take a look. Name of the patient?"

"Todd Kelly."

"Okay, hold on for a moment." She visited the grease board and then the nursing desk before returning to them. "Yes, I see. I'm sorry. It shouldn't be much longer."

"Well, how much longer?"

She let loose a long, exasperated sigh. "Look, sir. We've got some very ill people here tonight. Life-threatening illnesses in some cases. Mr. Kelly is not going to die. He can wait. The others can't."

Brad was not satisfied. "But you need to understand, Nurse. This man was fine a few hours ago, and then suddenly he was acting like a raving lunatic. Maybe it *is* life or death. Maybe he's had a stroke or something. I don't know, but he needs to see a doctor—and soon. He just might walk out of here. He might do anything. I don't know if I can control him."

"Sir, we'll get to him as soon as we can. That's all I can tell you. We're doing our best."

Yeah, well, your best sucks, Brad thought as he turned away. Then he saw that the chair that had previously contained Todd now contained only his coat. Frantically scanning the room, he caught sight of Todd walking out the door.

"No, no," he said, chasing Todd out into the freezing night air. "Where are you going?"

"I can't stay here any longer. They'll find me here. It's the first place they'll look," Todd said, walking away, oblivious to the cold. "It stinks in there. It smells like church."

"No, Todd. We need to stay. The doctor needs to check you out, remember? Like you said." Brad steered him back through the automatic door.

Just then, the nurse approached them. "Oh, there you are. The doctor can't see you if you wander around the hospital. Please follow me."

She led them through metal doors to an even more brightly lit cubicle in the exam area, furnished with only a gurney and two chairs and sectioned off from other cubicles by opaque plastic curtains. Ten minutes later, a white-coated man walked through the drape, dramatically pushing them aside, as if he were a performer stepping onto a stage.

"Well, gentlemen," he said, flopping in one of the chairs, flipping through a manila folder, "I am Dr. Marbury. What seems to be our problem here?"

"Maybe I should go," Brad said, starting to leave.

"No! Please stay with me," Todd pleaded.

Brad looked at the doctor, who shrugged and said, "Well, it's okay with me if it's okay with Mr. Kelly." Turning pages in Todd's file, the doctor said, "Looks like you haven't been feeling well."

Todd sat up from the gurney. "Yes, that's true. I've been a little more depressed lately. I think it may be the holidays."

"Yeah, I know what you mean. It gets kind of crazy this time of year, doesn't it?" Dr. Marbury responded.

"You said it, Doc!" Todd said and they both chuckled, as if they were longtime friends talking about the weather.

Brad was speechless. A short time ago, Todd was a mumbling madman; now he was responding as if nothing had happened.

As Dr. Marbury listened to Todd's heart and lungs through his stethoscope, a technician came through the curtains, wordlessly placed a tourniquet around Todd's arm, and began extracting several small tubes of blood. Brad looked away.

"You appear to be physically healthy," said Dr. Marbury, placing his stethoscope in his coat pocket, "but we're going to need a social worker to evaluate you psychiatrically."

"How long is *that* going to take?" Brad asked angrily. He didn't mean to sound impatient, but he could not control himself. He wasn't sure if he was more irritated with the hospital, Dr. Marbury, or Todd for his sudden miraculous recovery.

"It's okay, Brad. They're doing the best they can," Todd reassured him. "You just have to be patient. I really appreciate your staying with me all this time. I know I ruined your family's Christmas, but I should be fine now. You don't have to wait with me any longer. Why don't you go on home!"

Brad was tired and frustrated but felt, after all that had happened, he couldn't leave Todd now. Besides, he still wasn't sure *what* had happened.

Was Todd faking it now? Or was he suddenly better? "That's okay. I'm staying with you until we get things settled. Besides, you have no way to get home. Your car is at our house."

"Right. I forgot. This whole evening is kind of hazy to me."

"Me, too!" Brad responded.

"I really need to apologize to you and your family. I think I got a little loony back there. You know, that happens with me. Sometimes I act crazy."

"What happened?" Brad asked, but just then the social worker debuted through the curtain.

"Hello, Mr. Kelly. My name is Kelly, too. Kelly Friedman. I'm a social worker. I'm here to evaluate you." She looked at Brad, who started to get up again.

"He's my friend. Is it okay if he stays with me?" Todd asked.

"If you prefer." She shrugged. Then she turned to Todd. "So, what happened?"

"I thought I was doing okay. I moved here a few months ago. I really miss my kids."

"How many children do you have?" Kelly asked.

"Three."

"Three?" Brad said too loudly. "You said you had two!" Sheepishly, Brad glanced at the social worker, realizing he should not have interrupted.

Todd turned to Brad. "I have two with my last wife. I have an older son with my second wife."

"How many times have you been married?" Kelly asked.

"Three," Todd answered.

As the interview progressed, Brad tried to excuse himself several times, but Todd insisted that he stay. Over the next hour, Brad learned more about Todd than he wanted to know.

Todd was born in Edwardsville, Illinois, where his father was a professor at Southern Illinois University. His parents divorced when he was three, spurring his mother to take Todd along on a wandering journey that would have been the envy of a band of gypsies. In half a dozen years they moved to California, and from there to Colorado, and then to Richmond, Virginia. Contact with his father became less frequent, especially after he remarried. Christmas vacation was the only opportunity to see him, but after his father remarried and had children with his second wife, these visits stopped as well. In each new community his increasingly religious mother became a stalwart of the local parish. She often found work as the church secretary or in some other church-related job. She dragged Todd to every Mass, every church service. She guided him to the priest for every problem, from homework to social alienation. His mother was either constantly controlling his activity or pawning him off on the local priest. Naturally, he was an altar boy at each church.

The abuse started when he was about ten, in Richmond. He liked the new youth minister, Father Reilly, who took an active role in arranging activities for the altar boys. The first time was on a camping trip, in which they shared a tent. Later, when Father Reilly replaced the retiring priest, he frequently invited Todd to his quarters, to discuss Todd's "problems." Fondling turned to mutual masturbation and eventually anal intercourse.

Todd could tell no one. Mother worshiped Father Reilly. Friends were few. And confession became horribly uncomfortable as Father Reilly controlled the interchange, blocking any real disclosure. Still, Todd attended church regularly with his mother and acceded to her adoring comments about the priest and Catholicism.

At fourteen he started cutting himself. Father Reilly suggested he see a doctor whom the priest recommended. Medicine helped Todd fall asleep, but he would still awaken, crying out with nightmares of the heavy breathing and grunting of Father Reilly. Todd never told the doctor about his spiritual leader's activities. But when he was sixteen, he began working; bought a car; and, to his mother's frustration, ceased his activities at church.

Todd married his first wife at eighteen, when she became pregnant. He was mortified when the priest counseled them regarding their sin and the need to marry. Her parents and his mother hastily orchestrated the small, quiet wedding, and all were secretly relieved when Denise miscarried in her fourth month. After a year more of playing house, Todd and Denise accepted that they did not love each other and amicably and with great relief agreed to divorce. No longer able to tolerate the constant disapproval of his mother and the oppression of his community, Todd left Richmond for Denver.

A brief second marriage produced a son, now fifteen, whom he rarely saw. Indeed, the last time was the previous Christmas. A job reassignment transported him to Chicago, where he met his third wife at a support group for divorcing spouses. She was very open about her chronic depression and long psychiatric history, but Todd kept his past a secret from her and everyone else.

After he and his third wife began having problems, he finally sought therapy for himself and began seeing Dr. Max regularly. After several months Todd was able to tell the doctor about his painful abuse. Talking and medication helped some. Over the years the nightmares diminished but never fully ceased. And sometimes, especially when confronted by religious symbols, he felt that his spirit left his body. At such times he felt in a dream, detached, just as he had felt during the painful relations with Father Reilly. At such times he became afraid, petrified that others would learn of his past sins and damn him to hell.

Throughout the monologue, Brad shifted in his chair, desperately wanting to leave, yet fascinated by the story. This man, his coworker, was a much more complicated person than Brad had ever imagined. Brad wondered about the job. Was it too stressful for Todd? Should he tell someone about tonight's adventure? No! Tonight would stay confidential. Still, he would watch Todd a little more closely from now on. But what if something happened later? Would someone look back at this and blame Brad for not informing the company about a potential problem? Would Todd blame him for not insisting on a change? Brad's brain was overwhelmed. He would consider it all later.

At the end, the social worker seemed perplexed. "You seem fine now, yet it sounds like you were much worse earlier today. I'm not sure what to do now. I don't think you meet any criteria of danger to yourself or anyone else that would make you eligible for insured hospitalization."

"We've got great insurance," Brad interjected. "The company insurance covers just about everything."

"Mental health coverage is much different," Kelly responded. "And your coverage isn't as good as you think."

"Well, it doesn't matter," said Todd. "I really think I'm doing better and don't need to stay in the hospital any longer. Besides, I need to get going. I've got a lot of files on my desk at work."

"But you are going to need follow-up," Kelly said. "I think you need to see a psychiatrist for medication and therapy as well."

"I will look into that," Todd said.

Brad awoke from his reverie. "Don't worry about the job, Todd. Take the time you need. It'll be there for you."

Todd smiled. "Thanks, Brad. I really need to hear you say that."

Kelly frowned at her notes.

"What's wrong?" Todd asked.

"Oh, nothing," she responded, still frowning. "It's just, I'm still not sure what to put on your sheet as a diagnosis. Did your doctor in Chicago ever say what your diagnosis was? Schizophrenia? Bipolar? Schizoaffective?"

"No. He just said I was on the border of everything. And then he said he wasn't interested in labels anyway. He just said I needed to get better."

"So, are you?" she asked. "Better, I mean."

"I guess I'm still on the border. But I know I was doing better when I was seeing Dr. Max in Chicago. So maybe I can get back into it."

"Good," said Kelly.

"Good," said Todd.

"Let's get out of here," said Brad.

Psychosis and BPD

Severe regression to primitive and unrealistic thinking was noted in borderline patients for many years, but it was not included as a defining criterion for BPD until *DSM-IV* was published in 1994. Interestingly, Gunderson and Singer included brief psychotic experiences as one of the primary descriptive characteristics of BPD in one of the first attempts to behaviorally define the disorder in their seminal 1975 paper. Although this research became the primary model in developing the BPD concept for *DSM-III* five years later, reality distortion was not included in the official definition for another twenty-four years. This delay may have been caused by the preference to categorize a psychotic episode as a more severe Axis I illness, such as schizophrenia or bipolar disorder. Nevertheless, an increasing body of evidence has confirmed that lapses in connection to reality are observed in BPD frequently enough to mandate inclusion as a defining characteristic. Gunderson collated a number of studies examining the prevalence of cognitive/perceptual symptoms in borderline patients. Although there was a wide range of experience, paranoid ideations was the most prominent of these symptoms. Feelings of unreality and visual illusions were less common.

Psychosis in BPD is often more terrifying to others because it is so unexpected. People with chronic psychotic illnesses such as schizophrenia usually display eccentricities that presage or signal an acute exacerbation. However, many borderlines, like Todd, function at a very high level and interact appropriately on a surface level most of the time. When such an individual unexpectedly exhibits a dramatic reality break, others are shocked, puzzled, and unprepared, like Brad and his family. The outburst may also cause self-doubt and self-recrimination in others, who question why they were unable to predict the wildly disparate behavior. Afterward they may even question their own perceptions of the event—whether it happened at all—as the borderline reverts to normal functioning.

This criterion includes experiences of suspiciousness, paranoia, illusions (distorted perceptions of real external sensory stimuli), hallucinations (false sensory perceptions unassociated with reality), confused thinking and talking, and feelings of unreality. These distortions may include any or all of the five senses. The borderline may feel that his surroundings and/or he himself are not real. He may experience frightening distortions in perception, as when Todd felt he was being poisoned. Similarly, hallucinatory smells may signify poison gas; tactile hallucinations may suggest bug infestation. These episodes come on suddenly, are generally brief in duration (hours or days, rather than weeks or months), and often are precipitated by feelings of abandonment or other stressors. Often this symptom is present when other illnesses, especially dissociative identity disorder (DID, or "multiple personality"), substance abuse disorder, or major depressive disorder with psychosis, are concurrent. Borderlines with comorbid psychotic thinking generally experience longer hospital stays.

Dissociation

Borderlines often experience feelings of dissociation, which may be defined as a disruption in the usually integrated functions of consciousness, memory, external perception, identity (or internal perception), and physical action. Most of us have experienced dissociation for brief periods. For example, as you pull into your driveway after the familiar ride home from work, you may notice that you have no memory of the drive. As your thoughts drifted, you were able to negotiate the vehicle on a kind of "automatic pilot" but without conscious thought or memory. Some individuals in severe crises, who have exhibited superhuman strength, or daring yet calm heroism, report feeling in an "unreal" state in which time and events have slowed or seem different from ordinary consciousness. They also may be amnesic for these events. A sensory reexperiencing of a past event, or "flashback," is still another example of dissociation.

Dissociation also is observed in hypnosis. Persons who can achieve a trance state are able to segregate their senses and, in some cases, focus attention to either remember or forget specific experiences, or to more comfortably endure significant pain. Since dissociative phenomena require a "splitting" process, separating conscious experiences, it is not surprising that borderlines are vulnerable to dissociation and usually are extremely hypnotizable.

Although dissociation occurs in other disorders, especially depression, it is more common in BPD and in women. Some borderlines describe a kind of internal splitting in which they invoke different elements of their personality to function in different situations. However, unlike in DID— the most severe form of dissociation in which there is complete schism of personalities—these individuals are conscious of their behavior. For example, one borderline woman, an executive in a large company, drafted her "professional side" to evoke a serious, businesslike demeanor when in formal meetings; when on pleasure trips out of town, she consciously assumed her "slutty," promiscuous persona, exhibiting a completely different wardrobe, vocabulary, and demeanor. Nevertheless, despite conscious awareness, borderline impulsiveness can sometimes allow such behaviors to spin out of control, as when an intentionally assertive posture mutates into unchecked, angry outbursts.

In DID, two or more distinct personalities control behavior. Usually there are periods of amnesia, during which an alternate personality is controlling actions, outside the individual's usual consciousness. DID and less severe forms of dissociation are frequently observed in BPD. The overlapping symptoms of BPD and DID, which intersect at the phenomenon of splitting, and often share a common association with childhood trauma, suggest that the disorders are closely linked.

One recent study of the relationship between BPD and dissociative experiences examined potential genetic links. These researchers confirmed the significant connection of BPD to dissociation and to a history of suicide attempts. (Surprisingly, and in contradiction to other studies, they could not confirm a link with childhood trauma history.) They were able to demonstrate that specific chromosomal locations that are related to serotonin effects are associated with high scores on tests measuring dissociation phenomena in borderline patients.

Neuroimaging PET studies, investigating metabolic changes in the brain during dissociation, demonstrate altered activity in regions that connect perception of external events with internal emotional response. This may explain the emotional detachment of dissociation. Additionally, altered brain circuits, particularly in the frontal area, may explain the indifference to pain when borderlines self-mutilate, which is often during a dissociative state.

Treatment Considerations

Todd experienced severe paranoia and dissociation during his transient reality lapse. His acute symptoms mimicked those of schizophrenia, bipolar disorder, or even drug intoxication. However, unlike in these other illnesses, the dramatic psychotic behaviors can dissipate within hours. Accurate diagnosis is important, since treatment approaches will differ. While formal psychotherapy is the primary treatment approach for BPD, it is less often invoked in these other illnesses. Schizophrenia and bipolar disorder are considered primarily chronic, biologically based diseases, often impervious to traditional psychotherapy, and most responsive to medication management and basic behavioral support.

Antipsychotic drugs (neuroleptics) are specifically indicated in BPD for the treatment of distortions of reality (see chapter 11). The dosages of these medications used for treating the chronic psychotic diseases are usually substantially higher than those used to treat BPD. In relatively low doses, neuroleptics not only relieve distorted thinking but also may decrease anxiety and depression in borderlines.

Some have postulated that dissociative symptoms are associated with the body's internal opioid (endorphin) system. In times of severe physical or emotional stress, the brain triggers secretion of opiatelike substances, which provide relief of pain and sometimes of anxiety. Self-mutilation in borderlines is often accompanied by dissociative feelings, but the connection to biochemical processes is unclear. Perhaps opioid induction *precedes* self-inflicted pain, thus affording analgesia for the activity; or, perhaps, opioids, with attendant tension relief, are released *following* self-injury. Application of drugs that increase endorphin release in nonpsychiatric volunteers for a study replicates symptoms suggestive of dissociation and sensory distortion. Drugs that block release of these opiates, such as ReVia (naltrexone), decrease dissociative symptoms in some borderlines.

ACTION STEPS: DEALING WITH BORDERLINE PSYCHOSIS

1. *Talk the person down.* When the borderline experiences feelings of unreality or paranoia, logical discussion, as Brad quickly discovered, is fruitless. These episodes are similar in many ways to bad LSD trips, and much like the best course of action for handling a bad trip, gentle talking to calm the person down is the optimal early intervention.

2. *Maintain a comfortable environment.* Since fears of abandonment often precipitate these symptoms, the best environment for the borderline during the initial phase is a quiet, familiar surrounding with familiar, trusted people. Try to keep interactions calm and nonthreatening. Keep your voice low, even if the borderline is screaming.

3. *Ensure safety.* Minimizing the potential for danger during a paranoid episode should be the highest priority. All weapons or ordinary objects that can easily be used as weapons (knives, guns, letter openers, etc.) should be removed from the area. (In some cases it might be more efficient to lead the borderline out of a room containing these weapons or potential weapons.) Always position yourself between the borderline and the door, and be sure you can readily exit the room if you feel threatened.

4. *Get help.* If you are alone, seeking the assistance of nonthreatening friends or family can help maintain a safe environment. If violence is threatened, call an emergency service. Although the borderline may threaten escalation of violence or complete dissolution of contact with you if an ambulance or the police are called, the potential danger outweighs any other considerations. Threats to reject any future contact with you, made during a time of great stress, are unlikely to be sustained. Often the arrival of enforcement or medical personnel has a therapeutic, sobering effect on the borderline.

    Because these symptoms are often transient, they may gradually or abruptly diminish over a short period. Like Brad, others may be puzzled by the sudden transition. Psychotic episodes are more common during times of stress. The stressors may be a result of current pressures and/or of reminders of past traumas. For Todd, work pressures, combined with the inundation of religious symbols harking back to his abuse, precipitated his paranoia. Once calmed, in a nonthreatening environment, he was able to quickly recover his reality contact. Because many borderlines are resilient, it is impossible to predict which, if any, specific stressors will precipitate a psychotic crisis.

11

Treatment Strategies and Communication Techniques

I admit I've always had trouble accepting responsibility for my actions. But I blame my parents for that.

—MIKE PETERS, "Mother Goose and Grimm"

With regard to all human traits, the middle of the road is the right path. . . . Avoid both hysterical gaiety and somber dejection, and instead be calmly joyful always, showing a cheerful countenance. Act similarly with regard to all the dispositions. This is the path followed by the wise.

—MOSES MAIMONIDES

It is one thing for a victim to *understand* his devastating mental illness; it is quite another to *get well*. Analyzing, seeking, and participating in the correct treatment for BPD can be a painstaking journey, and this chapter attempts to guide the BPD sufferer and family through the available options. Several psychopharmacological and psychotherapeutic approaches that have shown promise in treating the disorder, including the author's "SET" system of communication, are described in detail. Strategies for communicating with the borderline and the qualities to look for in a therapist are described.

Psychotherapy

"The primary treatment for borderline personality is psychotherapy, complemented by symptom-targeted pharmacotherapy," states the *Practice Guidelines* of the American Psychiatric Association. The two types of therapy are meant to complement each other: psychotherapy aims for alteration in the functioning of the whole person and is an essential component in helping borderlines achieve stability; pharmacotherapy and other physical interventions are intended to resolve specific symptoms.

Treatment can be conducted in a range of settings. When treatment is conducted completely in a hospital setting—the most intensive form of treatment—several professionals may be involved, including psychiatrists, nurses, and social workers. The treatment program also may involve psychologists; dieticians; and art, music, and recreational counselors. In the hospital, patients are closely monitored and usually engage in daily individual and group sessions.

A step down in intensity is partial (or day) hospitalization, which usually involves regular attendance in therapy programs at the hospital but without overnight residence. Appropriate patients require intense, daily therapy but are not acutely dangerous to themselves or others and do not need twenty-four-hour supervision.

For most borderlines, treatment is conducted on an outpatient basis. Regular visits are typically scheduled once or twice a week, or less often. Many patients engage in "split" therapy, in which they see a counselor for regular, one-on-one sessions, and a physician periodically for medication supervision. They also may consult regularly with still another professional, who may offer group or family therapy or another specialized treatment (such as art therapy). Unified therapy may be conducted with a psychiatrist who is experienced in pharmacotherapy and psychotherapy techniques.

Although there are a variety of theoretical approaches to psychotherapy, most treatment models require one-on-one sessions. Family therapy can be a supportive adjunct when the individual is significantly involved with family members. Group therapy is often a component of specialized hospital-based programs and is an essential feature of dialectical behavioral therapy (DBT) (see later). Community, self-help support groups also can be valuable adjuncts.

Principles of Psychotherapy

The adventure of psychotherapy is a collaboration between client and caregiver. The process is directed by a professional who must establish a trusting relationship with his patient. The following is a typical psychotherapeutic progression that a patient should expect in the initial stages of treatment:

1. A thorough and complete evaluation, reflecting an understanding of the patient.

2. Identification of specific problems and mutually acceptable goals in confronting them.

3. Prioritization of issues to be examined, particularly the need to ensure safety and maintain the therapeutic alliance.

4. Development of a therapeutic plan for addressing problems.

5. Acceptance of mutual expectations and limitations, especially regarding behavioral, time, and financial commitments.

6. Confirmation of trust, confidentiality, and safety within the therapy setting.

7. Clear explanations and relevant education about the illness and its treatment.

8. Coordination and cooperation with all those involved in the treatment process, including payers.

Qualities for Treating and Relating to the Borderline

The qualities that define a professional who can successfully treat individuals with borderline characteristics are the same qualities needed by people who wish to sustain a relationship with them.

• *Consistency* in style and behavior is an important component. For many borderlines, chaos rules. Unreliability and betrayal often taint their experiences with others. Recognizing that the relationship will furnish constancy and reliability is necessary for the creation and growth of trust.

• *Honesty* is another component necessary to maintain trust. If one colludes with the borderline to cheat others, then the borderline will expect to be cheated eventually. The therapist, particularly, must be incorruptible and steadfast. Since many borderlines have a history of being exploited, interacting with others who exhibit integrity, who "do the right thing," energizes the hope that the world contains trustworthy people.

• *Commitment* to the relationship must be conveyed. Borderlines fear—yet often expect—abandonment. Stuck in black-or-white, splitting perceptions of others, a borderline can find it difficult to grasp that a therapist or a friend can be disappointed, annoyed, frustrated, or even angry with him, yet still remain committed to the relationship.

• *Flexibility* and openness contribute to healthier interactions. Borderlines often plead for direction from others, since they are so often confused about their own identity and feelings. Indeed, borderlines are frequently attracted to others who seem self-assured and confident. Unfortunately, such partners may have their own narcissistic issues, which will doom the relationship (see Patty in chapter 3). One who is tempted to rigidly control or direct the borderline's behavior may eventually become the object of blame when disappointment sets in. He will also become the target of rage when the other side of the need-to-be-controlled coin—the fear of engulfment—emerges.

• *Perspective* is important to maintain when interacting with borderlines. The tendency to perceive the world in extremes frequently propels the borderline to react in desperation. Refusing to book passage on the borderline's cruise to dramatic excess helps keep matters in proportion. Patience, unflappability, and carefully timed humor can assist in sustaining a priority of values that leads to more appropriate responses.

• *Respect* and even admiration for the borderline's courage and strength to confront pain and initiate growth is a necessary component of the relationship. Just as the borderline must attain incipient trust and confidence in a therapist or a friend, so the other must feel a connection to the borderline.

• *Empathy* for borderline pain is essential. Because many borderlines function at a very high level, it is sometimes difficult for others to understand their regression to more primitive levels of conduct. When an intelligent, attractive, competent individual indulges in repetitive self-destructive actions, such as pursuing harmful relationships or using drugs, others may have difficulty comprehending the underlying motivation. Repugnant or frightening behaviors, such as self-mutilation or the paranoia or dissociation of acute psychosis, can be formidable obstacles to sustaining empathic contact with others. Maintaining emotional connection with the borderline and working with him to understand and control his behavior allows the relationship to grow.

• *Detachment* is a necessary and important balance to empathy. Immersion in the cauldron of BPD emotions can be draining. Attempts to totally satisfy all of the borderline's needs are doomed to fail and only reinforce unrealistic expectations. Firm boundaries must be maintained. The borderline will be disappointed and fling guilt at the therapist who takes a vacation or the boyfriend who spends time with his other friends, but such respite time is important for all parties. It is unhealthy for the therapist or friend to sacrifice his own interests in response to borderline demands; this will only fuel resentment, which, in turn, will threaten calm and accepting consistency. The pressure to feel responsible for the borderline must be resisted. Personal time to refresh will allow more patience for potential future upheavals. The borderline can learn and grow from the need to more realistically respond to frustration and place less responsibility on others to provide her comfort. Conforming to predictable limitations also helps the borderline adapt to healthy relationships.

Qualities of a Successful Therapist

"Whoever fights monsters," wrote Friedrich Nietzsche, "should see to it that in the process he does not become a monster." The therapist treating BPD should possess skill, experience, and interest in confronting these complex issues, especially dependency, anger, impulsivity, and self-destructiveness. Active engagement is usually more successful in therapy than a passive "uh-huh" style. The practitioner should have at least several years of experience dealing with borderline patients. Ideally, she will already have been "around the block" with a few patients and so will have experience in recognizing patient manipulation. Past therapeutic mistakes and frustrations are the therapist's best teacher for future patients.

The therapist should have access, either directly or through a colleague, to various treatment modalities, including a hospital and medications. She should be willing to adapt to the needs of her patient and be open to collaboration with other professionals. She should be confident enough in her own abilities to follow through with a treatment plan, yet secure enough to question progress and be receptive to a second opinion if progress is stalled. A therapist who practices alone in an isolated venue, without benefit of formal or collegial supervision or consultation, or who does not pursue continuing education is more vulnerable to the vicissitudes of the therapeutic relationship. She may have more difficulty maintaining proper limits and adherence to the treatment plan. Because of the potential turbulence and demands of working with borderlines, the therapist should be satisfied in her life beyond the office and possess outside interests and support systems.

A primary task of therapy is to moderate the ricocheting extremes of emotional entropy into a more tranquil equilibrium. This requires a professional to demonstrate to the borderline how to embrace paradox. F. Scott Fitzgerald said the mark of a first-rate mind is the ability to hold two opposing ideas at once. It is also the mark of a first-rate therapist who treats BPD. The therapist must accept the patient for who he is, while simultaneously promoting change (the primary paradox of DBT; see later). She must establish a trusting, unconditionally accepting setting while challenging the borderline's distorted perceptions. She must understand her patient's self-pity and projection of blame on others while urging assumption of more responsibility. Ultimately, the therapist must teach the borderline to do what she does—support and accept the other person despite his frustrating behavior.

Considerations for choosing a therapist were explored in our previous book and elsewhere. The qualities described in this chapter also are important factors. Most important, there must be a sense of connection to a professional who exhibits empathy, wisdom, and confidence. The patient must like his doctor. Gunderson has suggested that successful therapists exude charisma, which instills indefinable feelings of encouragement and confidence.

Because of the time or emotional commitment or complexity of the process, many therapists try to avoid treating patients with a known diagnosis of BPD. Unfortunately, since the correct diagnosis is often missed or delayed, many practitioners, whether they like it or not, become "stuck" with unwanted borderline patients, to the detriment of both the patient and the therapist. In such situations, transfer of care may best serve both parties.

ACTION STEPS: *Finding the Right Therapist*

1. Gather a list of referrals from your doctors, family, neighbors, friends, and support group members. A nearby medical school or university may be able to recommend a competent practitioner. Don't rely exclusively on a list of professionals from your insurer, who may not be as committed to finding the best practitioner for your needs.

2. Know the limits of your insurance benefits and of your own resources. Be sure your therapist is aware of these limitations. If your plan limits visits to twenty per year, and you are unable to afford supplementation outside the plan, then you and your doctor must devise a treatment strategy that can be accomplished within these parameters.

3. Ask your doctor about his experience and treatment approach. Inquire about his availability (by phone, office appointment, exchange, e-mail, etc.).

4. Observe the efficiency of the office. Is it a comfortable setting? Are secretaries and other personnel courteous and friendly?

5. Look for the qualities we have described above, such as consistency, commitment, connection, and empathy.

Psychotherapy Strategies

For many years, until federal and insurance cutbacks in funding placed severe limits on treatment for the mentally ill in the 1990s, several therapy strategies for treating BPD were developed. Although primitive measures and plentiful anecdotal data supported the efficacy of these programs, only in the past decade have more substantial measures of improvement been developed. Use of these rigorous research tools in controlled trials has revealed that two structured therapeutic approaches are efficacious for borderline patients: psychodynamic (based on psychoanalytical principles) therapy and dialectical behavior therapy (DBT). Both of these therapy paradigms, as well as most other intensive supportive programs (and antecedent models), feature regular, weekly individual and group sessions, close consultation and supervision among treating professionals, and sustained treatment for periods of at least a year. No single organized therapy approach has shown consistent superiority over any other. All successful therapies emphasize the need to maintain safety; build a robust therapeutic alliance; and promote thoughtful reflection in place of impulsive action.

PSYCHODYNAMIC PSYCHOTHERAPY

Psychodynamic psychotherapy for borderlines usually involves an ongoing mixture of internal exploration supplemented with therapist support. The goals of self-exploration include recognizing maladaptive unconscious behaviors and consciously correcting them, learning to better tolerate painful feelings, and avoiding impulsive actions. During exploratory interactions the therapist is generally passive, allowing the patient to struggle with these issues. Insight about and understanding of the self produce self-reliance and acceptance of the self. In supportive exchanges, the therapist is more active, providing advice, encouragement, and affirmation. Goals include bolstering self-esteem, validating affective experiences, and strengthening necessary coping mechanisms.

A long-term Australian assessment of seriously afflicted borderline patients evaluated the effects of twice-weekly, individual psychodynamic therapy. Compared to their functioning a year prior to instituting the therapy, these patients exhibited less violence, less drug abuse, less self-harm, less work absenteeism, less psychiatric hospitalizations, less need for general medical care, less severe symptoms, and less BPD symptoms. The cost for medical care of these patients decreased significantly after instituting the psychodynamic treatment, mostly due to decreased hospital expense. After one year, the average savings per patient was more than U.S. $4,000. When this group of patients was compared to other, less seriously impaired borderline patients who received cognitive and supportive treatment, those administered psychodynamic psychotherapy displayed fewer BPD symptoms a little over a year later. Indeed, 30 percent of the psychodynamic group no longer presented enough symptoms to satisfy the BPD diagnosis, while none of the patients in the cognitive group qualified for a change in diagnosis.

Individual psychodynamic psychotherapy usually requires more time for BPD than for nonborderline conditions. One analysis of several outcome studies demonstrated that 50 percent improvement could be expected from this treatment for uncomplicated anxiety or depression after eight to thirteen psychotherapy sessions. For BPD, however, this level of improvement required twice as many sessions. Nevertheless, this study indicated that 75 percent of borderlines improved after a year, and up to 95 percent of patients improved after two years.

Researchers also have studied the efficacy of psychodynamic psychotherapy for BPD in a partial hospitalization setting. A British group compared an intensive psychodynamic program, consisting of individual and group therapies combined with other techniques, with standard partial hospital care. The average treatment period was eighteen months. Within the first six months, the intensive therapy group exhibited less suicidal behavior and less borderline symptoms. However, only in the last six months did these patients demonstrate less need for hospital-based care, confirming the need for long-term therapy.

DIALECTICAL BEHAVIOR THERAPY (DBT)

DBT, a form of cognitive-behavioral treatment, is the most systematically investigated treatment for BPD. This therapeutic stance is based on the assumption that psychological distress stems from habitual distortions in thinking (cognitions) that lead to maladaptive behaviors. According to DBT theory, BPD symptoms result from an inability to regulate emotions, which emanates from the collision of a vulnerable individual with a harsh, invalidating environment.

DBT's tightly structured format follows specific guidelines listed in a training manual developed by Marsha M. Linehan, the primary architect of DBT. Treatment includes regular, weekly individual and group psychotherapy to build skills and motivation. Telephone consultations between the patient and the therapist within specific guidelines also are encouraged, to generalize learned skills to the individual's environment. All therapy team members are mandated to consult weekly to maintain and enhance their own skills and motivation. The issue-focused phone calls and mandatory team meetings are two of the unique features of DBT.

After gaining mutual commitment and agreeing on goals, the patient and therapists proceed through four primary stages of treatment. Stage 1 focuses on developing skills to establish better behavioral control. Stage 2 concentrates on past traumas and helps the individual work through them. Stage 3 addresses self-esteem. In stage 4, the objective is to increase personal happiness.

Several studies comparing DBT with standard, nonspecific supportive treatment show that DBT results in better treatment compliance and fewer self-harming behaviors and hospital admissions. Modifications of DBT to treat people suffering from substance abuse and bulimia also have revealed promising results. However, some studies have demonstrated that DBT is not superior to standard care therapy in achieving improvement in depression and anger symptoms. Like the investigations of efficacy in psychodynamic psychotherapy, most studies continued for at least a year. Whether symptom improvement can be sustained for significant periods after treatment termination is not yet established.

One interesting modification of the cognitive-behavioral approach to treatment of BPD emphasizes the importance of others in the borderline's life. This program is called STEPPS (Systems Training for Emotional Predictability and Problem-Solving), developed at the University of Iowa. Like DBT, STEPPS focuses on the borderline's inability to modulate emotional intensity. Also, like DBT, the program follows a structured, manual-directed program. The unique element of STEPPS is its emphasis on the borderline's social system, including family, friends, romantic partners, and health professionals. Treatment takes place primarily in educational group "seminars," which provide information to borderlines and their significant others about BPD and skills training for changing maladaptive behaviors. Training others in the borderline's "system" educates them about the illness and helps them to help the borderline.

Providing adequate training and facilities for professionals desiring to offer standardized treatments, such as psychodynamic psychotherapy or DBT, is severely impeded by cost considerations in both public and private institutions. Despite strong inferences that specialized programs for BPD offer superior and cost-effective treatment, current financial constraints on the treatment of psychiatric disorders in this country inhibit optimal therapeutic approaches.

Other Therapeutic Techniques

Eye movement desensitization and reprocessing (EMDR) is a technique developed for the treatment of post-traumatic anxiety, panic, substance abuse, and other disorders. This approach requires the patient to rapidly move his eyes while discussing or thinking of disturbing past experiences. Many borderlines have a history of post-traumatic stress disorder (PTSD) and drug abuse and therefore could be considered candidates for this therapy. However, its efficacy remains unsubstantiated by large, controlled studies.

Some techniques have been suggested to confront specific behaviors, especially self-mutilation. Borderlines who gain tension relief from self-inflicted pain can sometimes achieve similar assuagement from holding ice cubes. This allows tactile sting without permanent harm to the flesh. Those who gain gratification from the sight of their blood can sometimes attain relief by marking up their limbs with a red Magic Marker (see chapter 6). Such substitute activities can help the borderline move away from self-harm. However, ultimately, more satisfying methods for self-soothing are necessary to abandon these destructive but reliable methods of comfort.

Pharmacotherapy (Medications)

Until the mid-1980s, the conventional wisdom insisted that there was no place for medications in the treatment of personality (Axis II) disorders; personality disorders were considered to be deeply ingrained character traits that were elicited by individual reactions to environmental traumas and were amenable only to psychotherapy. However, since that time, research has demonstrated that medications are useful in treating specific symptoms of BPD. Nevertheless, according to the APA's official *Practice Guidelines,* "cure is not a realistic goal—medications do not cure character." Symptom-specific medicines, however, can alleviate a great deal of borderline pain and disability, even if they are not an inoculation or panacea that cures the illness. (In some cases, medications can eliminate enough of the defining symptoms that an individual no longer qualifies for the formal borderline designation; in these situations the person is indeed "cured" of BPD.) Although many of these medicines have proven useful for BPD, none has been officially certified by the Food and Drug Administration (FDA) specifically for treatment of the disorder. Therefore, like many drugs utilized by physicians, these medications are employed for "off-label" usage.

Antidepressants

Because of the high comorbidity of BPD with depression, antidepressants are the most commonly used medicines with this illness. Of the antidepressants, serotonin reuptake inhibitors (SRIs) are the most studied and utilized. They are the primary drugs used in most cases of BPD. Although most research specifically examined the older SRIs, especially Prozac (fluoxetine) and Zoloft (sertraline), recent studies and extrapolations confirm that the other SRIs should be equally efficacious. These include Paxil (paroxetine), Luvox (fluvoxamine), Celexa (citalopram), Lexapro (escitalopram—related to citalopram), and Effexor (venlafaxine, which also has direct effects on the neurotransmitter norepinephrine). Often, when one SRI is ineffective, a trial of another may produce positive results.

Predictably, SRIs have been effective for mood instability and associated symptoms of depression, such as feelings of emptiness. Studies also indicate that related impulsive-aggressive behaviors also respond. Intense anger, self-destructive impulsivity, and suicidal and self-mutilating behaviors often benefit from SRI treatment. Interestingly, one study demonstrated that symptoms of aggression and impulsivity responded within a week to an SRI, much faster than the drug's effect on depression. Indeed, this positive result was independent of the drug's effects on depression or anxiety.

Older antidepressants, such as tricyclic antidepressants (TCAs) and monoamine oxidase inhibitors (MAOIs), also have been studied. Both groups have more side effects and can be toxic in overdose. Studies of TCAs (such as Elavil [amitriptylene] or Tofranil [imipramine]) have shown them to be less effective for BPD than other antidepressants. In some cases, TCAs worsened emotional control. People on MAOIs (such as Nardil [phenelzine] or Parnate [tranylcypromine]) must follow dietary and concurrent medication restrictions, or risk hypertensive reactions. Although MAOIs have demonstrated efficacy comparable to that of SRIs, the potential toxicity of MAOIs limits their use.

Mood Stabilizers

This group of medications includes lithium and several antiseizure drugs. They help control impulsivity and temper outbursts. Also, these medicines—alone or more often in combination with antidepressants—are known to improve mood changes. Indeed, they were first exploited for treatment of bipolar disorders. Lithium and the anticonvulsants Tegretol (carbamazepine) and Depakote (valproate) are the most studied in this class. However, newer anticonvulsants such as Trileptal (oxcarbazepine—chemically related to Tegretol), Topamax (topiramate), Lamictal (lamotrigene), Neurontin (gabapentin), Gabitril (tiagabine), and Zonegran (zonisamide) also may prove to be useful.

Antipsychotics (Psychotropics or Neuroleptics)

These medicines were originally developed to treat psychoses of schizophrenia and mania. Research confirms their utility in treating thought disorders and dissociation in BPD, although usually in doses lower than those used in the Axis I psychotic illnesses. Additionally, these medications, like the mood stabilizers, have proven useful for borderline symptoms of anger and impulsivity. Furthermore, usually in combination with other medicines, they have exhibited antidepressant effects. They also may lessen anxiety symptoms. Unlike antianxiety drugs (see below), they are not addictive or disinhibiting.

Most research has centered on older drugs such as Thorazine (chlorpromazine), Stelazine (trifluoperazine), Trilafon (perphenazine), Haldol (haloperidol), Navane (thiothixene), Loxitane (loxapine), and others. However, the newer "atypical" psychotropics possess fewer side effects and complications and, in preliminary trials, appear to be as effective for BPD as the older drugs. These more recent medicines include Clozaril (clozapine), Risperdal (risperidone), Zyprexa (olanzapine), and Seroquel (quetiapine). (Little information is available for the latest medicines in this group, Geodon [ziprasidone] and Abilify [aripiprazole], but indications are that they also may be useful.)

Antianxiety Drugs

Anxiety is a common component of BPD. Anxiety over abandonment concerns, disturbed relationships, and feelings of emptiness may be prominent, though it may be a factor in mood changes as well. Impulsivity and self-mutilation sometimes mitigate anxiety. The most common tranquilizers used to treat anxiety are benzodiazepines including Xanax (alprazolam), Ativan (lorazepam), Valium (diazepam), Librium (chlordiazepoxide), Tranxene (chlorazepate), and Klonopin (clonazepam), among others. As these medicines can be addictive and sometimes increase impulsivity, their use is limited. Longer-acting benzodiazepines such as Klonopin and Tranxene appear to be safer. Buspar (buspirone) is a nonaddictive, nonbenzodiazepine used for anxiety but its utility in BPD has not been demonstrated.

Opiate Antagonists

Preliminary reports suggest that these medicines lessen self-mutilating behaviors and destructive impulsivity. They appear to work by blocking the release of the body's own endorphins, which are secreted after self-mutilating tissue damage and which may provide analgesia and relief of tension. Most research has investigated the drug Revia (naltrexone).

Other Physical Treatments

Electroconvulsive therapy (ECT) remains one of the most reliable treatments for depression. When depression complicates BPD, and antidepressants and other drugs are unsuccessful, ECT may be considered. There are few studies examining the effect of ECT on BPD with depression. Most suggest that when any personality disorder complicates affective disorder, prognosis is less favorable.

Repetitive transcranial magnetic stimulation (RTMS), a new technique designed for treatment of depression and auditory hallucinations, is less disruptive and incurs fewer side effects than ECT. In this procedure, magnetic waves are directed at targeted areas of the brain. Only one small study has investigated the use of RTMS in BPD. Hyperarousal and impulsivity were examined. The procedure displayed moderate efficacy compared to fake treatment and appeared to be safe, with few side effects.

Attempts to treat BPD with homeopathic or "natural" herbs have been unsuccessful, with one exception: Omega-3 fatty acid ethyl-eicosapentaenoic acid, commonly found in seafood, has been associated with lower rates of bipolar and depressive disorders. One small study examined its utility in borderline women. The compound was found to significantly diminish aggressiveness and depressive symptoms in these subjects.

Communication Techniques

Interacting with the borderline can be an arduous and frustrating exercise—for therapists as well as for others important in the borderline's world. The borderline's coping mechanisms of black-or-white thinking, splitting, projective identification, and idealization alternating with devaluation inevitably lead to contradictory communications that are difficult to resolve.

ACTION STEPS: *General Approaches to Communication*

1. *Maintain boundaries.* Lacking a consistent sense of identity, the borderline easily merges with another. It is therefore necessary for both parties to maintain their separateness, despite the temptation to become twins of the soul, joined at their emotions, excluding the rest of the world. Recognize and embrace differences. Encourage the borderline to pursue his own distinct interests and talents.

2. *Don't assume responsibility.* If boundaries are not clearly sustained, the borderline's therapist or partner may feel responsible for the borderline's emotions or behaviors. Trying to change, protect, or be responsible for the borderline is the trap often referred to as codependency.

3. *Plan for safety.* The companion and the treating therapist should hold the safety of all parties as the highest priority and so should be prepared for action, especially if there is a past history of violence. If the borderline has threatened to hurt herself or someone else, she must be informed, calmly and in a matter-of-fact way, that future threats will result in specific measures, such as calling the police, leaving the house, etc. Do not attempt to logically reason with the borderline in times of crisis. Debating with her about such issues as your commitment to the relationship or the reasons for her suicide attempt is a waste of precious time. Since words and actions may be contradictory anyway, it is more appropriate to respond to the potentially dangerous action. Remind the borderline of your previous understanding that you would call for help if she tried to hurt herself, and proceed with the plan.

4. *Clarify contradictions.* Companions often face contradictory demands from their borderline partners that place them in an apparent "no win" situation. In nonemergency situations these paradoxes can often be resolved by hitting the ball back to the partner's court:

   Example A: Annette complains that John never helps around the house. But when he insists on making dinner that evening, she claims that he is too controlling. John calmly points out the contradiction to

Annette and asks her advice on how he should handle his confusion. In this way he puts responsibility for handling the paradox on Annette.

Example B: Lilly, sixteen years old, confesses to her mother, Joan, that she has just ingested a bottle of aspirin but swears she will not go to the hospital. Lilly threatens never to speak to Joan again if her mother calls 911, as Joan had informed her daughter she would do if such a crisis arose. Joan reflects her dilemma for her daughter: "If I call for help against your wishes, you'll say I don't care about you and be angry. On the other hand, if I abide by your wishes, you could become seriously ill and even die. That also would be pretty uncaring! Since you're going to perceive me as uncaring either way, I must take the course of action that will protect your safety and call for help."

5. *Prepare for the predictable.* Once a partner learns about borderline behavior patterns and knows what to look for, preparing for them can short-circuit maladaptive responses.

Example: On Tuesday, Lori calmly predicts to her husband, Rich, that if he goes out with his buddies on Friday night, he may possibly drink too much again, and his subsequent hangover will cause him to miss their son's Little League game and their neighbor's bar mitzvah on Saturday and then feel guilty all weekend. She explains that she will go to these activities without him, and if people ask about him, she will tell them the truth. Lori's preparatory "script-reading" may alter Rich's behavior in two ways. First, it reassures Rich that even though he perceives his behavior as wildly chaotic, it can be understandable and predictable. Second, it might arouse Rich's contrariness in such a way that he will avoid the predicted behavior, just to show Lori!

SET/UP

In our previous book we described in detail the SET system of communication. SET—an acronym for **S**upport, **E**mpathy, and **T**ruth—is a simple, practical approach to interacting with borderlines, especially in times of crisis. In each communication, all three elements should be invoked. SET is how one attempts to communicate with the borderline. UP—which stands for **U**nderstanding and **P**erseverance—is the goal that both parties try to achieve.

Support, Empathy, Truth

It is helpful to view this system as an equilateral triangle. The Support side employs an *"I"* statement of personal concern and a pledge to help, such as *"I* am very concerned about how you are feeling," or *"I* want to try to help."

The Empathy side is a *"You"* statement that acknowledges and accepts the borderline's anguish: "How painful this must be for *you."* Emphasis is on how the *borderline* is feeling, not the speaker. Empathy is not sympathy ("I feel so sorry for you"), nor is it identification ("I know just how you feel: I went through the same thing"). Sympathy declarations typically provoke annoyance, and identification statements often invite angry responses challenging the speaker's real understanding of the borderline's experience. When Support and Empathy assertions are delivered and heard adequately, communication usually proceeds without conflict.

The Truth segment represents a realistic appraisal of the situation and recognizes the borderline's accountability in solving the problem. While Support and Empathy are subjective affirmations describing the feelings of the partner *("I")* and the borderline *("You"),* Truth is an objective *"It"* statement, describing the current dilemma and challenging the borderline to deal with it. Emphasis is on individual responsibility. Although close relations can be supportive and understanding, the borderline must ultimately be responsible for his own life. Truth is best expressed in a neutral, matter-of-fact fashion that avoids blame or punishing: "This is what happened. . . . These are the consequences. . . . This is what I can and can't do to help. . . . What are you going to do about resolving it?" The Truth side of the SET triangle is the most important, since it stimulates practical problem-solving. It also is the most difficult for the borderline, since, by demanding individual responsibility without the distraction of blame, it confronts borderline splitting and the temptation to wallow in feelings of victimization.

Much like following a complex recipe, the quantity of the ingredients should be precise: all three levels of SET should be expressed in equal proportions. When Truth is conveyed without Support and Empathy, a distorted kind of "tough love" is communicated, which will only anger the borderline and cause him to reject help. Further communication will be dismissed. Imparting Support and Empathy without Truth colludes with the borderline in avoiding responsibility for his behavior and ultimately discourages change.

When Elements of SET Are Missing

Just as you cannot be sure that everyone will like your dish, even when you include all three ingredients in the right proportions, the borderline may not eat what you dish out, by simply blocking one from consciousness. "You don't care about me" is a common refrain when the borderline does not absorb the Support message. In response, you should reiterate Support messages. But you must be careful not to go too far. When it is clear that the borderline has heard these repeated statements, avoid immersion in a struggle to convince him:

"You don't care about me."

"Yes, I do."

"No, you don't."

"Yes, I do."

"No . . ." and so on.

Instead, acknowledge his doubts, integrating them into your Empathy statements: "It must be hard for you to believe that anyone cares about you after all you have gone through."

When Empathy is not assimilated, the borderline typically expresses feelings of being misunderstood: "You don't know how I feel." When this refrain is heard, further communications acknowledging the borderline's anguish can be helpful, though, again, it usually is a mistake to try to *prove* you care by being manipulated into taking over responsibility for the borderline's problems. Insisting that you *do* know how she feels or have experienced similar circumstances will only lead to unproductive debate.

When Truth statements are inadvertently omitted or inadequately interpreted, a surprising and uncharacteristic period of quiescence may result. If interactions are proceeding perhaps too well, the borderline may not be receiving enough Truth. In order not to "rock the boat," others may acquiesce to borderline demands, thus promoting distorted perceptions that reinforce the borderline's avoidance of examining her own behavior and responsibilities. Inevitably, when unrealistic expectations are dashed and overly protective relationships are disappointed, the boat will capsize. For example, Jeff and Janet are afraid to confront their seventeen-year-old son, Adam, whose violent temper has recurred since a fight with his girlfriend, resulting in more punched holes in the wall and drunken driving. While expressing their loving support and understanding of the reasons for his temper outbursts, they are intimidated by his rage, thus joining him in ignoring the gaping cracks in the living room wall and a subsequent warrant for his arrest. Calm, sympathetic discussion transforms into angry agitation when they try to discuss how to handle his legal problem; thus they all avoid the topic. Yet by abdicating control of the home situation, Jeff and Janet are only postponing a more extreme explosion when Adam is inevitably confronted with Truth and is arrested. Confronting Truth in the beginning—by setting limits, assuming more actively responsible parental roles, and directly confronting Adam's anger—will result in more manageable conflict that has less chance of escalating to more violent explosions later on.

SETting UP Examples

Bruce, diagnosed with BPD, and Amy have been married for six years. Bruce's company has been suffering lately due to a recession and he has been informed that he will soon be laid off, causing both partners anxiety. After another in a long series of fights with her husband, Amy inflames the situation:

> BRUCE: Nothing I ever do is good enough for you. I'm sick of this. I'm sick of you. I need a drink. I'll see you later. [He starts to leave the house.]
>
> AMY: Sure, that's right. Every time we try to talk, you take off. You're a coward, Bruce! You know that? You're a coward!
>
> BRUCE: I don't need to stay here and listen to your crap!
>
> AMY: Fine. Go get drunk! Get another DWI. This time I hope they put you in jail!
>
> Bruce storms out.

This time Amy utilizes SET principles to guide the conversation:

> BRUCE: Nothing I ever do is good enough for you. I'm sick of this. I'm sick of you. I need a drink. I'll see you later. [He starts to leave the house.]
>
> AMY: I really don't like it when we fight. I really want us to get along [Support]. I know you're angry and I can understand why you get mad at me [Empathy].

BRUCE: Then why do you keep nagging me?

AMY [Avoiding the temptation to strike back or be defensive] I know you're mad at me about all this. And I know you're still on edge about the stress from your job. You must feel a lot of pressure not knowing what they're going to do about your position [Empathy]. But we're two adults. We ought to be able to figure this out [Truth].

BRUCE: I don't know how to reason with you.

AMY: Well, for starters, let's just talk about it. You know how you used to handle it in the old days. You'd get pissed, storm off, go to a bar and get drunk, come home, throw up, and then we'd start fighting all over again [Predicting]. Remember that time your boss called you early to come in on a Saturday morning after we had a blowout the night before? You were so sick, you wanted to die! But you put on your suit and faked it. [Bruce laughs sheepishly.] Hell, if you could get through that, you can get through anything! [Amy uses carefully chosen levity.]

BRUCE: I said I'd never drink again after that.

AMY: [Ruefully] Yeah, you did. And we both know another DWI will cost you your license, and maybe your job [Truth]. But look, we've got a problem and we need to solve it—together. I love you very much [Support] and I know you've been under a lot of stress [Empathy]. But taking it out on me doesn't solve your concerns about the job. It just hurts my feelings and we both end up feeling lousy. Let's be a team and work together, like we always have. Let's look in the paper and start preparing for the next job [Truth].

Understanding and Perseverance

On first glance, the scenarios presented above might seem forced or "programmed," a "sugarcoated" tactic for dealing with an immediate crisis. But they are not intended to be "scripts" you need to rehearse or a program you need to memorize. SET is merely a basic, easily understood framework in which to fit your individual personality and emotional reactions; it is a structure for managing emotions while striving for productive communication. SET is designed to help all parties in a crisis setting maintain a sense of balance: When you get angry, balance your frustration with Supportive and Empathic statements. When you sense stagnation, think of the need to interject objective reality with Truth.

With productive communication comes Understanding and Perseverance. Understanding, both of the principles involved and of your partner, leads to more productive, nondefensive interchange. Perseverance is necessary for all involved to stay the course.

12

Prognosis and Directions of Future Research

It is the future that creates his present.
All is an interminable chain of longing.

—ROBERT FROST, "Escapist—Never"

For I dipt into the future, far as human eye could see,
Saw the Vision of the world, and all the wonder that would be;

—ALFRED LORD TENNYSON, "Locksley Hall"

Despite continued economic, societal, and political obstacles, the prognosis for borderline patients is more optimistic than in years past. This chapter explores the individual characteristics that improve short-term and long-term outcomes. Recent discoveries in the fields of brain physiology, genetics, and biotechnology increase the prospects for further advances and suggest future areas of exploration. Finally, we propose an idealized model for the treatment of BPD.

At the time of publication of our first book, the BPD diagnosis had been defined and accepted in *DSM-III* for fewer than ten years. Studies on the course and prognosis of the disorder at that time were marked by confusion about the diagnosis and lack of long-term assessments. Because of the serious ramifications of the illness, including a suicide rate approaching 10 percent, and its resistance to short-term treatment, many felt that the prognosis was dismal. Indeed, some managed care insurers limited therapeutic coverage, insisting, as one physician-reviewer for the insurance company declared, "Everyone knows that borderlines never get better!"

Prognosis: Borderlines Do Get Better

Long-term follow-up studies over the past decade have indicated that even though the course of BPD varies considerably among individuals, the overall prognosis is much better than many previously thought. General impairment and risk of suicide are greatest in the young adult years (men are more than twice as likely as women—18 percent versus 8 percent—to commit suicide), but over time, many borderlines "mature out" of their symptoms. By their midthirties and forties, most borderline patients improve significantly with or without treatment (although treatment clearly accelerates the process). A recent British study demonstrated that over a period of twelve years, patients diagnosed with a personality disorder in the dramatic (Cluster B) group—which includes borderline, narcissistic, antisocial, and histrionic personality disorders—were more likely to make positive life changes than those with diagnoses in the eccentric (Cluster A) or anxious (Cluster C) groupings of personality disorders.

Connection to Physical Health

Individuals with BPD exhibit not only coexisting psychiatric illnesses but also other physical disorders, which require medical attention. A general medical practice sees a much higher percentage of patients diagnosed with BPD than is observed in the general population. One study followed borderline patients for six years and compared the health of those who demonstrated persistent BPD symptoms with those whose symptoms diminished. Symptomatic BPD patients were more likely to suffer from diabetes, arthritis, hypertension, back pain, and obesity. They were more likely to use cigarettes and alcohol, less apt to exercise, more likely to have suffered household accidents, and more likely to have visited a hospital for medical care.

Socioeconomic Factors

Most longitudinal studies of borderlines involve middle- or upper-class patients who initiated treatment in their late adolescence or early twenties.

Most of this research, inaugurated in the 1980s, was performed in private institutions, to which the poor had less access. The few studies done with the economically disadvantaged reveal a more tortured background, with a higher incidence of abuse, less education, and less successful relationships. Those individuals from a more depressed socioeconomic background have a strikingly worse prognosis.

Gender Differences

When first tracked in the longitudinal studies, women are more likely to be married, to have children, to complain of depression, and to feel overwhelmed by life events. Men are more likely to have a history of legal problems and substance abuse. Women frequently turn to relationships—which often fail—for solace. Symptoms worsen when a relationship degenerates. Men more often turn to work for comfort and support. Membership in other organizations such as religious groups or treatment programs (like Alcoholics Anonymous) also improves the prognosis for men. However, personal intimacy for them is much more elusive.

Short-Term Results

Most studies do not show significant improvement in BPD symptoms during the first year of treatment, and dropout rates are substantial during this period. Even when there is measurable improvement of symptoms within the first two years, day-to-day functional impairment persists. However, patients followed over longer times, with or without therapy, demonstrate gradually improving living skills and are less likely to satisfy criteria for a BPD diagnosis. Prior impaired functioning and severe impulsivity are two of the most negative short-term prognostic indicators. Even in those borderlines who improve to a point where they no longer satisfy criteria for the BPD diagnosis, these two qualities predict a generally lower level of overall functioning.

Long-Term Outcomes

Most large, long-term studies find that on average, about 66 percent of patients initially hospitalized with a diagnosis of BPD achieve an adequate level of functioning after ten years regardless of further therapy interventions. About 40 percent of all patients are considered "cured" (defined as no longer meeting criteria for the BPD diagnosis). Usually, vocational stability is achieved more often than social success. Most are successfully working, but fewer (especially men) have satisfactory relationships or families.

The Role of Treatment

Most borderlines engage in some kind of therapy for several years. The type of therapy may range from brief, intermittent contacts for support and medication management, to regular, intensive psychotherapy. Compared to patients with major depression or several other personality disorders, individuals with BPD utilize more treatment modalities (such as hospitalization, individual psychotherapy, and pharmacotherapy) in greater amounts. However, over time, the intensity of care sought by individual patients declines. The rate of hospitalization and rigorous psychotherapy diminishes, while the utilization of intermittent medication checks increases. Active therapy increases remission rates sevenfold. Over several years, almost 26 percent of actively treated patients per year experience some level of recovery (versus fewer than 4 percent of untreated individuals), up to a remission rate of 75 percent. Full recovery occurs in more than 50 percent of patients engaged in regular treatment after fifteen months. In groups of untreated patients, 10.5 years are required to achieve the 50 percent recovery rate. In one six-year study of recovering borderline patients, serial improvement in individual symptoms was noted. Impulsivity resolved most quickly, followed by improvement in cognitive distortions and interpersonal relating. Mood instability was more chronic and took longer to resolve completely. Although many patients considered to be in remission experienced some minor residual symptoms, less than 6 percent suffered relapses severe enough to again re-fulfill BPD criteria.

Prognostic Predictors

Short-Term Predictors

A number of factors have been found to correlate with favorable and unfavorable outcomes of BPD patients over the short term (two to four years).

Factors correlating to a positive prognosis include:

- Early and rapid progress in treatment
- Supportive relationships with parents, spouse, and friends
- Friendliness and likability

Factors correlating to a negative prognosis include:

- *Chronicity.* The longer the symptoms persist, the more likely they will continue to persist.

- *Severity.* The more serious the symptoms, the less likely they are to remit.

- *Comorbidity.* The presence of other disorders, such as depression or substance abuse, worsens the prognosis.

- *Impulsivity.* The more persistently and severely this symptom is expressed, the less likely full recovery can be achieved.

- *Age of onset at the extremes.* When initial symptoms are observed either in the patient's early adolescence or in his thirties or forties, rates of recovery diminish.

- *Impaired relationships with parents.* Poor relationships with parents, as a child and later as an adult, predict a poor outcome.

- *Disability.* Patients receiving disability payments have a worse prognosis than those who are financially self-supporting.

Long-Term Predictors

Studies that follow the course of borderlines for ten or more years yield specific characteristics that affect prognosis.

Positive prognostic signs include:

- Higher intelligence
- Physical attractiveness
- Artistic talent
- Self-discipline
- Involvement in a twelve-step program (AA or NA) if there is a history of substance abuse
- Early, rapid improvement

Negative indicators are:

- Chronic hostility and irritability
- History of antisocial behavior (more prevalent in men)

- History of severe parental abuse (incest occurs seven times more often in female borderlines than in males)

- Severe, pathological jealousy

- Eccentric, alienating behavior

- Poverty

- History of substance abuse without involvement in a twelve-step program

After ten or more years, more than 90 percent of individuals who evidenced one or more of the positive prognostic indicators and none of the negative ones were rated as doing well. Among those who exhibited one or more of the negative indicators without any of the positive characteristics, only 35 percent attained a minimally satisfactory level of functioning.

Future Frontiers of Research

The last half of the twentieth century witnessed tremendous advances in medical research and methodology. Research into the physiology of the brain has revealed possible biological causes of mental illness and confirmed mind-body connections that were previously mere conjecture. The psychiatric profession has undertaken painstaking investigation into classifying and defining mental disorders and refining treatment approaches. New medications have been developed to treat specific symptoms. Innovative psychotherapy strategies have been devised, with attempts to standardize their utilization. Although obstacles and challenges remain, the future holds great promise for understanding and treating disabling psychiatric illnesses.

Brain Physiology and Genetic Research

Discoveries about the workings of the brain have contributed to the development of new medicines. Current research focuses on neurotransmitters, which carry electrical messages between neurons (brain cells). Thus far, our understanding of psychiatric syndromes approaches the gates to these neurons, but we have only been able to peek inside. We do not yet fully comprehend what transpires inside the neuron after the neurotransmitter delivers its message, much less understand how this cascade of whistling and crackling electrophysiological impulses results in the emotional experiences of what we label depression, mania, psychosis, or borderline personality disorder.

Implications for Biotechnology

Over the next several decades, researchers will continue to pursue this biochemical trail as it leads into the nucleus—the very core of the cell. The nucleus contains our chromosomes, our inherited, programmed vulnerabilities and attributes. This human blueprint, we have learned, can be tweaked. Genes cannot be transformed (at least not yet), but they can be turned on and off, producing more or less of the ingredients of what makes our individuality. Perhaps the ultimate comprehension of human responses lies here. With this understanding, we may someday be able to graphically display an individual's neuronal vulnerabilities and strengths. We may learn how to adjust one's own genetic resources naturally to better cope with stresses. A little more serotonin here, a little less P-factor there, and suicidal depression or disabling psychosis, in response to a severe trauma, may be avoided. The implications for the biotechnology and pharmaceutical industries are at once obvious and enormous. In the not too distant future, it may be possible to tailor medications not just for a specific symptom or condition but also for an *individual patient* with the symptom/condition.

The Interface of Nature and Nurture

Genetic research also may lead to environmental adjustments that have powerful preventive and treatment potential. The development of BPD is dependent on the convergence of the many factors that constitute temperament and character. It has been shown that heritability of general personality characteristics permeates future generations at an average rate of about 50 percent, so BPD almost certainly has significant genetic components. Probably, multiple gene loci contribute to biochemical vulnerabilities for the development of BPD, which is expressed when these dispositions are exposed to severe environmental stressors. Cloninger, for example, has suggested that inborn features of "high reward dependence" (strong craving for reassurance) and "low harm avoidance" (constant pursuit of danger) constitute many BPD behaviors and are correlated with specific chromosomal activities. Genetic predispositions to mood, aggression, and impulse dysregulation also may result in vulnerability to the development of BPD.

The character component of personality is commonly accepted to be shaped by the environment. Early exposure to abandonment or to emotional, physical, or sexual abuse may contribute to the development of BPD behaviors. Recurrent frustrations; feelings of alienation; lack of healthy, mutually satisfying relationships; and the inability to establish a healthy connectedness to a spiritual system, profession, or organization may also, when converging with biological vulnerabilities, induce BPD.

If someday genetic loci, which can be correlated with biochemical interactions that are related to BPD behaviors, can be identified, we may then be more sensitized to careful monitoring of environmental dangers. For example, when genetic markers identify a child as having a temperamental vulnerability to BPD, precautions can be taken—on several levels—at a much earlier stage of development. This greater attentiveness at home and school may prevent future unhappiness and even may be lifesaving.

Future Directions of Psychotherapy

Although someday we may be able to custom-design medications for the individual, it is much more difficult to custom-design a therapist for the individual. When medication is helpful, it really does not matter *who* prescribes it. If Prozac cures your depression, the administrator of the pill (after monitoring the correct dosage) is irrelevant; the result is invariably the same. The effect of psychotherapy, on the other hand, *does* vary, depending on the practitioner.

Since Freud's development of psychoanalysis, the professional psychotherapeutic community has attempted to standardize psychotherapy. The goal has been to approach the consistency of dispensing medication so it would similarly not matter who administered the treatment. Traditional psychoanalysts attempt to achieve this through a form of apprenticeship: candidates are closely supervised on their own cases, while undergoing their own personal analysis. Other psychotherapy approaches, such as interpersonal therapy (IPT), cognitive behavioral therapy (CBT), and dialectical behavioral therapy (DBT), have published training manuals that attempt to standardize the principles involved and instruct the practitioner in the particular therapy techniques.

However, people are not chemicals and are, for better or worse, less predictable. Therapists, like patients, have a personality—a mixture of temperament and character. Character, primarily a product of life experiences, cannot be elicited from a manual. Temperament, primarily a product of inheritance, cannot be taught. Although an educated, motivated practitioner can learn techniques, his personal qualities (such as flexibility, empathy, and charisma) will have a greater contribution to success as a therapist. Yet even a talented therapist will not connect with every patient. Multiple determinants characterize the ideal patient-therapist "fit." What can best be taught is the ability to recognize when this "fit" is or is not working.

Research has demonstrated some commonalities of successful psychotherapy for BPD. Consistent psychotherapy over an extended period of at least a year, utilizing multiple resources with close coordination and collaboration, is a significant component of successful treatment. Such a strategy can result in relief from, and possibly a cure of, great suffering. It can improve overall health. In some cases it can be lifesaving. It is also expensive. Although lifetime medical expenses will be lower for a patient experiencing successful treatment, the short-term investment in resources can be costly.

Economic, Societal, and Political Challenges

Continuing trends from the twentieth century, we are a society in which individuals and families move a great deal (many times for job-related reasons); divorce almost half the time; and have less connection to stabilizing anchors such as entrenched neighborhoods, churches, and schools. As entropy continues to trump constancy, we should expect expression of more BPD pathology in our culture.

Confronting these social issues, mending the torn social fabric, is one of the great challenges to our civilization. When scientists discovered that the spread of bubonic plague could be controlled by the elimination of rats and improved sanitation, they directed the appropriate environmental corrections. If we can identify the heritable and environmental factors that increase the prevalence of BPD and other psychiatric illnesses, we should likewise be able to initiate appropriate "social hygiene" that will minimize this spreading psychiatric plague. We are not describing *1984*-type mind control; only the potential to develop immunity in people against psychiatric disease, just as we can vaccinate children to protect them from developing polio.

Another major obstacle to continuing medical progress is determining how to finance it. For decades in this country, many population segments have been insulated from the true costs of medical care by the traditional coverage of private and government insurance. However, over the past twenty years, as the prices for medical research and treatment have soared, we are now faced with the crisis of financing their continuation. Limitations on expenditures have become necessary, but one of the "solutions" to the problem, "managed care," is neither managing very well, nor dedicated to care. Instead, managed care seems to be devolving into "cut cost."

Inevitable cutbacks in medical care have hit mental illness the hardest for a variety of reasons. Until recently, psychiatric syndromes were harder to define than other medical diseases, and treatment was less systematic and less successful. Happily, these concerns have been addressed. However, there remains a lingering societal prejudice that psychiatric illnesses, unlike physical disorders, are somehow "the patient's fault" or the result of a weak will. With several exceptions, personal culpability does not usually attach to physical disorders in the same way that it does to mental illness. A ramification of this stigma prevents many who suffer from psychiatric disorders to lobby openly and effectively for better care in the local or national political arenas.

Social Stigma

The stigma of mental illness remains a profound influence. Despite advances in thinking, most people are far less likely to confess their battle against depression than their struggle with arthritis. The "shame" of mental illness reflects a continued misperception that, unlike other diseases, it can be willed away. The Woody Allen stereotype of a psychiatric patient as a silly neurotic who just needs a kick in the pants and admonishment to stop feeling sorry for himself remains prominent. Even in our enlightened era, psychiatrists are often disparaged as "headshrinkers"— that is, for not being "real doctors." (Have you ever heard the label "bodyshrinker" applied to an internist or an orthopedics specialist?) Indeed, within the Medicare payment scheme for physicians (replicated by most insurers), "cognitive services" (talking to a patient) are paid at a rate much lower than surgical procedures.

If, indeed, this stigma makes psychiatry the stepchild of medicine, then surely BPD is the orphan of the stepchild. Many practitioners avoid treatment of BPD despite its prevalence in the landscape of psychopathology. Borderline patients are disparaged for their exhaustive needs and resistance to improvement. BPD sometimes is a diagnosis of countertransference, at times more representative of the practitioner's frustration with the patient than an accurate description of the patient's symptoms. The economic pressure for immediate response to treatment impacts the position of managed care and other payers, who are often unwilling to provide the adequate, longer-term care needed for the patient. Thus the borderline, perhaps more than almost any other patient, is least likely to be allowed the treatment necessary for cure. If a true indicator of a civilization's principles is how it aids its most helpless citizens, then this country's care of the mentally ill compromises its nobility.

Treatment Model Visions

The prevalence of BPD in the psychiatric care system and the intricacies of its adequate treatment require special considerations. Gunderson and others have proposed specialty centers for treatment of BPD. Such idealized facilities should embrace these features:

1. Treatment is pursued along a continuum, individualized for the patient's needs. Hospitalization, partial hospitalization, and outpatient facilities are utilized. Also, supervised halfway and less monitored quarterway housing are available.

2. Therapists are experienced and trained in treating BPD. More important, they *want* to treat these patients.

3. Treatment includes access to individual, group, and family therapies.

4. Multiple modalities of care are represented, such as art therapy, music therapy, movement therapy, psychodrama, bibliotherapy (reading and discussion of books, plays, poetry, videos, etc.), exercise techniques, and dietary consultations.

5. Contemporary pharmacotherapy must be available and coordinated with psychotherapy.

6. Coordination of care among the specialties requires regular team meetings and collaboration.

7. Internal training and supervision are ongoing. Contacts with other programs allow expansion of useful techniques.

8. Research is continuous and published for the benefit of patients and for other programs.

9. Borderline support groups are established in the community, with an emphasis on education for patients and their families and loved ones.

10. A cooperative, not adversarial collaboration must be established with managed care organizations and other payers. For this to be achieved, there must be mutual recognition of the advantages and cost benefits of early recognition and treatment of BPD. Early investment in treatment reduces more expensive, continuous "revolving door" utilization of medical facilities. But there must also be accountability and demonstration of efficacy to those who pay the bills.

11. There must be acknowledgment and appreciation of the differentiation of specialized care within the insurance industry and the public. Currently, within a community, private and government payers compensate all practitioners and facilities the same, without recognition of specialized training, expertise, or quality. Under this system of reimbursements, there is no incentive to develop higher-quality facilities. Ultimately, if we are to fulfill our obligations to those in need of adequate medical treatment, we must accept that specialized health care may be more costly.

Resources

Publications

General Overviews

"Borderline Personality Disorder." *Journal of the California Alliance for the Mentally Ill* 8, no. 1 (1997). A collection of articles by prominent experts and by individuals and families who have struggled with BPD.

Cauwels, Janice. *Imbroglia: Rising to the Challenges of Borderline Personality Disorder.* New York: W. W. Norton, 1992. A comprehensive overview detailing definition, causes, and treatment of BPD.

Gunderson, John G. *Borderline Personality Disorder: A Clinical Guide.* Washington, D.C.: American Psychiatric Publishing, 2001. Though directed primarily for practitioners, this review is accessible for nonprofessionals.

Heller, Leland M. *Life at the Border: Understanding and Recovering from the Borderline Personality Disorder.* Okeechobee, FL: Dyslimbia Press, 1991. A perspective of BPD from a family physician who emphasizes the medical aspects of the disorder.

Kreisman, Jerold J., and Hal Straus. *I Hate You—Don't Leave Me: Understanding the Borderline Personality.* New York: Avon Books, 1991. A detailed, readable overview of BPD, with recommended strategies to improve communication with those contending with BPD.

Mason, Paul T., Randi Kreger, and Larry Siever. *Stop Walking on Eggshells: Coping When Someone You Care about Has Borderline Personality Disorder.* Oakland, Calif.: New Harbinger Publications, 1998. A practical, very helpful guide for those who are close to someone with BPD. Also contains firsthand accounts and is accompanied by a workbook.

Moscovitz, Richard A. *Lost in the Mirror: An Inside Look at Borderline Personality Disorder.* Dallas: Taylor Publications, 1996. A compassionate description of the borderline experience.

217

Personal Accounts

Paxton, Laura. *Borderline and Beyond.* White Tiger Press, 2001. Order at www. powells.com. A detailed description of one woman's recovery with helpful tips and encouragement.

Thorton, Melissa F., Eric W. Peterson, and William D. Barley. *Eclipses: Behind the Borderline Personality Disorder.* Monte Sano Publishing, 1997. Order at www.powells.com. A description of one person's recovery from BPD by utilizing a particular treatment approach, dialectical behavioral therapy (DBT).

Walker, Anthony. *The Courtship Dance of the Borderline.* Writers Showcase Press, 2001. Order at www.powells.com. A psychiatrist's reflection on his own marriage to a person with BPD, and the effects of the illness on the relationship.

Audio and Video Programs

The Infinite Mind Explores Borderline Personality Disorder. 1999. Originally aired on National Public Radio. Hosted by Fred Goodwin, M.D. (former director of the National Institute of Mental Health), and featuring Marsha Linehan, Ph.D., Valerie Porr, M.A. (president of Treatment and Research Advancements Association for Personality Disorder), and Sally Bedell Smith (author of *Diana: Portrait of a Troubled Princess*) (60-min. audiotape; tape and transcript are free upon joining TARAAPD; see below).

Integrated Treatment of Borderline Personality Disorder: Pharmacotherapy and Psychotherapy. 1995. Based on material presented by Glenn O. Gabbard, M.D., at a conference sponsored by the American Psychiatric Association (75-min. VHS, 8378, ISBN 0-88048-378-4, from American Psychiatric Publishing, Inc. www.appi.org).

Understanding Borderline Personality Disorder: The Dialectical Approach. 1995. An introduction for therapists on BPD and DBT. (37-min. VHS and 36-page manual, 567-X, Cat. no. 2567 (order from Guilford Press, 72 Spring Street, New York, NY 10012).

Organizations

New England Personality Disorder Association, Inc. (NEPDA)
McLean Hospital, 115 Mill Street, Belmont, MA 02478
Phone: 617-855-2680

Provides educational resources; sponsors support groups, lectures, and newsletters; and lobbies health insurance and managed care companies for fairness in funding the treatment of personality disorders.

Treatment and Research Advancements Association for Personality Disorder
   (TARAAPD)
www.tara4bpd.org
TARAAPD@aol.com
Phone: HELPLINE 888-4-TARA APD
National, nonprofit organization advocates for individuals with BPD and their families, sponsors workshops and seminars, operates a national resource and referral center, and articulates BPD issues to congressional legislators.

Web Sites

Borderline Personality Disorder Research Foundation
www.borderlineresearch.org
Funds research projects.

Borderline Personality Disorder Sanctuary
www.mhsanctuary.com/borderline
Provides education, books, support, and a state-by-state listing of physicians and therapists.

BPD Central
bpdcentral.com
One of the original and largest sites about BPD; includes many resources for those with BPD and their families.

International Society for the Study of Personality Disorders
www.isspd.com
Sponsors international meetings on BPD.

National Education Alliance for Borderline Personality Disorder (NEA-BPD)
borderlinepersonalitydisorder.com/
Support and education regarding family issues for relatives, consumers, and professionals.

National Institute of Mental Health—Borderline Personality Disorder
www.nimh.nih.gov/publicat/bpd.cfm
Fact sheets for BPD.

Soul's Self-Help Central
www.soulselfhelp.on.ca/borderpd.html
Supportive contacts for those with BPD.

Welcome to Oz
www.egroups.com/community/welcometooz
Bulletin board for family members and loved ones of persons with BPD.

Welcome to Oz—Professionals
groups.yahoo.com/group/wtoprofessionals
Bulletin board and e-mail communication for practitioners working with BPD.

Notes

CHAPTER 1: BORDERLINE BASICS

2 *plagued Princess Diana*   Sally B. Smith, *Diana in Search of Herself* (New York: Random House, 1999).

2 *Our previous book . . . one of the first attempts*   Jerold J. Kreisman and Hal Straus, *I Hate You—Don't Leave Me: Understanding the Borderline Personality* (New York: Avon Books, 1991), 4–9.

4 *defining psychiatric illnesses*   American Psychiatric Association: *Diagnostic and Statistical Manual of Mental Disorders, Fourth Edition, Text Revision* (Washington, D.C.: APA, 2000), 706–710; American Psychiatric Association: "Practice Guideline for the Treatment of Patients with Borderline Personality Disorder," *American Journal of Psychiatry* (October Supplement) 158 (2001).

4 *Patients with the diagnosis of BPD are more likely*   "Practice Guideline," p. 158; American Psychiatric Association: *Diagnostic and Statistical Manual of Mental Disorders, Third Edition* (Washington, D.C.: APA, 1980), 346–347; Glen O. Gabbard, "BPD and Rational Managed Care Policy," symposium presented at the annual meeting of the American Psychiatric Association, Philadelphia, 1994; John G. Gunderson and Mary C. Zanarini, "Current Overview of the Borderline Diagnosis," *Journal of Clinical Psychiatry* (Supplement) 48 (1987): 5–11.

4 *One large study indicated*   Scott Snyder, Walter A. Goodpaster, Wesley M. Pitts Jr., et al., "Demography of Psychiatric Patients with Borderline Personality Traits," *Psychopathology* 18 (1985): 38–49.

6 *more severe functional impairment*   Andrew E. Skodol, John G. Gunderson, Thomas H. McGlashan, et al., "Functional Impairment in Patients with Schizotypal, Borderline, Avoidant, or Obsessive Compulsive Personality Disorder," *American Journal of Psychiatry* 159 (2002): 276–283.

7 *A collaborative, longitudinal study*   Charles A. Sanislow, Carlos M. Grilo, Leslie C. Morey, et al., "Confirmatory Factor Analysis of DSM-IV Criteria for Borderline Personality Disorder: Findings from the Collaborative Longitudinal Personality Disorders Study," *American Journal of Psychiatry* 159 (2002): 284–290.

9 *Rather than concluding . . . these authors argue*   Kurt A. Heumann and Leslie C. Morey, "Reliability of Categorical and Dimensional Judgments of

Personality Disorder," *American Journal of Psychiatry* 147 (1990): 489–500; Timothy J. Trull, Thomas A. Widiger, and Pamela Guthrie, "Categorical versus Dimensional Status of Borderline Personality Disorder," *Journal of Abnormal Psychology* 99 (1990): 40–48.

10 *All of these illnesses are found* Mary C. Zanarini, Frances R. Frankenburg, Elyse D. Dubo, et al., "Axis I Comorbidity of Borderline Personality Disorder," *American Journal of Psychiatry* 155 (1998): 1733–1739; James J. Hudziak, T. J. Boffeli, Jerold J. Kreisman, et al., "Clinical Study of the Relation of Borderline Personality Disorder to Briquet's Syndrome (Hysteria), Somatization Disorder, Antisocial Personality Disorder, and Substance Abuse Disorders," *American Journal of Psychiatry* 153 (1996): 1598–1606; Dawn M. Johnson, M. Tracie Shea, Shirley Yen, et al., "Gender Differences in Borderline Personality Disorder: Findings from the Collaborative Longitudinal Personality Disorders Study," *Comprehensive Psychiatry* 44 (2003): 284–292.

11 *Physiological distinctions suggest* Christian G. Schmahl, Bernet M. Elzinga, Thomas H. McGlashan, et al., "Psychophysiological Reactivity to Stressful Scripts in BPD and PTSD," symposium presented at the annual meeting of the American Psychiatric Association, New Orleans, 2001.

11 *Primary care physicians . . . less than half the time* Raz Gross, Mark Olfson, Marc Gameroff, et al., "Borderline Personality in Primary Care," *Archives of Internal Medicine* 162 (2002): 53–60.

11 *Thus many doctors avoid . . . managed care companies* Donna S. Bender, Regina T. Dolan, Andrew Skodol, et al., "Treatment Utilization by Patients with Personality Disorders," *American Journal of Psychiatry* 158 (2001): 295–302.

13 *explored in our previous book* Jerold J. Kreisman and Hal Straus, *I Hate You—Don't Leave Me: Understanding the Borderline Personality* (New York: Avon Books, 1991), 41–58.

13 *A significant subgroup* Robert van Reekum, Chris A. Conway, David Gansler, et al., "Neurobehavioral Study of Borderline Personality Disorder," *Journal of Psychiatry and Neuroscience* 18 (1993): 121–129.

13 *Further, specific temperaments* Stefano Pallanti, "Personality Disorders: Myths and Neuroscience," *CNS Spectrums* 2 (1997): 53–63.

13 *such sensitivity is seen more frequently in women* Marie-Louise de Vegvar, Larry J. Siever, and Robert L. Trestman, "Impulsivity and Serotonin in Borderline Personality Disorder," *Biological and Neurobehavioral Studies of Borderline Personality Disorder,* ed. Kenneth R. Silk (Washington, D. C.: American Psychiatric Press, 1994), 23–40.

13 *One study utilized PET scanning* Marco Leyton, Hidehiko Okazawa, Mirko Diksic, et al., "Brain Regional α-[^{11}C]Methyl-L-Tryptophan Trapping in

Impulsive Subjects with Borderline Personality Disorder," *American Journal of Psychiatry* 158 (2001): 775–782.

13   *Other neurotransmitters*   Regina Pally, "The Neurobiology of Borderline Personality Disorder: The Synergy of 'Nature and Nurture,'" *Journal of Psychiatric Practice* 8 (2002): 133–142.

14   *The neurotransmitters acetylcholine . . . mood*   Bonnie J. Steinberg, Robert L. Trestman, and Larry J. Siever, "The Cholinergic and Noradrenergic Neurotransmitter Systems and Affective Instability in Borderline Personality Disorder," in *Biological and Neurobehavioral Studies of Borderline Personality Disorder,* ed. Kenneth R. Silk (Washington, D.C.: American Psychiatric Press, 1994), 41–62.

14   *Some researchers . . . autoimmune disorders*   Thomas D. Geracioti, Mitchel A. Kling, Robert M. Post, et al., "Antithyroid Antibody-Linked Symptoms in Borderline Personality Disorder," *Endocrine* 21 (2003): 153–158.

14   *These authors demonstrated . . . decreased volume*   Martin Driessen, Jorg Herrmann, Kerstin Stahl, et al., "Magnetic Resonance Imaging Volumes of the Hippocampus and the Amygdala in Women with Borderline Personality Disorder and Early Traumatization," *Archives of General Psychiatry* 57 (2000): 1115–1122.

14   *Some BPD researchers . . . specific genes*   C. Robert Cloninger, R. Adolfsson, and N. Svrakic, "Mapping Genes for Human Personality," *Nature Genetics* 12 (1996): 3–4.

14   *For example . . . strong hereditary components*   Stefano Pallanti, "Personality Disorders: Myths and Neuroscience," *CNS Spectrums* 2 (1997): 53–63.

15   *Interestingly, some studies . . . chemical dysregulation*   J. Benjamin, L. Li, C. Patterson, et al., "Population and Familial Association between D4 Dopamine Receptor Gene and Measures of Novelty Seeking," *Nature Genetics* 12 (1996): 81–84.

15   *other studies with a gene locus*   R. P. Ebstein, R. Segman, J. Benjamin, et al., "5-HT2C Serotonin Receptor Gene Polymorphism Associated with the Human Personality Trait of Reward Dependence: Interaction with Dopamine D4 Receptor (D4DR) and Dopamine D3 Receptor (D3DR) Polymorphisms," *American Journal of Medical Genetics* 74 (1997): 65–72.

15   *Family members of borderlines*   Jerold J. Kreisman and Hal Straus, *I Hate You—Don't Leave Me: Understanding the Borderline Personality* (New York: Avon Books, 1991), 99–117.

15   *Thus an individual may be born*   Regina Pally, "The Neurobiology of Borderline Personality Disorder: The Synergy of 'Nature and Nurture,'" *Journal of Psychiatric Practice* 8 (2002): 133–142.

16 *Both individual and group therapies* American Psychiatric Association: "Practice Guideline for the Treatment of Patients with Borderline Personality Disorder," *American Journal of Psychiatry* (October Supplement) 158 (2001): 4–6.

16 *Our use of SET techniques* Jerold J. Kreisman and Hal Straus, *I Hate You—Don't Leave Me: Understanding the Borderline Personality* (New York: Avon Books, 1991), 97–115.

16 *Pharmacotherapy is an important* American Psychiatric Association, "Practice Guideline for the Treatment of Patients with Borderline Personality Disorder," *American Journal of Psychiatry* (October Supplement) 158 (2001): 14–18.

16 *about 8 percent of BPD patients commit suicide* American Psychiatric Association, "Practice Guideline for the Treatment of Patients with Borderline Personality Disorder," *American Journal of Psychiatry* (October Supplement) 158 (2001): 24.

CHAPTER 2: FEARS OF ABANDONMENT

29 *The desperate fear of abandonment* John G. Gunderson, "The Borderline Patient's Intolerance of Aloneness: Insecure Attachments and Therapist Availability," *American Journal of Psychiatry* 153 (1996): 752–758.

30 *As explained in our first book* Jerold J. Kreisman and Hal Straus, *I Hate You—Don't Leave Me: Understanding the Borderline Personality* (New York: Avon Books, 1991), 49–53.

30 *soothe herself in times of stress* Ibid., 28; Charles P. Cohen and Vance R Sherwood, "Becoming a Constant Object for the Borderline Patient," *Bulletin of the Menninger Clinic* 53 (1989): 287–299.

31 *In one study of psychiatric patients* William Cardasis, Jamie A. Hochman, and Kenneth R. Silk, "Transitional Objects and Borderline Personality Disorder," *American Journal of Psychiatry* 154 (1997): 250–255.

33 *In this investigation* Christian G. Schmahl, Bernet M. Elzinga, Eric Vermetten, et al., "Neural Correlates of Memories of Abandonment in Women with and without Borderline Personality Disorder," *Biological Psychiatry* 54 (2003): 142–151.

CHAPTER 3: UNSTABLE INTERPERSONAL RELATIONSHIPS

44 *One study found ... two most discriminating criteria* H. George Nurnberg, Marjorie Raskin, Philip E. Levine, et al., "Hierarchy of DSM-III-R Criteria Efficiency for the Diagnosis of Borderline Personality Disorder," *Journal of Personality Disorders* 5 (1991): 211–224.

44 *Anger and paranoia are* Frank E. Yeomans, James W. Hull, and John C. Clarkin, "Risk Factors for Self-Damaging Acts in a Borderline Population," *Journal of Personality Disorders* 8 (1994): 10–16.

45   *Villains can be perceived*   Jerold J. Kreisman and Hal Straus, *I Hate You— Don't Leave Me: Understanding the Borderline Personality* (New York: Avon Books, 1991), 10–11, 50.

46   *"At the outset of close relationships"*   Sally B. Smith, *Diana in Search of Herself* (New York: Random House, 1999), 366.

47   *Adult BPD is frequently associated*   Andrea Fossati, Lilliana Novella, Deborah Donati, et al., "History of Childhood Attention Deficit/Hyperactivity Disorder Symptoms and Borderline Personality Disorder: A Controlled Study," *Comprehensive Psychiatry* 43 (2002): 369–377.

47   *Subtle abnormalities*   Mary C. Zanarini, Catherine R. Kimble, and Amy A. Williams, "Neurological Dysfunction in Borderline Patients and Axis II Control Subjects," in *Biological and Neurobehavioral Studies of Borderline Personality Disorder,* ed. Kenneth R. Silk (Washington, D.C.: American Psychiatric Press, 1994), 159–175.

48   *The usual communication*   René J. Muller, "Is There a Neural Basis for Borderline Splitting?" *Comprehensive Psychiatry* 33 (1992): 92–104.

49   *Psychiatric patients with BPD*   Thomas G. Gutheil, "Borderline Personality Disorder, Boundary Violations, and Patient-Therapist Sex: Medicolegal Pitfalls," *American Journal of Psychiatry* 146 (1989): 597–602.

50   *Borderline patients in intensive psychotherapy*   James W. Hull, Robert C. Lane, and Jean Okie, "Sexual Acting Out and the Desire for Revenge," *Psychoanalytic Review* 76 (1989): 313–328.

50   *Similarly, Princess Diana*   Sally B. Smith, *Diana in Search of Herself* (New York: Random House, 1999), 245.

CHAPTER 4: IDENTITY DISTURBANCE

65   *While the other eight criteria*   Dawn M. Johnson, M. Tracie Shea, Shirley Yen, et al., "Gender Differences in Borderline Personality Disorder: Findings from the Collaborative Longitudinal Personality Disorders Study," *Comprehensive Psychiatry* 44 (2003): 284–292.

65   *The earlier version required "uncertainty about"*   American Psychiatric Association, *Diagnostic and Statistical Manual of Mental Disorders, Third Edition* (Washington, D.C., APA, 1980), 346–347.

65   *DSM-IV . . . requires only "unstable self-image"*   American Psychiatric Association: *Diagnostic and Statistical Manual of Mental Disorders, Fourth Edition, Text Revision* (Washington, D.C.: APA, 2000), 706–710.

66   *Role (or identity) confusion*   Erik Erikson, *Childhood and Society,* 2nd ed. (New York, W. W. Norton, 1963), 261–263.

66 *"identity diffusion"* Otto Kernberg, *Borderline Conditions and Pathological Narcissism* (New York, Jason Aronson, 1975), 39.

67 *Some researchers have subcategorized* Tess Wilkinson-Ryan and Drew Westen, "Identity Disturbance in Borderline Personality Disorder: An Empirical Investigation," *American Journal of Psychiatry* 157 (2000): 528–541.

68 *"Lacking any firm identity"* Sally B. Smith, *Diana in Search of Herself* (New York: Random House, 1999), 365.

CHAPTER 5: DESTRUCTIVE IMPULSIVITY

81 *Impulsivity is frequently associated with* F. Gerard Moeller, Ernest S. Barratt, Donald M. Dougherty, et al., "Psychiatric Aspects of Impulsivity," *American Journal of Psychiatry* 158 (2001): 1783–1793.

81 *Disruption in serotonin metabolism* Josephine Elia, David M. Stoff, and Emil F. Coccaro, "Biological Correlates of Impulsive Disruptive Behavior Disorders: Attention Deficit Hyperactivity Disorder, Conduct Disorder, and Borderline Personality Disorder," *New Directions for Mental Health Services* 54 (1992): 51–57.

81 *Of all the defining criteria* Paul S. Links, Ronald J. Heslegrave, and Robert van Reekum, "Impulsivity: Core Aspect of Borderline Personality Disorder," *Journal of Personality Disorders* 13 (1999): 1–9.

81 *older borderline patients exhibit less impulsivity* Janine Stevenson, Russell Meares, and Anne Comerford, "Diminished Impulsivity in Older Patients with Borderline Personality Disorder," *American Journal of Psychiatry* 160 (2003): 165–166.

82 *Anger, restlessness, guilt, and suicidal tendencies* Robert van Reekum, Paul S. Links, M. Janice E. Mitton, et al., "Impulsivity, Defensive Functioning, and Borderline Personality Disorder," *Canadian Journal of Psychiatry* 41 (1996): 81–84.

83 *Indeed, one study investigating BPD patients . . . in Italy* James J. Hudziak, T. J. Boffeli, Jerold J. Kreisman, et al., "Clinical Study of the Relation of Borderline Personality Disorder to Briquet's Syndrome (Hysteria), Somatization Disorder, Antisocial Personality Disorder, and Substance Abuse Disorders," *American Journal of Psychiatry* 153 (1996): 1598–1606.

83 *However, swift, impulsive actions* John G. Gunderson and Glen O. Gabbard, *Psychotherapy for Personality Disorders* (Washington, D.C.: American Psychiatric Press, 2000), 76–79.

84 *These studies indicate a blunting of serotonin discharge* Paul H. Soloff, Carolyn C. Meltzer, Phil J. Greer, et al., "A Fenfluramine-Activated FDG-PET Study of Borderline Personality Disorder," *Biological Psychiatry* 47 (2000): 540–547; Larry J. Siever, "Biology of Borderline Personality Disorder," *The Eco-*

nomics of Neuroscience (TEN) 3 (2001): 41–47; Marco Leyton, Hidehiko Okazawa, Mirko Diksic, et al., "Brain Regional α-[^{11}C]Methy1-L-Tryptophan Trapping in Impulsive Subjects with Borderline Personality Disorder," *American Journal of Psychiatry* 158 (2001): 775–782.

85   *Those who suffered the most abuse*   Thomas Rinne, Herman G. M. Westenberg, Johan A. den Boer, et al., "Serotonergic Blunting to meta-Chlorophenylpiperazine (m-CPP) Highly Correlates with Sustained Childhood Abuse in Impulsive and Autoaggressive Female Borderline Patients," *Biological Psychiatry* 47 (2000): 548–556.

85   *Some scientists have proposed*   Emil F. Coccaro, "Biological Correlates of BPD," symposium presented at the annual meeting of the American Psychiatric Association, New Orleans, 2001; Frederick G Moeller, research presented at the World Psychiatric Association International Congress, Madrid, 2001.

85   *one theoretical model proposes*   C. Robert Cloninger, "A Systematic Method for Clinical Description and Classification of Personality Variants," *Archives of General Psychiatry* 44 (1987): 573–588.

85   *Some have suggested that psychiatric patients*   Kreisman and Straus, *I Hate You, Don't Leave Me,* 60–82; Joel Paris, "Social Risk Factors for Borderline Personality Disorder: A Review and Hypothesis," *Canadian Journal of Psychiatry* 37 (1992): 510–515.

86   *"social factors interact with other risk factors"*   Paris, "Social Risk Factors," 513.

86   *Data also indicate*   American Psychiatric Association, "Practice Guideline for the Treatment of Patients with Borderline Personality Disorder," *American Journal of Psychiatry* (October Supplement) 158 (2001): 14–15.

CHAPTER 6: SUICIDAL BEHAVIORS AND SELF-MUTILATION

103   *Further, a recent study indicated*   Randy A. Sansone, "Diagnostic Approaches to Borderline Personality and Their Relationship to Self-Harm Behavior," *International Journal of Psychiatry in Clinical Practice* 5 (2001): 273–277.

103   *And yet, many BPD patients . . . remain undiagnosed*   Stig Söderberg, "Personality Disorders in Parasuicide," *Nordic Journal of Psychiatry* 55 (2001): 163–167.

103   *Studies reveal*   "Nonfatal Self-Inflicted Injuries Treated in Hospital Emergency Departments—United States, 2000," *Morbidity and Mortality Weekly Report* (Office of Statistics and Programming, National Center for Injury Prevention and Control, Centers for Disease Control) 51 (2002): 436–438.

103 *In the high-risk group* Paul H. Soloff, Judith A. Lis, Thomas Kelly, et al., "Risk Factors for Suicidal Behavior in Borderline Personality Disorder," *American Journal of Psychiatry* 151 (1994): 1316–1323.

103 *More than 70 percent of all BPD patients* Mary C. Zanarini, John G. Gunderson, Frances R. Frankenburg, et al., "Discriminating Borderline Personality from Other Axis II Disorders," *American Journal of Psychiatry* 147 (1990): 161–167.

104 *It is almost a thousand times the suicide rate* Barbara Stanley, Marc J. Gameroff, Venezia Michalsen, et al., "Are Suicide Attempters Who Self-Mutilate a Unique Population?," *American Journal of Psychiatry* 158 (2001): 427–432.

104 *Although many BPD symptoms ameliorate . . . the risk of suicide persists* Randy A. Sansone, George A. Gaither, and Douglas A. Songer, "Self-Harm Behaviors across the Life Cycle: A Pilot Study of Inpatients with Borderline Personality Disorder," *Comprehensive Psychiatry* 43 (2002): 215–218.

104 *A number of factors further heighten the risk* Paul H. Soloff, Judith A. Lis, Thomas Kelly, et al., "Risk Factors for Suicidal Behavior in Borderline Personality Disorder," *American Journal of Psychiatry* 151 (1994): 1316–1323; Beth S. Brodsky, Kevin M. Malone, Steven P. Ellis, et al., "Characteristics of Borderline Personality Disorder Associated with Suicidal Behavior," *American Journal of Psychiatry* 154 (1997): 1715–1719; Paul H. Soloff, Kevin G. Lynch, Thomas M. Kelly, et al., "Characteristics of Suicide Attempts of Patients with Major Depressive Episode and Borderline Personality Disorder: A Comparative Study," *American Journal of Psychiatry* 157 (2000): 601–608; Beth S. Brodsky, Maria Oquendo, Steven P. Ellis, et al., "The Relationship of Childhood Abuse to Impulsivity and Suicidal Behavior in Adults with Major Depression," *American Journal of Psychiatry* 158 (2001): 1871–1877; Jessica Gerson and Barbara Stanley, "Suicidal and Self-Injurious Behavior in Personality Disorder: Controversies and Treatment Directions," *Current Psychiatry Reports* 4 (2002): 30–38; Paul S. Links, Brent Gould, and Ruwan Ratnayake, "Assessing Suicidal Youth with Antisocial, Borderline, or Narcissistic Personality Disorder," *Canadian Journal of Psychiatry* 48 (2003): 301–310; Michael T. Lambert, "Suicide Risk Assessment and Management: Focus on Personality Disorders," *Current Opinion in Psychiatry* 16 (2003): 71–76.

105 *Its prevalence has been rising* Barent W. Walsh and Paul M. Rosen, *Self-Mutilation: Theory, Research, and Treatment* (New York: Guilford Press, 1988) 11–14.

105 *In a study of almost two thousand* E. David Klonsky, Thomas F. Oltmanns, and Eric Turkheimer, "Deliberate Self-Harm in a Nonclinical Population: Prevalence and Psychological Correlates," *American Journal of Psychiatry* 160 (2003): 1501–1508.

105 *From 55 to 85 percent of self-mutilators* Barbara Stanley, Marc J. Gameroff, Venezia Michalsen, et al., "Are Suicide Attempters Who Self-Mutilate a Unique Population?," *American Journal of Psychiatry* 158 (2001): 427–432.

105 *Sometimes there is a contagion effect* Ronald M. Winchel and Michael Stanley, "Self-Injurious Behavior: A Review of the Behavior and Biology of Self-Mutilation," *American Journal of Psychiatry* 148 (1991): 306–317.

105 *Self-mutilation also is often observed . . . eating disorders* Ronald W. Pies and Anand P. Popli, "Self-Injurious Behavior: Pathophysiology and Implications for Treatment," *Journal of Clinical Psychiatry* 56 (1995): 580–588.

106 *But suicide attempters with a past history of SIB* Barbara Stanley, Marc J. Gameroff, Venezia Michalsen, et al., "Are Suicide Attempters Who Self-Mutilate a Unique Population?" *American Journal of Psychiatry* 158 (2001): 427–432.

106 *Self-mutilation . . . may serve several different functions* Ibid.; Armando R. Favazza, "Why Patients Mutilate Themselves," *Hospital and Community Psychiatry* 40 (1989): 137–145; Jerold J. Kreisman and Hal Straus, *I Hate You—Don't Leave Me: Understanding the Borderline Personality* (New York: Avon Books, 1991), 31–32.

107 *A borderline with a history of childhood sexual abuse* Paul H. Soloff, Kevin G. Lynch, and Thomas M. Kelly, "Childhood Abuse as a Risk Factor for Suicidal Behavior in Borderline Personality Disorder," *Journal of Personality Disorders* 16 (2002): 201–214.

107 *A European study documented* David Owens, Judith Horrocks, and Allan House, "Fatal and Non-Fatal Repetition of Self-Harm," *British Journal of Psychiatry* 181 (2002): 193–199.

107 *A discouraging British investigation* Olive Bennewith, Nigel Stocks, David Gunnell, et al., "General Practice Based Intervention to Prevent Repeat Episodes of Deliberate Self-Harm: Cluster Randomised Controlled Trial," *British Medical Journal* 324 (2002): 1254–1257.

108 *For them, SIB may represent . . . "anger turned inward"* Stig Söderberg, "Personality Disorders in Parasuicide," *Nordic Journal of Psychiatry* 55 (2001): 163–167; Paul H. Soloff, Judith A. Lis, Thomas Kelly, et al., "Risk Factors for Suicidal Behavior in Borderline Personality Disorder," *American Journal of Psychiatry* 151 (1994): 1316–1323; Barbara Stanley, Marc J. Gameroff, Venezia Michalsen, et al., "Are Suicide Attempters Who Self-Mutilate a Unique Population?," *American Journal of Psychiatry* 158 (2001): 427–432.

108 *However, no consistent studies* Mark J. Russ, "Self-Injurious Behavior in Patients with Borderline Personality Disorder: Biological Perspectives," *Journal of Personality Disorders* 6 (1992): 64–81.

108 *One tantalizing case report from the Far East* Y. C. Lim and B. K. Seng, "Self-Mutilation in a Family: Case Report," *Singapore Medical Journal* 26 (1985): 482–484.

109 *Medicines that modify ST levels (SRIs)* Thomas Rinne, A. J. Ernststraat, Wim Brink-Vanden, et al., "Childhood Abuse and the HPA Axis in Adult Female Patients," symposium presented at the annual meeting of the American Psychiatric Association, New Orleans, 2001; Ulrich Sachsse, Susannne Von Der Heyde, and Gerald Huether, "Stress Regulation and Self-Mutilation" (Letter to the Editor), *American Journal of Psychiatry* 159 (2002): 672.

110 *frequent or prolonged hospitalizations* Joel Paris, "Chronic Suicidality among Patients with Borderline Personality Disorder," *Psychiatric Services* 53 (2002): 738–742.

111 *Research confirms that treatment for BPD* American Psychiatric Association, "Practice Guideline for the Treatment of Patients with Borderline Personality Disorder," *American Journal of Psychiatry* (October Supplement) 158 (2001): 5.

112 *Two psychotherapeutic approaches have submitted* Ibid., 5.

113 *DBT consists of four components* Marsha M. Linehan, *Cognitive-Behavioral Treatment of Borderline Personality Disorder* (New York: Guilford Press, 1993); Marsha M. Linehan, *Skills Training Manual for Treating Borderline Personality Disorder* (New York: Guilford Press, 1993).

113 *"benevolent demanding"* Marsha M. Linehan, *Treating Borderline Personality Disorder: The Dialectical Approach. Program Manual* (New York: Guilford Press, 1995).

113 *as we described in our St. Louis program* Jerold J. Kreisman, "CTU: The Systematic Inpatient Treatment of the Borderline Patient," *Res Medica* 3 (1986): 19–26.

113 *"Stylistically, DBT blends"* Marsha M. Linehan, *Skills Training Manual for Treating Borderline Personality Disorder* (New York: Guilford Press, 1993).

113 *One adapted model, MACT* Maria Ridolfi and John G. Gunderson, "A New Cognitive Behavioral Approach to Self-Harm Behavior," symposium presented at the annual meeting of the American Psychiatric Association, New Orleans, 2001.

CHAPTER 7: MOOD INSTABILITY

122 *some have suggested that BPD should be classified as a subtype* Michael H. Stone, "Contemporary Shift of the Borderline Concept from a Sub-Schizophrenic Disorder to a Subaffective Disorder," *Psychiatric Clinics of North America* 2 (1979): 577–594; Hagop S. Akiskal, "Subaffective Disorders: Dys-

thymic, Cyclothymic, and Bipolar II Disorders in the 'Borderline' Realm," *Psychiatric Clinics of North America* 4 (1981): 25–46.

123   *"due to a marked reactivity of mood"*   American Psychiatric Association; *Diagnostic and Statistical Manual of Mental Disorders, Fourth Edition, Text Revision* (Washington, D.C.: APA, 2000), 710.

123   *Studies have demonstrated that borderlines have more frequent*   Rex W. Cowdry, David L. Gardner, K. M. O'Leary, et al., "Mood Variability: A Study of Four Groups," *American Journal of Psychiatry* 148 (1991): 1505–1511.

123   *72 percent accuracy*   Harold W. Koenigsberg, Philip D. Harvey, Vivian Mitropoulou, et al., "Characterizing Affective Instability in Borderline Personality Disorder," *American Journal of Psychiatry* 159 (2002): 768–788.

123   *the congruence between ratings by both the patient and clinician*   Katherine A. Comtois, Deborah S. Cowley, David L. Dunner, et al., "Relationship between Borderline Personality Disorder and Axis I Diagnosis in Severity of Depression and Anxiety," *Journal of Clinical Psychiatry* 60 (1999): 752–758.

124   *Compared to depressed patients*   Steven M. Southwick, Rachel Yehuda, and Earl L. Giller, "Psychological Dimensions of Depression in Borderline Personality Disorder," *American Journal of Psychiatry* 152 (1995): 789–791.

124   *Patients with dysthymic disorder*   Carolyn M. Pepper, Daniel N. Klein, Rochelle L. Anderson, et al., "DSM-III-R Axis II Comorbidity in Dysthymia and Major Depression," *American Journal of Psychiatry* 152 (1995): 239–247.

124   *Further, the likelihood of depression*   Jeremy M. Silverman, Lynn Pinkham, Thomas B. Horvath, et al., "Affective and Impulsive Personality Disorder Traits in the Relatives of Patients with Borderline Personality Disorder," *American Journal of Psychiatry* 148 (1991): 1378–1385.

124   *Conversely, patients with a diagnosis of dysthymia*   Lawrence P. Riso, Daniel N. Klein, Tova Ferro, et al., "Understanding the Comorbidity between Early-Onset Dysthymia and Cluster B Personality Disorders: A Family Study," *American Journal of Psychiatry* 153 (1996): 900–906.

124   *It can coexist with other disorders, and it can camouflage*   Jerold J. Kreisman and Hal Straus, *I Hate You—Don't Leave Me: Understanding the Borderline Personality* (New York, Avon Books, 1991), 21–26; John G. Gunderson, *Borderline Personality Disorder: A Clinical Guide* (Washington, D.C.: American Psychiatric Publishing, 2001), 38–61.

126   *PTSD patients showed more profound physiological reactions*   Christian G. Schmahl, Bernet M. Elzinga, Thomas H. McGlashan, et al., "Psychophysiological Reactivity to Stressful Scripts in BPD and PTSD," paper presented to the annual meeting of the American Psychiatric Association, Philadelphia, 2002.

127 *Bulimia . . . is the most common* John G. Gunderson, *Borderline Personality Disorder: A Clinical Guide* (Washington, D.C.: American Psychiatric Publishing, 2001), 38–61.

127 *Binge eating leading to obesity* Ibid., 47.

127 *Only half of these patients were receiving* Raz Gross, Myrna M. Weissman, Mark Olfson, et al., "BPD in Primary Care," paper presented to the annual meeting of the American Psychiatric Association, Philadelphia, 2002.

128 *probably associated with these unhealthy habits* Frances R. Frankenburg, Mary C. Zanarini, John Hennen, et al., "BPD, Medical Illness, Lifestyle Choices, and Health Care Utilization," paper presented to the annual meeting of the American Psychiatric Association, Philadelphia, 2002.

128 *Most patients with a diagnosis of DID* Richard P. Horevitz and Bennett G. Braun, "Are Multiple Personalities Borderline?," *Psychiatric Clinics of North America* 7 (1984): 69–87.

129 *read "hidden demeaning or threatening meanings into"* American Psychiatric Association, *Diagnostic and Statistical Manual of Mental Disorders, Fourth Edition, Text Revision* (Washington, D.C.: APA, 2000), 694.

129 *"unusual perceptual experiences, including body illusions"* Ibid., 701.

129 *An individual with a diagnosis of avoidant personality disorder* Ibid., 721.

129 *Someone with dependent personality disorder* Ibid., 725.

129 *HPD is characterized by excessive emotionality* Ibid., 714.

130 *"But I'm not a serpent, I tell you!"* Lewis Carroll, *Alice's Adventures in Wonderland* (New York: Macmillan, 1962), 70.

CHAPTER 8: EMPTINESS

146 *Gunderson has suggested that* John G. Gunderson, *Borderline Personality Disorder: A Clinical Guide* (Washington, D.C.: American Psychiatric Publishing, 2001), 75.

146 *DSM-IV deleted boredom . . . because more specific research* James H. Rogers, Thomas A. Widiger, and Anthony Krupp, "Aspects of Depression Associated with Borderline Personality Disorder," *American Journal of Psychiatry* 152 (1995): 268–270.

146 *Indeed, some researchers have previously proposed* Michael H. Stone, "Contemporary Shift of the Borderline Concept from a Sub-Schizophrenic Disorder to a Subaffective Disorder," *Psychiatric Clinics of North America* 2 (1979): 577–594; Hagop S. Akiskal, Bohgos I. Yerevanian, Glenn C. Davis, et al., "The Nosologic Status of Borderline Personality Disorder: Clinical and

Polysomnographic Study," *American Journal of Psychiatry* 142 (1985): 192–198.

147 *In contrast, people suffering from major depression* John G. Gunderson and Katharine A. Phillips, "A Current View of the Interface between Borderline Personality Disorder and Depression," *American Journal of Psychiatry* 148 (1991): 967–975; Drew Westen, Jay Moses, Kenneth R. Silk, et al., "Quality of Depressive Experience in Borderline Personality Disorder and Major Depression: When Depression Is Not Just Depression," *Journal of Personality Disorders* 6 (1992): 382–393; Laura Bellodi, Marco Battaglia, Mariangela Gasperini, et al., "The Nature of Depression in Borderline Depressed Patients," *Comprehensive Psychiatry* 33 (1992): 128–133.

147 *As an adult, the individual is unable* Gerald Adler, *Borderline Psychopathology and Its Treatment* (New York: Jason Aronson, 1985).

149 *Linehan's DBT model* Marsha M. Linehan, *Cognitive-Behavioral Treatment of Borderline Personality Disorder* (New York: Guilford Press, 1993).

CHAPTER 9: ANGER

159 *A study of domestic violence by men* LaTina Else, Stephen A. Wonderlich, William W. Beatty, et al., "Personality Characteristics of Men Who Physically Abuse Women," *Hospital and Community Psychiatry* 44 (1993): 54–58.

159 *Another investigation confirmed that rage* David L. Gardner, Ellen Leibenluft, Kathleen M. O'Leary, et al., "Self-Ratings of Anger and Hostility in Borderline Personality Disorder," *Journal of Nervous and Mental Disease* 179 (1991): 157–161.

159 *other studies of depressed psychiatric patients note* Maurizio Fava, "Depression and Anger Attacks," symposium presented at the annual meeting of the American Psychiatric Association, Philadelphia, 2002.

159 *One study monitored persistence of specific* Tracie Shea, Robert L. Stout, Shirley Yen, et al., "Two-Year Stability of Personality Disorder Criteria," symposium presented at the annual meeting of the American Psychiatric Association, Philadelphia, 2002.

160 *Kernberg . . . "excessive nature of primary aggression"* Otto Kernberg, "Borderline Personality Organization," *Journal of the American Psychoanalytic Association* 15 (1967): 673.

160 *The prefrontal cortex* Eric Hollander, Nicole Posner, and Scott Cherkasky, "Neuropsychiatric Aspects of Aggression and Impulse Control Disorders," in *The American Psychiatric Publishing Textbook of Neuropsychiatry and Clinical Neurosciences,* 4th ed., ed. Stuart C. Yudofsky and Robert E. Hales (Washington, D.C.: American Psychiatric Publishing, 2002), 579–596.

161   *PET . . . has demonstrated abnormalities in these regions*   Antonia S. New and Larry J. Siever, "Neurobiology and Genetics of Borderline Personality Disorder," *Psychiatric Annals* 32 (2002): 329–336.

161   *Interestingly, one study demonstrated . . . administration of an SRI*   Brian Knutson, Owen M. Wolkowitz, Steve W. Cole, et al., "Selective Alteration of Personality and Social Behavior by Serotonergic Intervention," *American Journal of Psychiatry* 155 (1998): 373–379.

CHAPTER 10: REALITY DISTORTIONS: PARANOIA AND DISSOCIATION

176   *Gunderson and Singer . . . in their seminal 1975 paper*   John G. Gunderson and Margaret T. Singer, "Defining Borderline Patients: An Overview," *American Journal of Psychiatry* 132 (1975): 1–9.

176   *Gunderson collated a number of studies*   John G. Gunderson, *Borderline Personality Disorder: A Clinical Guide* (Washington, D.C.: American Psychiatric Publishing, 2001), 14–15.

177   *These episodes come on suddenly*   American Psychiatric Association, *Diagnostic and Statistical Manual of Mental Disorders, Fourth Edition, Text Revision* (Washington, D.C.: APA, 2000), 706–710.

177   *Borderlines with comorbid psychotic . . . longer hospital stays*   Frank T. Miller, Toni Abrams, Rebecca Dulit, et al., "Psychotic Symptoms in Patients with Borderline Personality Disorder and Concurrent Axis I Disorder," *Hospital and Community Psychiatry* 44 (1993): 59–61.

178   *Although dissociation occurs in other disorders*   Kenneth R. Silk, Naomi E. Lohr, Drew Westen, et al., "Psychosis in Borderline Patients with Depression," *Journal of Personality Disorders* 3 (1989): 92–100.

178   *DID and less severe forms of dissociation*   Glenn N. Saxe, Bessel A. van der Kolk, Robert Berkowitz, et al., "Dissociative Disorders in Psychiatric Inpatients," *American Journal of Psychiatry* 150 (1993): 1037–1042.

179   *They were able to demonstrate that specific chromosomal locations*   Marianne Goodman, Harold W. Koenigsberg, Lawrence Sprung, et al., "Pathological Dissociation in BPD," symposium presented at the annual meeting of the American Psychiatric Association, Philadelphia, 2002.

179   *Additionally, altered brain circuits*   Regina Pally, "The Neurobiology of Borderline Personality Disorder: The Synergy of 'Nature and Nurture,'" *Journal of Psychiatric Practice* 8 (2002): 133–142.

180   *Drugs that block release of these opiates*   Martin J. Bohus, G. Bernhard Landwehrmeyer, Christian E. Stiglmayr, et al., "Naltrexone in the Treatment of Dissociative Symptoms in Patients with Borderline Personality Disorder: An Open-Label Trial," *Journal of Clinical Psychiatry* 60 (1999): 598–603.

CHAPTER 11: TREATMENT STRATEGIES AND COMMUNICATION
            TECHNIQUES

184 *"The primary treatment"* American Psychiatric Association, "Practice Guideline for the Treatment of Patients with Borderline Personality Disorder," *American Journal of Psychiatry* (October Supplemnet) 158 (2001): 4.

184 *Family therapy can be a supportive adjunct* Judith K. Kreisman and Jerold J. Kreisman, "Marital and Family Treatment of Borderline Personality Disorder," in *Family Treatment of Personality Disorders: Advances in Clinical Practice,"* ed. Malcolm M. MacFarlane (Binghamton, N.Y.: Haworth Press, forthcoming).

188 *Considerations for choosing a therapist* Paul Mason, Randi Kreger, and Larry J. Siever, *Stop Walking on Eggshells: Coping When Someone You Care about Has Borderline Personality Disorder* (Oakland, Calif.: New Harbinger, 1998); Paul Mason and Randi Kreger, "Walking on Eggshells: When Someone You Care About Has Borderline Personality Disorder," BPDCentral@aol.com (1996), 47; Jerold J. Kreisman and Hal Straus, *I Hate You—Don't Leave Me: Understanding the Borderline Personality* (New York: Avon Books, 1991), 130–132.

188 *Gunderson has suggested that successful therapists* John G. Gunderson, *Borderline Personality Disorder: A Clinical Guide* (Washington, D.C.: American Psychiatric Publishing, 2001), 252–254.

189 *antecedent models* Jerold J. Kreisman, "CTU: The Systematic Inpatient Treatment of the Borderline Patient," *Res Medica* 3 (1986): 19–26.

189 *No single organized therapy* Falk Leichsenring and Eric Leibing, "The Effectiveness of Psychodynamic Therapy and Cognitive Behavior Therapy in the Treatment of Personality Disorders: A Meta-Analysis," *American Journal of Psychiatry* 160 (2003): 1223–1232.

190 *All successful therapies emphasize* American Psychiatric Association, "Practice Guideline for the Treatment of Patients with Borderline Personality Disorder," *American Journal of Psychiatry* (October Supplement) 158 (2001): 11–14.

190 *Compared to their functioning one year prior* Janine Stevenson and Russell Meares, "An Outcome Study of Psychotherapy for Patients with Borderline Personality Disorder," *American Journal of Psychiatry* 149 (1992): 358–362.

190 *After one year, the average savings* Janine Stevenson and Russell Meares, "Psychotherapy with Borderline Patients, II: A Preliminary Cost Benefit Study," *Australia-New Zealand Journal of Psychiatry* 33 (1999): 473–477.

190 *Indeed, 30 percent of the psychodynamic group* Russell Meares, Janine Stevenson, and Anne Comerford, "Psychotherapy with Borderline Patients, I: A

Comparison between Treated and Untreated Cohorts," *Australia-New Zealand Journal of Psychiatry* 33 (1999): 467–472.

190 *Nevertheless, this study indicated* Kenneth I. Howard, S. Mark Kopta, Merton S. Krause, et al., "The Dose-Effect Relationship in Psychotherapy," *American Psychologist* 41 (1986): 159–164.

191 *A British group compared* Anthony Bateman and Peter Fonagy, "Effectiveness of Partial Hospitalization in the Treatment of Borderline Personality Disorder: A Randomized Controlled Trial," *American Journal of Psychiatry* 156 (1999): 1563–1569.

191 *DBT's tightly structured format* Marsha M. Linehan, *Skills Training Manual for Treating Borderline Personality Disorder* (New York: Guilford Press, 1993).

192 *However, some studies have demonstrated that DBT* Charles R. Swenson, William C. Torrey, and Kelly Koerner, "Implementing Dialectical Behavior Therapy," *Psychiatric Services* 53 (2002): 171–178.

192 *One interesting modification . . . emphasizes the importance of others* Nancee Blum, Bruce Pfohl, Don St. John, et al., "STEPPS: A Cognitive-Behavioral Systems-Based Group Treatment for Outpatients with Borderline Personality Disorder: A Preliminary Report," *Comprehensive Psychiatry* 43 (2002): 301–310.

192 *EMDR is a technique* Francine Shapiro, Silke Vogelmann-Sine, and Larry F. Sine, "Eye Movement Desensitization and Reprocessing: Treating Trauma and Substance Abuse," *Journal of Psychoactive Drugs* 26 (1994): 379–390.

193 *"cure is not a realistic goal"* American Psychiatric Association, "Practice Guideline for the Treatment of Patients with Borderline Personality Disorder," *American Journal of Psychiatry* (October Supplement) 158 (2001): 14.

194 *Interestingly, one study . . . responded within a week to an SRI* Emil F. Coccaro and Richard J. Kavoussi, "Fluoxetine and Impulsive Aggressive Behavior in Personality-Disordered Subjects," *Archives of General Psychiatry* 54 (1997): 1081–1088.

194 *In some cases, TCAs worsened emotional control* American Psychiatric Association, "Practice Guidelines for the Treatment of Patients with Borderline Personality Disorder," *American Journal of Psychiatry* (October Supplement) 158 (2001): 36–37.

196 *RTMS, a new technique* Adrian Preda, "Repetitive Transcranial Magnetic Stimulation for BPD," symposium presented at the annual meeting of the American Psychiatric Association, Philadelphia, 2002.

196 *Attempts to treat BPD with homeopathic* Mary C. Zanarini and Frances R. Frankenburg, "Omega-3 Fatty Acid Treatment of Women with Borderline

Personality Disorder: A Double-Blind, Placebo-Controlled Pilot Study," *American Journal of Psychiatry* 160 (2003): 167–169.

198 *In our previous book* Jerold J. Kreisman and Hal Straus, *I Hate You—Don't Leave Me: Understanding the Borderline Personality* (New York, Avon Books, 1991), 130–132.

CHAPTER 12: PROGNOSIS AND DIRECTIONS OF FUTURE RESEARCH

206 *General impairment and risk of suicide* Michael H. Stone, *The Fate of Borderline Patients: Successful Outcome and Psychiatric Practice* (New York: Guilford Press, 1990).

206 *A recent British study . . . patients diagnosed . . . in the Cluster B group* Helen Seivewright, Peter Tyrer, and Tony Johnson, "Change in Personality Status in Neurotic Disorders," *Lancet* 359 (2002): 2253–2254.

206 *A general medical practice sees a much higher percentage* Raz Gross, Myrna M. Weissman, Mark Olfson, et al., "BPD in Primary Care," symposium presented at the annual meeting of the American Psychiatric Association, Chicago, 2000.

206 *One study followed borderline patients for six years* Frances R. Frankenburg, Mary C. Zanarini, John Hennen, et al., "BPD, Medical Illness, Lifestyle Choices, and Health Care Utilization," symposium presented at the annual meeting of the American Psychiatric Association, Philadelphia, 2002.

207 *Those individuals from a more depressed socioeconomic* Michael H. Stone, "Long-Term Outcome in Patients with Borderline Personality Disorder," *The Economics of Neuroscience* 3 (2001): 48–56.

207 *Even in those borderlines who improve* Paul S. Links, Janice E. Mitton, and Meir Steiner, "Predicting Outcome for Borderline Personality Disorder," *Comprehensive Psychiatry* 31 (1990): 490–498; Andrew E. Skodol II, Thomas H. McGlashan, M. Tracie Shea, et al., "Course of Diagnoses and Impairment in Patients with BPD," symposium presented at the annual meeting of the American Psychiatric Association, Philadelphia, 2002; Mary C. Zanarini, Frances R. Frandenburg, John Hennen, et al., "A Six-Year Symptomatic and Functional Course of BPD," symposium presented at the annual meeting of the American Psychiatric Association, Philadelphia, 2002.

207 *Usually, vocational stability is achieved* Michael H. Stone, "Long-Term Outcome in Patients with Borderline Personality Disorder," *The Economics of Neuroscience* 3 (2001): 48–56.

208 *Compared to patients with major depression* Donna S. Bender, Regina T. Dolan, Andrew E. Skodol, et al., "Treatment Utilization by Patients with Personality Disorders," *American Journal of Psychiatry* 158 (2001): 295–302.

208   *The rate of hospitalization and rigorous psychotherapy diminishes*   Mary C. Zanarini, Frances R. Frankenburg, and John Hennen, "Psychiatric Treatment of Borderline Patients Followed for Four Years," symposium presented at the annual meeting of the American Psychiatric Association, New Orleans, 2001.

208   *In groups of untreated patients, 10.5 years*   J. Christopher Perry, Elisabeth Banon, and Floriana Ianni, "Effectiveness of Psychotherapy for Personality Disorders," *American Journal of Psychiatry* 156 (1999): 1312–1321; J. Christopher Perry and Michael Bond, "Empirical Studies of Psychotherapy for Personality Disorders," in *Psychotherapy for Personality Disorders,* ed. John G. Gunderson and Glenn O. Gabbard (Washington, D.C.: American Psychiatric Press, 2000), 14–31.

208   *In one six-year study*   Mary C. Zanarini, Frances R. Frankenburg, John Hennen, et al., "The Longitudinal Course of Borderline Psychopathology: 6-Year Prospective Follow-up of the Phenomenology of Borderline Personality Disorder," *American Journal of Psychiatry* 160 (2003): 274–283.

208   *Short-term predictors*   Paul S. Links, Janice E. Mitton, and Meir Steiner, "Predicting Outcome for Borderline Personality Disorder," *Comprehensive Psychiatry* 31 (1990): 490–498; Paul S. Links, M. Janice E. Mitton, and Meir Steiner, "Stability of Borderline Personality Disorder," *Canadian Journal of Psychiatry* 38 (1993): 255–259; Mary C. Zanarini and Frances R. Frankenburg, "Predictors of Improvement for Borderline Patients," symposium presented at the annual meeting of the American Psychiatric Association, Chicago, 2000.

210   *After ten or more years*   Michael H. Stone, "Long-Term Outcome in Patients with Borderline Personality Disorder," *Economics of Neuroscience* 3 (2001): 48–56.

211   *It has been shown that heritability*   W. John Livesley, Kerry L. Jang, Douglas N. Jackson, et al., "Genetic and Environmental Contributions to Dimensions of Personality Disorder," *American Journal of Psychiatry* 150 (1993): 1826–1831.

211   *Cloninger . . . has suggested that inborn features*   C. Robert Cloninger, "A Systematic Method for Clinical Description and Classification of Personality Variance," *Archives of General Psychiatry* 44 (1987): 573–588.

215   *proposed specialty centers for the treatment of BPD*   John G. Gunderson, *Borderline Personality Disorder: A Clinical Guide* (Washington, D.C.: American Psychiatric Publishing, 2001), 300–304.

Index